ALL THE QUEEN'S MEN

The Household Cavalry
and
The Brigade of Guards

by

RUSSELL BRADDON

The Badge of the Household Division

HAMISH HAMILTON
LONDON

First published in Great Britain 1977
by Hamish Hamilton Ltd
90 Great Russell Street London WC1B 3PT

Copyright © 1977 by Russell Braddon

SBN 241 89431 X

Design by Patrick Leeson

Filmset and printed in Great Britain by
BAS Printers Limited, Wallop, Hampshire

ALL THE QUEEN'S MEN

BY THE SAME AUTHOR

Fiction

Those in Peril
Out of the Storm
Gabriel Comes to 24
The Proud American Boy
The Year of the Angry Rabbit
Committal Chamber
The Inseparables
When the Enemy is Tired
Will You Walk a Little Faster?
Prelude and Fugue for Lovers
The Progress of Private Lilyworth
End Play

Non-fiction

The Piddingtons
The Naked Island
Cheshire VC
Nancy Wake
End of a Hate
Joan Sutherland
Roy Thomson of Fleet Street
The Siege
Suez
The Hundred Days of Darien

To Debby, Bill and Jim

Contents

CONTENTS

Plates in colour

Plates in black and white

PLATES IN BLACK AND WHITE

Acknowledgments

THE VIEWS of more than three hundred officers, NCO's and men of the Household Division of 1974/75 have been incorporated in this book. Normally (if only to impress the critics) each of them would be acknowledged by name; but none is so acknowledged here.

The reason for this is twofold. First, many of them will have been promoted since I talked to them, and nothing is more discourteous to a corporal (or a major) than referring to him as Guardsman (or Captain). Second, many of them may disagree with the manner in which I have deployed their words, and at least they should be able to console themselves with the axiom that where there are no names there can be no pack drill.

Nevertheless, to all those who did help me, from the Major General to Troopers and Guardsmen, I hereby offer my thanks and the hope that this book will not make any of them regret their courtesy and generosity.

Introduction

'WHAT A COSY title it is, The Household Division,' a colonel warned. 'But once you start to find out just what an intricate, convoluted and interlocking relationship of seven regiments over a period of more than three hundred years the history of this Household Division really is, you'll probably decide, Christ, it can't be done.'

Researching this book, it soon became evident that the colonel had a point. Not only are there seven regiments and more than three hundred years involved in any history of the Household Division, there are sixteen sovereigns, dozens of statesmen, scores of wars, hundreds of dates and thousands of distinguished military names. Obviously many more facts would have to be omitted than included if the work was to be limited to a single volume: selectivity would have to be ruthless.

Names were the first to go. Apologies are extended to all those of all ranks whose exploits from 1660 to today have been described, or whose words have been quoted, but almost without exception to have included their names would merely have confused the reader.

Next went most of the battles. Gallantly though the regiments now known as the Household Division almost invariably performed in action, their battalions and squadrons did tend tactically to repeat themselves, and such repetitions would merely have bored the reader.

Next went most of the esoteric details about uniforms. Uniforms were changed at the behest first of colonels and then of kings, varied for a long time from regiment to regiment, and could anyway be described only by using medieval tailoring terms, which would merely have irked the reader.

And finally acknowledgments were discarded. To have acknowledged every source of every quotation or fact would have involved a dozen footnotes a page, and excessive footnotes would merely have distracted the reader—who may nevertheless rest assured that nothing that follows is invented, all of it having been taken from regimental histories, archives and museums, from interviews with hundreds of officers, NCO's and men, from visits to Ulster, Germany and the Household barracks in England, from newspapers, diaries, letters, novels, biographies, memoirs and reports in the library of the House of Commons.

These arbitrary limits to the subject matter having been imposed, what remained to be examined was a body of 'Household' troops whose double task it has always been to protect the Sovereign and fight the Sovereign's wars. This body, at any given point in its history, was simply the product of the society and era from which it sprang, the king it was serving, the London in which it was guarding him, the wars it was fighting on his behalf, and all previous wars as far back as 1640.

For this reason I have attempted not a single vast canvas densely packed with every available detail, but rather a series of tolerably uncluttered transparencies, the one to be superimposed, in the reader's mind, upon the other until an impression emerges of the whole. No single transparency—such as the London of George II, or the Guards at War in the Eighteenth Century—is presented as being definitive; but it is hoped that collectively they will create in the reader's mind an impression of something perennially patrician, precocious and indestructible, that being the impression created by the Household Division in the mind of the author.

The Badge of the Household Division

ALL THE QUEEN'S MEN

1 *The Guards on Parade*

ONE WET showery morning in October 1684, just before he died, Charles II reviewed 4,100 of his Foot and Horse Guards on Putney Heath. To the beating of drums they 'successively exercised the military posture of pike, sword and musket, every man dexterously discharging his duties, with an exact general readiness, to the great delight and satisfaction of Their Majesties and Royal Highnesses.' Nowadays such Royal reviews take place not on Putney Heath but on Horse Guards Parade, and not in October (when, as in 1684, the weather is more than likely to be 'an impediment') but early in the summer.

It is a Saturday in early June, therefore, and crowds stand under the trees on either side of a be-flagged Mall, waiting for the Queen. The roadway itself is empty, except for the motionless Guardsmen who line both kerbs. Escorted by her Household Cavalry, the Queen will ride side-saddle almost to the end of the Mall between those two lines of Guardsmen, then turn right, briefly, down to Horse Guards.

Where sit thousands of spectators in tiered stands built along three sides of the rectangular Parade, the west side—just across the road from the park—being open. Two long ranks of Guardsmen—more than five hundred NCO's and men —stand in an L-shaped formation beneath the spectators on the north side and across the open west side; and the massed bands of the Household Brigade—three

H.M. Queen Elizabeth II at a Birthday Parade

hundred and sixty strong—are formed up beneath the spectators on the south side. When the Queen arrives, she will take up her position in front of the arch on the east side.

Looking back along the Mall towards the Palace, the scene is one of perfect symmetry—a straight pink ribbon of road, flanked on either side first by Guardsmen in navy blue trousers, scarlet tunics, white belts and black bearskins, then by a bank of spectators, over whom curls a green wave of gleaming foliage punctuated at regular intervals by poles on each of which there flutters a flag.

A clatter of unseen hooves is heard as the Sovereign's Escort of the Household Cavalry, swords at the slope, comes down Constitution Hill. Of this escort, one section enters the Palace forecourt, another halts at the entrance to the Mall, the Mounted Band—gorgeously caparisoned in coats of gold—halts in front of the Queen Victoria Memorial, facing the Palace forecourt, and the remaining divisions wheel round the Memorial and halt by the Palace South Gate.

A brief flurry of orders—'*Household Cavalry, Eyes Centre, Dress . . . Household Cavalry, Steady . . . Household Cavalry, Eyes Front . . . Household Cavalry, Slope*

Swords'—precedes the departure of the Queen Mother and other members of the Royal Family in their respective carriages.

As the Queen Mother's carriage emerges from the Palace archway the order *'Household Cavalry, Royal Salute, Carry Swords'* is given. As she rides past, the Standard is lowered and the band plays the National Anthem.

Then comes the remainder of the Royal Family, and as all their carriages move briskly towards Horse Guards the band rides up and halts fifty yards behind the section waiting at the head of the Mall. At the same time, the First Division moves up to halt twenty-five yards behind the band, and the Second Division moves up to halt fifty yards behind the First Division.

The Queen rides into the Palace forecourt, is greeted by the order *'Household Cavalry, Royal Salute, Carry Swords,'* and takes up her position twenty-five yards behind the Second Division.

Royal Colonels of Regiments, personal Aides de Camp and two grooms of the Royal Household follow her; behind whom ride the Field Officer of the Escort, the Escort Commander, the Standard and a bevy of senior officers; who are followed, at an interval of twenty-five yards, by the Third and Fourth Divisions; behind whom, bringing up the rear, bearing wicked-looking axes, are two farriers.

Into the perfect symmetry of the Mall there thus processes an equally symmetrical Cavalry formation, marvellously designed both to protect and to display the Queen at its centre. Beneath the waves of foliage and the fluttering of flags, between the presses of crowds and the scarlet tunicked Guardsmen, along the centre of the pink ribbon of roadway clatters, jingles and chinks a column of huge black horses mounted by beplumed, helmeted, cuirassed and jack-booted troopers, backs straight as their vertical swords and expressions stiff as the flared cuffs of their white gauntlets. Not so much astride their mounts as voluptuously ensconced in the sheepskins that cover their saddles, chins jutting, eyes bleak beneath helmet rims, aglitter with brass and steel and waxed leather, they are the epitome of martial splendour. In the midst of whom, austerely side-saddle and solitary, the woman who is their Colonel in Chief contrives to look both soldierly and regal.

Meantime that double line of Guardsmen which was drawn up across the west side of Horse Guards, facing the Archway, has parted to form a corridor through which the carriages of the Queen Mother and other Royals have passed: and, having admitted them, has swung inwards again, to re-form the original line and await the arrival of the Queen.

Whose escort is soon thrusting its way down from the Mall. As she reaches the nearest corner of Horse Guards Parade she leaves her escort and rides steadily and diagonally across the Parade toward the Archway.

By the time she reaches that Archway, her entire mounted escort must have formed up on the opposite side of the road from the Foot Guards on the west side of the Parade.

Exactly as the silver throated clock in the tower above the archway begins to strike eleven, the last trooper is slotting his horse into place, and the Queen is turning to face all those assembled in honour of her official birthday. The chimes of the clock die away and the Massed Band plays the National Anthem.

The Queen then begins her inspection—which carries her along the two front rows of the L-shaped formation, down the back rows, past her Cavalry Escort and back to the Archway, where she will sit motionless on her horse for the next hour and twenty minutes.

Now it is time for the Massed Band to perform. Twenty abreast, in eighteen ranks, they play, and at the same time execute a slow march across the Parade and half-way back again, counter marching as they turn about. Then they quick march, counter marching again on the about-turn, and halting at the centre.

Next those Guardsmen on the right flank of the west side of the Parade begin to quick march. The band breaks into an accompanying march, and somehow, as it plays, so pivots upon itself that it vacates the centre of the parade and allows the Guardsmen to move past it and receive the Colours they are to troop.

These Colours at their head, the Colour escort slow march through the twin and stationary ranks of all the other Guardsmen, the band playing the while and wheeling again, the Colour passing between the last two Guardsmen and coming to a halt exactly as the clock strikes 11.30.

Now all the Foot Guards form into eight separate Guards and, led by the Colour Escort, march in slow time up the south side, across the east side past the Queen, down the north side and back along the west side.

They march in slow time and, as they march, something about the slight pause in each pace, some combination of music, discipline, colour and occasion grips the spectators and generates a sense of extraordinary corporate emotion.

As the Colour passes the Queen, it is lowered in salute; but, as it passes each stand, the seated spectators rise to it—not so much because the programme has asked them to as because it seems impossible not to respond (as audiences do in an opera house) to a great performance. And as if prompted by that response to an encore, the Guards surge briskly from melancholic slow time into exhilarating quick time, and swing boldly past all the spectators and their Queen again.

Watching them, the casual onlooker revels in a performance as symbolic as a Coronation, as stunningly costumed and sound-tracked as an American musical, and as intricately choreographed as a ballet. But to the informed spectator the Birthday Parade depicts three centuries of Royal, British and military history as well.

H.M. Queen Elizabeth II among her troops

The bearskins signify victory at Waterloo, the cuirasses and helmets are the contribution of George IV; the mounted musicians' coats of gold stem from the reign of Charles II, the slow march from the reign of George II; the Guards stand in two ranks because that is how they confronted the cream of Napoleon's Imperial Army; every intricate piece of drill is an ordinary battle manoeuvre from the past; the Trooping the Colour was once a means of ensuring that everyone knew to which standard he must rally in the coming battle; Horse Guards has been the parade ground of Sovereigns' Guards and Escorts since 1660; and upon Horse Guards Parade, since George III's time (except during two World Wars) a birthday tribute to the reigning Sovereign has always been paid.

With the Foot Guards at last motionless again, the moment arrives for the mounted men of the Sovereign's Escort to pay *their* tribute, first walking the four sides of the Parade, then trotting, plumes bobbing above glittering helmets and cuirasses, orders conveyed by gracefully extended swords, and the Massed Mounted Band playing spendidly equestrian music throughout.

Their performance concluded, the National Anthem played a last time, they leave Horse Guards Parade, wait in the Mall for the Queen Mother (who has departed unobtrusively, via Whitehall and Trafalgar Square), follow her home, and take up their post on Constitution Hill, adjacent to Buckingham Palace. To which the Queen, riding at the head of her marching Guardsmen, now returns.

Arrived there, she takes the salute, from the centre gate, first of her Foot Guards (less those who will remain, as the New Queen's Guard, to relieve the Old Queen's Guard) then of those from her mounted Escort who are about to go on duty at Horse Guards, next of the Royal Horse Artillery (who, at eleven o'clock, in Hyde Park, have fired a forty-one gun salute) and finally of her Sovereign's Escort.

This done, she turns, rides across the forecourt between her Old and New Queen's Guards, passes under the Archway, dismounts and makes her way up to the balcony to acknowledge the Royal Air Force's fly-past at precisely one o-clock. For another year, the Birthday Parade is over and the crowds go home. That afternoon the Guards who entertained them will resume their normal duties.

2 *Attention to Detail*

I T W I L L surprise no-one to learn that all those who participate in the Birthday Parade prepare for it most rigorously. Accomplished horsewoman though she is, the Queen trains for weeks in the riding school at Buckingham Palace, while her Household troops practise just as arduously on barrack squares, on dawn marches over the actual course and at several full-dress rehearsals, the video tapes of which are discussed by everyone from the Major General, who is all powerful, to the Garrison Sergeant Major, who is all knowing.

These discussions are called De-briefs, and the one held immediately after the First Rehearsal is the most revealing of them all. 'In general terms,' remarked the Major General of the 1975 occasion, 'a very fair parade, a much better first rehearsal, in fact, than last year's.'

Glancing round the table at the splendidly uniformed adjutants who would pass on his comments to their respective battalions, and recognizing the impassive expression of men determined to die with dignity, he then began the executions.

'But no better than very fair! The Sovereign's Escort rather held us up at the Palace, and coming down the Mall they were weaving horribly. Perhaps'— looking directly at the Blues and Royals adjutant—'it could be filtered back to them that they really must keep their dressing and line. And once they arrived at Horse Guards, they took an awful time dressing, which is bad from the point of view of the rhythm of the parade as a whole, so do please tell everyone to get a move on.'

He looked at his notes before continuing. 'One hates to single *any*one out for criticism, but it's what we're here for, and *your* Guard'—looking at an adjutant at the end of the table—'were awful. They seemed to get into the most frightful flap and panic. Perhaps,' solicitously, 'there's difficulty hearing the Field Officer?'

The Field Officer being a Lieutenant Colonel, the adjutant concerned was not about to accuse him of inaudibility; but it was the Field Officer himself who answered the question.

'I think that at that point the Massed Band may have been playing just a little too loudly,' he murmured.

The Senior Director of Music, a major, hastened to volunteer to play more quietly at that point in future.

'*Would* you?' begged the Major General.

'Of course, sir,' promised the Major.

The Major General made a few more observations, as perceptive as they were succinct, then passed the commentary on to the Brigade Major (who is, of course, another Lieutenant Colonel) with the final remark, '*He* will deal with the more

The Irish Guards march past H.M. the Queen at the Birthday Parade

detailed points: I'll just repeat that it was very fair. I won't say good; but after the next rehearsal, it will, I'm sure'—smiling menacingly—'be very good.'

Once again the videotape was run; and the Brigade Major's comments were clinical and cruel. 'Seven and Eight Guards there, too many men looking about . . . When marching, men *must* swing their arms. So must officers. Otherwise— stop the film there—otherwise they look—see *him*—like bloody ponces . . . The Queen Mother's coach arrived a good thirty seconds late . . . And at this point, yes, there it is, *those* Guardsmen were blatantly asleep . . . That drum major's staff just ruined everything; and there's a drummer in there—go back, will you. Thank you. Yes, a drummer in there, one file in from the Queen, who simply can*not* march.'

And so it went on, with gentlemanly venom, until the Brigade Major exploded, 'Just *look* at that. That gap is awful.'

'I'm afraid,' explained an adjutant, 'that was someone who'd fainted, sir, right at the beginning.'

No further mention was made of the gap or of the Guardsman who had caused it by fainting; but the march past itself was dismissed as 'not good'—partly because the drums were too slow to break everyone from a slow to a quick march, partly because too many Guardsmen were looking down as they came into line after forming ('and in bearskins it's disastrously noticeable,') and partly because of those who led them. Of them the Brigade Major said icily, '*Bloody* officers!'

Back with their battalions, the various adjutants passed on the points made at the de-briefing.

'There are all sorts of anti-fainting devices,' the Foot Guards were told. 'Wriggle your toes, flex your knees, avoid tight bearskins, and think what the R.S.M.'ll do to you if you do faint.'

'Generally better than last year's first rehearsal,' the Household Cavalry were told, 'but there are still one or two who think they can get away with anything.'

'Officers' sword drill was not up to scratch . . . Wheeling round the Wedding Cake'—a Household colloquialism for Queen Victoria's big, white circular memorial in front of the Palace—'divisions must keep as far out as possible . . . Going down the Mall, the left-hand file failed to line themselves up, which shouldn't be too difficult, even for them, with the pavement to guide them. As it was, the Major General said we were "weaving horribly", which didn't exactly delight Silver Stick, who was displeased enough already because all the horses, according to him, were bad news.

'To revert to the Mall, each division was weaving in a rather ghastly way . . . At Horse Guards the Band *must* fit into its alloted space, with every man closing up to a six inch interval, otherwise the following divisions won't have enough room. They didn't today. . . .

'A few good points. There was very little fidgeting; only two troopers were seen reaching for their helmets. And although that's two too many, it's an improvement.

'The walk was a little too slow, the trot a little too fast. And returning from Horse Guards there were no criticisms, so I presume it was all right. Now . . . any questions?'

'Yes,' said the Director of Music. 'Could the divisions behind us leave a bigger gap between themselves and us?'

'You mean they rode too quickly?' the adjutant enquired.

'Actually,' interrupted one of the Division Commanders, 'the Band rode dreadfully slowly.'

'The Band,' retorted the Director of Music, 'can proceed no faster than the Royals and the Brigade Major who follows them.'

'Is anyone suggesting,' enquired the adjutant blandly, 'that the Royals be either overtaken or asked to get a move on?' No one, it seemed, was suggesting that. 'Then perhaps the Band will ride as quickly as possible and the divisions will follow as slowly as possible?'

Everyone nodded, allowing the adjutant to bring his de-briefing to an elegant conclusion. 'The Foot Guards,' he reminded, 'take enormous pains to get themselves word and movement perfect. It is up to us not just to do as much as they, but to do better: in fact, to show that touch of class that distinguishes us from them. That's all.'

Looking decidedly smug about their distinguishing touch of class, the officers and N.C.O.'s of the Sovereign's Escort adjourned, while, half a mile away, at Chelsea Barracks, the Massed Band of the five regiments of Foot Guards rehearsed yet again the seventeen tunes and the complicated drill that were to be their contribution to the Birthday Parade. As they performed the spin wheel, watching Guardsmen (for whom drill holds few terrors) shook their heads in wonder.

Just to prove that it was no fluke, the Massed Band repeated the manoeuvre it has made peculiarly its own; and the watching Guardsmen departed, lest their cherished illusion that all Household bandsmen are idiots be destroyed forever.

Eventually the rehearsals stop, because the day of the Parade itself has dawned. And with the dawn arise those who must travel to London from distant Pirbright and Caterham. They do half an hour's P.T. (which will wake them up and move their bowels), eat a substantial breakfast, shower, shave, dress and leave by coach at 7.15 a.m. They take their dress uniforms and bearskins with them. Their capes follow in another vehicle. Should it rain in London, every man will miraculously receive his cape in time to save his uniform.

Those performing at Horse Guards go to Chelsea Barracks; those due to line the Mall go to Wellington Barracks; and both detachments arrive at 8.25. All are

Everyone, including the Queen, rehearses assiduously for the Birthday Parade

offered tea or orange squash before they change. Once in their dress uniforms they are issued with barley sugar. At 9.45, Number Eight Guard marches out of Chelsea Barracks, heading for Horse Guards, led by its regimental band. Every two minutes, another Guard will set off, its band at its head. Thirty-seven minutes after its departure each Guard will arrive at Horse Guards, where its markers await it.

At 9.58, the street-lining troops march out of Wellington Barracks, so that they can all be posted down the Mall by 10.15. Not infrequently half of them will be recruits from the training depot at Pirbright standing in for those Guardsmen who are attending to some disagreeable emergency overseas. These recruits will have rehearsed their role dawn after dawn (so as to leave their normal daily curriculum intact). Pretending that Brunswick Road, Pirbright, is the Mall, they will have marched to it and lined it every morning for weeks; and many a driver will have been mystified to see several hundred 'guardsmen' presenting arms to him. He would have been even more mystified to learn that to them he represented either the Queen or the Queen Mother. On the day itself, however, as they line the Mall, the rookies will perform as faultlessly as the Guardsmen who leaven their ranks.

At 10.22, Number Eight Guard will fall in on its mark at Horse Guards Parade. By 10.30 all the Foot Guards will have fallen in, and the five Regimental Bands that led them will have coalesced into one Massed Band.

They will all now stand motionless (except for invisible toe wriggling and knee-flexing) for about twenty minutes, when some of them, on the west side, will have the good fortune to swing backwards to form the corridor through which the Queen Mother and her Royal relatives will pass, then swing forward again to close the line. The rest must content themselves with presenting arms.

Another wait, then, till the Queen, accompanied by Princes and V.I.P.'s, arrives. As the last of her Mounted Escort nudges his way into position across the road from the Foot Guards on the west side, the Queen reaches the Archway and turns to face her assembled Household troops. The clock strikes eleven and the Anthem is played.

Then comes the Queen's inspection of every man, on foot or mounted, on the parade. It takes time; and the business of the Colour Escort receiving the Colour from the Regimental Sergeant Major, then trooping it, after which the Foot Guards march past the Queen, first in slow and then in quick time, seems interminable to the motionless mounted men of the Sovereign's Escort.

Who also had got up at dawn, to have breakfast, then saddle their horses and attach the bit and the brass headstall, the bright chain, the irons and leathers, the stirrup bosses and the packing that goes over the saddle and under the voluptuous sheepskin.

This done, their horses groomed, they had dressed, pulling on the buckskin breeches that are kept spotless with shoe whitener, then the blue webbing sword belt, and the tunic (red for the Life Guards, dark blue for the Blues and Royals) which conceals the sword belt.

The back of the cuirass was put on next, and laced to the front, brass scales over the shoulder linking front to back securely.

Then enormous trees were taken out of huge, thigh-length, beeswaxed, glossy jack boots, and feet and legs thrust home. Spurs were attached with a chain under the instep and a leather strap across it.

A white cross-belt was secured over the left shoulder, round the front of the cuirass, under the right shoulder. Hands were sheathed in stiff white gauntlets with wide cuffs reaching almost to the elbow.

Then, taking their plumes (white, and onion-shaped at the top for Life Guards; red for the Blues and Royals) out of their protective bags, they attached them to the spike on top of their helmets, and each man carefully placed his helmet on his head so that the centre of its rim lay precisely on the bridge of his nose, the scales of his chin-strap snugly under his lower lip (if he was a Life Guard) or under the point of his chin (if he was a Blue and Royal) and the strands of his plume fell evenly past each ear and round the back of his neck.

By this time, lashed into cuirasses, poured into buckskins and wedged into jack-boots, they had been able to move only with difficulty; but affixing scabbards and swords to the white leather loops that hang from their concealed blue webbing belts, they had waddled down to the barrack square, clambered on to mounting blocks and hoisted themselves into the snug groove of their built-up sheepskins. All that had then remained was their inspection.

Which was endless, horses and their ornamentation receiving as much attention as the troopers. But eventually they had ridden out of their Knightsbridge Barracks and clattered magnificently to Hyde Park Corner, jingled down Constitution Hill, circumnavigated the Wedding Cake and escorted the Queen to Horse Guards—where now, it seemed, the Foot Guards intended marching forever.

Suddenly, though, the Foot Guards are still, their once immaculate boots sheened with dust, a breeze from St. James's Park ruffling their black bearskins (but cooling them in their thick scarlet tunics not at all) and their faces flushed. They are not finished, however. Now *they* must endure the ammoniac dust and clatter of the Household Cavalry. Then they must march the Queen home; and finally—those of them not so unfortunate as to have immediately to mount guard at the Palace—they must march back to Chelsea.

Chins jutting beneath metal straps, eyes blinking beneath the bearskin's fringe, they hiss uncharitable asides about the Cavalrymen; and, when it's over, march back to the Palace, behind the Queen, in lines so impeccable that no onlooker could guess that each weary man is aware only of the rank and corporate stench of his comrades.

Arrived at the Palace, and the last march past acknowledged, the Queen is escorted to the Glass Screen in the quadrangle beyond the archway. Dismounting, she vanishes inside; and footmen appear, bearing silver salvers, on which are carrots for the horses.

For the men, however,—the Guardsmen and Troopers who provided the morning's marvellous spectacle—there are no carrots. Often in recent years their officers have suggested that there should be (or rather, that there should be beer and some kind of celebration) but the Regimental Sergeant Majors have invariably rejected the idea out-of-hand.

The job of protecting the Sovereign never ceases, they have always pointed out. The Birthday Parade is just part of that job. When it's done, there's the rest of the daily job still to be done. So back to Chelsea march the Guardsmen, back to Knightsbridge ride the Sovereign's Escort, back to Pirbright and Caterham in coaches drive those stationed out of town, and back to ordinary duties go they all.

But they are not merely accomplished public performers, these men of the Household Division, and many of their duties are far from ordinary. The role they have

A Drummer brushes down his ceremonial uniform, whilst dressed in rather unceremonial denims

just played and the duties they are about to perform have been evolving for more than three hundred years; there is much about them that is paradoxical; and all of them today are as professional as their officers in Wellington's time were dilettante.

Perhaps the best way to illustrate the colossal span of the Guardsman's history is to note that the first new weapon of war he used was the bayonet, which replaced the pike, while one of the most recent is an electronically-guided, solid-fuel missile fired from the belly of an armoured vehicle and capable of destroying an enemy tank.

Perhaps the best way to illustrate the paradoxical nature of the Household Division is to remark that not only did General Monck, the man whose political initiative made possible its creation, serve Cromwell most ably, he also led his Coldstream regiment so brilliantly against Bonnie Prince Charlie's supporters at the Battle of Dunbar that the *Lyfe Guards of Foot* (who subsequently became the Scots Guards) were comprehensively defeated.

No less paradoxically, the cavalry regiment that eventually became the Blues was originally formed (at the behest of Cromwell's Council of State) by Sir Arthur Heselrigg, whose attempted arrest, along with that of four other Parliamentarians, precipitated the Civil War. Known as Heselrigg's Lobsters, because of the shape of their helmets, the regiment fought Charles I with zest, passed to the command of

James Berry (who gave it a blue standard and a blue uniform to match) and enforced Cromwell's bleak republicanism with the utmost zeal. Due to be disbanded along with the rest of the Model Army upon the restoration of Charles II, it was resurrected after the revolt of the so-called Fifth Monarchy Men in 1661.

Perhaps the best way to demonstrate that it is most inadvisable to generalise about the Guards is to remark that the Scots Guards—conceded even by themselves to be the least whimsical of all the Household regiments—have had as their mascots over the centuries not only dogs (which is normal for the British) but a monkey (which is peculiar for anyone) and two cows called Bella and Bertha (which must surely be unique).

And perhaps the best way to illustrate how deeply the Household Division is rooted in history is to reflect on the fact that its Foot and Horse Guard components (formally united as recently as 1950) have, since 1660, been both ally and foe on the field of battle to France, Holland, Spain, Austria, Prussia, Russia, the United States of America, Italy, Egypt and Cyprus. Probably there are others. Certainly what is now known as the Household Division has fought both for and against more countries than it has merely opposed or supported. Indeed, of all the world's continents, Australia appears to be the only one in which it has not yet performed as a belligerent. But the Division is still little more than three centuries old, and Australia is even younger, so doubtless by the time each has reached maturity that omission will have been rectified. For Australia's sake, and also for that of the Sovereign, who will certainly still be Colonel in Chief of the one and very probably Head of State of the other, it is to be hoped that, when it happens, the two will be allies, not foes.

3 The Birth of the Guards

SOME TIME late in 1659 General George Monck, who commanded a compact but efficient force at Coldstream, on the Scottish River Tweed, conceived the idea of marching to London and restoring to Parliament the authority so long usurped from it by the late Oliver Cromwell and his Model Army. In so doing he became the father of today's Household Division—which, to those who believe in the influence of heredity, explains much about their subsequent temperament and behaviour.

George Monck started his military career after varying perods of service as a courtier with Charles I, a sailor, a soldier of fortune and finally, in 1642, as a colonel in the Earl of Leicester's Regiment in Ireland suppressing one of its incessant rebellions.

He was thirty-three years old after a year's service in Ireland and, having enjoyed a considerable military success there, must have been somewhat surprised, on his return to England, in 1643, to be arrested on suspicion of disloyalty to Charles I.

Or perhaps he was not surprised. Aged seventeen he had sought sanctuary in the Navy to escape prosecution for beating up the Under Sheriff of Devon; next he had served in the Dutch army as a mercenary; and history fills in few of the details, and none of his politics during those formative, unorthodox years. He may well have been thoroughly disloyal to his king and his subsequent career can certainly be taken as proof of his disloyalty (or equally of his loyalty) to all the protagonists of those tumultuous times.

Be that as it may, he persuaded the king that he was not disloyal and returned to service in the Royal Army until captured by Cromwell's Roundheads. Accused by them of disloyalty to Parliament, he was confined to the Tower for two years.

But was then released by Parliament and given the command of some Scottish troops in Ulster, where he enjoyed further military successes against the Irish until his force defected in favour of the imprisoned king. In spite of which Cromwell decided to give him yet another command, declaring him to be 'an honest general' and 'a simple hearted man.'

Monck having been about as simple hearted in 1650 as was Admiral Canaris during World War II, Cromwell can only be deemed a poor judge of men—the more so since his subordinates had vehemently protested the proposed appointment, their spokesman exclaiming, 'What! To betray us? We took him at Nantwich prisoner. We'll have none of him.' But the newly appointed Lord Protector, having just beheaded Charles I, felt strong enough to ignore their protests and gave Monck command of a regiment on the Scottish border.

This regiment Monck led to stunning effect in the battle of Dunbar which virtually destroyed the Scots' capacity even to resist Cromwell's cheerless authority any longer, let alone to restore Charles II. Monck then mopped up the last centres of Scottish resistance, at Stirling and Dundee, and Cromwell obliterated the rest of Charles II's supporters at Worcester.

His loyalty to the regicide army at last beyond dispute, Monck was appointed a General of the Fleet—to help fight Cromwell's only effective enemy, the formidable Dutch Navy. Probably no worse than other admirals of his day, Monck was certainly more military, his best remembered naval order being, 'Wheel to the right— Charge!' Commented a subservient speaker of the House of Commons, however, 'His natural sagacity supplied the place of practical experience, and his valour matched the sullen desperation of the Dutch Admirals.'

'In fact,' his enemies demur, 'he very nearly lost his ship in the first severe gale.'

In 1654, Scotland having ungratefully rejected the delights of her enforced union with Cromwell's England and begun another revolt, Monck found himself back on terra firma. His subjugation of the Scottish revolt was pitiless; his soldiers came to be feared and hated.

The Lord Protector died late in 1658 and General Monck's loyalty either to Cromwell's useless son or to Parliament's discredited Rump must have begun to waver the moment he got news of what Pepys described as 'the joyfullest funeral I ever saw, for there was none that cried but dogs.'

The fact that the troops attending Richard Cromwell at the Proclamation of his succession to the Protectorship were pelted with vegetables by Oxford's normally timid academics can have done nothing to bolster Monck's ebbing Republicanism. And the outbreaks of violence in London following Richard Cromwell's early abdication of power must positively have spurred him to action; for by January 1, 1660, he was leading his two regiments—one of Foot, the other of Horse—to London, to repress its rioters, restore order and, as he put it, 'avert the perpetuation of arbitrary government by the sword.'

This publicly asserted intent of Monck's to make England's Model Army—then the most impressive in Europe—the servant rather than the master of what had for years been an impotent Parliament had not been universally acclaimed by those he commanded; but removing the dissidents (five company commanders, three corporals and a gunsmith) from his regiment, he had nevertheless confidently led his 4,500 men south across the Tweed.

Marching steadily upon London he did not, however, proclaim any of the Royalist motives later attributed to him. At York, on the contrary, he publicly caned an officer who had declared, 'General Monck will at last let the King upon us,' and at Leicester he went even further, emphatically denouncing any who might even attempt to restore the monarchy. But all the time he marched relentlessly on London at the head of a small army that commanded universal admiration, one spectator reporting, 'The Foot had the best arms and were the likeliest men that ever I saw.'

Arrived in London, where his Foot Regiment was dubbed the Coldstream, Monck became the most powerful man in England. He led a force strong enough to control the city and restore order; that force was wholly loyal to him, and not a little fond of him; and Parliament was delighted to be recalled by him. No-one was likely even to gainsay him, still less to challenge him.

Nevertheless he allowed Parliament to make the first overt moves toward the restoration of the monarchy, although it is probable that he had for some time been corresponding with the exiled king. Once Parliament *had* moved, however, he lost no time in writing to Charles and convincing him that he should return to the throne on Parliament's terms, to become king of a Protestant country governed by Parliament rather than Palace.

★　　★　　★

General Monck, whose march on London ended the Commonwealth, made inevitable the restoration of the Monarchy, and set the scene for the birth of the Household Cavalry and the Brigade of Guards (Engraved by W. J. Fry after the original by Sir Peter Lely)

Charles had been on many despairing journeys since he had been obliged to flee first to the Scilly Isles, then to Jersey and finally to Paris to escape the Roundheads who were pursuing his father and all of the Royal family.

In Paris he had joined his mother, studied for two years and organised an abortive invasion of England. In 1649, advised of his father's impending doom, he had sent Parliament a piece of paper on which was nothing but his signature, above which, he had let it be known, England could insert any terms it wished if only his father's life would be spared. But to no avail. His father had been executed and even though Scotland and parts of Ireland and the Channel Islands had subsequently proclaimed him their new king—even though he was in fact *crowned* Scotland's king at Scone on 1 January, 1651—it had all come to nought when his army was decimated by Cromwell's in September, 1651.

Escaping capture then by such unregal exploits as hiding up a tree, he had made his way via Brighton to France, whence he and his advisers had plotted endlessly to procure Cromwell's assassination.

Far from succumbing to these machinations, however, Cromwell had negotiated an alliance with France, as a result of which Charles had been obliged to flee first to Germany and then to Belgium.

In 1656, at Bruges, he had formed those who had followed him into exile into the nucleus of a regiment of Guards. In 1659, he had unsuccessfully sought the help of France and Spain in mounting yet another invasion force. In 1660 General Monck had written to him and persuaded him to issue a declaration that he would never be so contemptuous of Parliament's authority as his late father had been. In anticipation of his return to England he had meanwhile appointed others of those who had gone into exile with him as the officers of three troops of Horse Guards. The Declaration of Breda having been accepted by Parliament, he had been proclaimed King of England; and on 26 May 1660 he had landed at Dover—there to be greeted by none other than General Monck 'with all imaginable love and respect.'

★   ★   ★

Charles was understandably delighted to be escorted from Dover to a joyful London by the General whose Coldstreamers he described as conspicuous for their 'beauty, discipline and martial appearance.' He at once acknowledged his debt of gratitude to Monck by awarding him the then colossal grant of £7,000 a year, appointing him Captain-General of the Army and creating him Baron Monck, Earl of Torrington and Duke of Albemarle.

The King's next and very willing step was to obey Parliament's request that he disband entirely the Model Army that had defeated his father's forces, made possible his father's execution and thwarted each of his own attempts to recapture his father's throne. Armies, Parliament insisted, were 'inconsistent with the happiness of every nation', and the new king was inclined to agree, the more so since his Treasury at that time contained only £11.2.10.

But before the final stages of that dismantling process could be effected, another revolt broke out in London the avowed aim of which was to 'bind the kings of the earth in chains and their nobles with links of iron'. It was Monck's two Regiments of Horse and Foot that promptly crushed this disagreeable uprising—in appreciation of which, having been mustered on Tower Hill, on 4 February 1661, and ordered to lay down their arms as Republican troops, the Regiment of Foot were then ordered to take them up again 'as an extraordinary guard to His Royal Person, whom God long preserve in health and happiness'.

At that moment, the Coldstream Regiment was reborn. Though subsequently christened the Second Regiment of Foot Guards, Coldstream is the only name they have ever used, and because they were created a regiment by Cromwell in 1650—as opposed to the First Foot Guards, who were created a regiment by Charles II only in 1656—*Nulli Secundus* is the motto they later assumed to ensure that the First Foot (or Grenadiers) never forgot it.

For the moment, though, Charles II found himself defended only by the Duke of Albemarle's Coldstreamers, the three Troops of Horse Guards he had formed in Holland, and the Royal Regiment of Guards he had created at Bruges. Alarmed by those who would have 'bound him in chains', he demanded from an equally alarmed Parliament an army of loyal but trained men to uphold his authority.

Parliament thereupon set aside £123,1150.0.8 a year to augment his existing troops with another Foot Regiment, a sufficiency of garrisons round the country and a Regiment of Horse to be commanded by the Earl of Oxford. That regiment—originally raised by Sir Arthur Heselrigg—had been recently disbanded, along with the rest of the Model Army. It now remustered as the Royal Horse Guards, presumably wearing the blue uniforms of its republican days, (there are no accounts to be found for the purchase of new uniforms anywhere in the regiment's archives) and, either because of that, or because of the Earl of Oxford's colours, or for some other reason long since forgotten, its eight Troops were promptly dubbed 'The Blues'.

In 1661 the Duke of Albemarle resumed his career as an admiral, sailing with Prince Rupert and engaging the Dutch fleet, who treated him with so little awe that he soon 'had all his tackle taken away by chain and his breeches to the skin were shot off'. Ever a practical and adaptable man, he had the sense to leave 'all things to the conduct and skill of' Prince Rupert. Thereafter, confessing himself to be 'no seaman', he confined his interests to those of a soldier and Captain General.

These were not inconsiderable, as the terms of the King's appointment make resoundingly clear. Until the day he died in 1670, Monck was 'Captain General of all our armies and land forces and men whatsoever, now levyed or raised, in or out of our realms of England, Scotland and Ireland, or dominion of Wales'.

With these forces it would be his duty 'to resist and withstand all invasions, tumults, seditions, conspiracies and attempts . . . to be made against our person, state, safety, crown and dignity'.

Armed with almost despotic powers, Albemarle did not fail his king, seeing to it that there were no invasions of England's soil, and that the Guards became immediately responsible for ensuring that there were as few tumults, seditions and conspiracies as possible.

Not content with this, it was also at Albemarle's instigation that five hundred men were raised in 1664 for *sea service* as part of the Coldstream Foot Guards. These five hundred were the founders of the corps which subsequently became the Royal Marines.

Also in 1664 a detachment of Foot Guards achieved a local victory overseas the effects of which remain incalculable. They seized from the Dutch the small settlement now known as New York. Had they not, would not the French most certainly have done so shortly afterwards as they waged endless war against William of Orange? Had the *French* captured New York, would the English settlements in seventeenth-century America even have survived, let alone flourished and eventually rebelled? Had they not . . .?

Useless to speculate; and yet probably not too much to say that the detachment despatched from the Captain General's Foot Guards to seize New York was a sine qua non of the United States of America of today—and that that depended upon Honest George Monck leading his Coldstreamers all the way from Scotland to London in the first few weeks of 1660.

4   *The Growing-up of the Guards: 1660–1691*

MONCK, SAY his critics, was an opportunist of the worst kind, guilty of 'dissimulation and insincerity', because he made it a prerequisite of his support for any restoration of the monarchy that he be granted the Lieutenancy of Ireland and because he was also guilty of regicide.

His apologists deny all these charges—none so shrilly as his official biographer of 1723 who protested that it was 'during Colonel Monck's employment *in Ireland* was committed the execrable murder upon the person of the late King; an action of so great Impudence and Villainy as can find no parallel in past ages'.

Of Monck's very effective soldiering on behalf of the Lord Protector, his bio-

Beating up for recruits (By Robert Dighton, 1781)

grapher explains, 'though he served the Party (he was) disposed of in an employment (in Ireland) of so much distance and privacy as he could hardly know of, much less be concerned in so great a guilt as was the murder of that excellent King'.

Perhaps; yet more probably—since eleven years later, equally distanced, he knew so well what was happening in London that he felt himself constrained to march upon it—he was as involved in the murder of King Charles I as any other of the colonels who fought with Cromwell.

And perhaps Monck's chameleon-like ability to assume the differing colours of one cause after another was bequeathed to the Guards, subsequently enabling them, almost without a tremor, to transfer their allegiance from Stuart James to Dutch William, from English Anne to German George, and from mad George to his unloving son the Prince Regent.

Perhaps Monck was guilty less of disloyalty as an individual than of professionalism as a soldier; and perhaps today's Household Division has merely inherited his professionalism, matching *his* willingness to go to war on foot or by ship with its own willingness to enter battle by parachute, helicopter, armoured carrier, tank,

Land Rover or Shanks's pony.

Demonstrably it has inherited the role Monck played when, as the King's most trusted officer, he moved into the cockpit apartments of Whitehall Palace, with his regiment quartered conveniently nearby. Household troops have mounted guards for the Sovereign's person and palaces at Whitehall, and have been quartered close to it, from that day to this.

Protected in London by his First Regiment of Foot Guards (which had been created round the nucleus formed at Bruges in 1656), by the Coldstreamers (who had become the Second Regiment of Foot Guards) and by the three skeletal troops of Horse Guards he had created in Holland in 1660 (and fleshed out after his Restoration with six hundred Private Gentlemen), Charles no doubt felt safe enough in his capital.

With the Blues at Oxford, the reincarnated Scottish Foot Guards at Edinburgh and Dunbarton, a fourth Troop of Horse Guards in Scotland and a scattering of small garrisons around England, he also no doubt felt safe enough within his three kingdoms. But he never felt strong enough—let alone rich or belligerent enough— to wage either a religious war against Catholic France or an aggressive war against Protestant Holland. So he appeased the one and engaged the other almost entirely at sea while enjoying the pleasures of being England's full-time resident king.

The Duke of Albemarle died in 1670, leaving Charles more than ever secure. In the remote north, Scottish Foot Guards had subdued the troublesome Covenanters; the First and Second Regiments of Foot Guards were policing London and England's more important southern towns and ports; and apart from forming three troops of mounted *infantrymen*, called the Horse Grenadier Guards, Charles was content to leave his new Regular Army as Monck had bequeathed it.

★   ★   ★

In the Middle Ages armies had consisted of armoured knights on horseback and their humble followers, who came on foot, carrying bows and arrows. The knight provided his own horse and armour, the common soldier his own bow and arrows. To bear a knight in armour, a horse needed to be bigger and stronger than those bred in England, so they were imported from Ireland and France. To find the most skilful bowmen in Europe, a warring king needed look no further than the nearest English village.

All this had changed, however, when the musket displaced the bow as the foot soldier's weapon of war. For one thing the vulgar musket ball destroyed the armoured knight's patrician invulnerability; for another, a musket's cost was beyond the purse of the English rustic required to bear it. Instead of part-time, self-supporting, feudal armies, therefore, there developed professional regiments of cavalry and foot soldiers, each of which was raised, equipped and paid by its colonel, who made it available to the king, who paid him a nominal sum per man for its services.

With the arrival of such professionalism came the demand for higher standards; and much as twentieth century tennis and golf have improved immeasurably under professionalism's influence, so did seventeenth-century soldiering. The rustic, villager or townsman who joined a foot regiment joined it for life and was transformed by it into an efficient fighting machine. Drills were created that made it possible to manoeuvre him swiftly and without confusion on the battlefield, and keep him steady when attacked. He was so effectively trained by non-commissioned officers, almost as brutish as himself, that not even the fact that he was led by officers who were completely untrained could destroy his efficiency. And acting corporately, as a company under a captain, or as a regiment under a colonel, he had become, by the time Oliver Cromwell took him over, a quite formidable foot soldier and a dashing cavalryman.

Having decapitated the King and abolished the concept of monarchy, Cromwell had welded all the colonels' regiments into a professional army which controlled England, Wales, Scotland and Ireland for eleven years. His troops in England and Wales numbered 14,400, and cost him £218,425.4.0 a year: his troops in Scotland numbered 10,640, and cost him £195,451.18.0 a year.

His men were fined a shilling for swearing (a shilling being more than the thriftiest of them would be likely to save in months; exclamations as mild as 'Upon my life' being regarded as swearing). Cromwell himself, of course, was much given to the use of phrases like 'In the bowels of Christ'; but that was not swearing, or, if it was, it ceased to be upon the lips of the Lord Protector. 'By God,' on the lips of a private, however, was sufficient to earn him a severe punishment.

As clean mouthed then as he was ill paid he could escape the army only by a court martial's discharge into the hands of the captain of a frigate, for use as a seaman; by request (which was seldom granted, but was a passport to any trade without the need to serve an apprenticeship if it were); or by disablement (in which case he would be treated at Ely House or the Savoy in London).

His rations were ample bread, or biscuit, and a quarter to half a pound of cheese a day; his uniform was stout, because it had to last a year unchanged; and his loyalty to his regiment was inexplicably profound.

For this reason alone, if not also for the sheer joy of putting the Puritan hell of Cromwell's regime forever behind him, he had experienced no difficulty in following his colonel into the camp of the restored monarchy; but Charles II distrusted the Colonels who had supported the man who had executed his father, so only Monck's regiment of Foot and another of Horse had survived intact from Cromwell's Model army.

The First Regiment of Foot Guards, the Second (or Coldstream) Regiment of

Foot Guards, the Horse Guards, the Horse Grenadier Guards and the Blues offered their soldiers neither an easier nor a harder life than had the Model Army. Soldiers still enlisted for life and they were still only paid sufficient a day to cover the deductions claimed for their daily upkeep.

At least, though, they could now swear, which they immediately began to do, shouting such frightful obscenities as *piss, a pox on it, strap me vitals* and *ods nigger noggers* with disgusting frequency. Less agreeably, when the King married Catherine of Braganza and received Tangier as part of his dowry, they were sent to Africa to defend it, wearing the same uniform as they had habitually worn in England. Constantly besieged, parboiled and homesick, they were delighted when the King decided that this was a portion of his dowry he could do without and four years later brought them home.

Small detachments were also sent to Virginia, towards which the English attitude was made abundantly clear when an official was urged to consider the colonists' souls. 'Souls!' he exploded. 'Damn their *souls*. Let them make *tobacco*.' Even less thought was given to the welfare of the Foot Guards despatched there for two years at a time, and it was a much hated posting.

For the most part, though, Charles kept his small army in England, quartering the bulk of his Foot Guards 'about the cities of London and Westminster,' sending small detachments of the rest to Berwick, Carlisle, Dover, Portsmouth, Harwich, Hull, Plymouth, Deal, Teignmouth, York, Windsor and Jersey, while scattering his Horse Guards round Canterbury, Reading, Salisbury, York, Uxbridge, Islington and Farnham. And so grateful was England to be rid of Cromwell's military rule that it allowed itself to be kept in order by these token garrisons.

For the soldiers, however, discipline was tight. 'No soldier,' ran an order of 3 November 1671, 'is to marry without the permission of his captain upon pain of being cashiered and losing the pay that might be due'—and was almost invariably overdue. And all the men and horse of the Horse Guards had to be billeted within trumpet sound of their Headquarters at Knightsbridge. Though a trumpet call at Knightsbridge could be clearly heard a mile away in Paddington, the implication was unmistakable—Charles expected to be protected, in London, at all times.

THE GUARDS, THEIR SOVEREIGN AND LONDON, 1660–1901

5   *Charles II*

THE LONDON in which Charles II created his Regiments of Foot and his Troops of Horse Guards was topographically the London of Queen Elizabeth, during whose reign its population had doubled to two hundred thousand and its narrow streets had been made muddier than ever by the introduction of the coach.

As early as 1174, Thomas à Becket's chaplain had complained of the 'immoderate drinking of foolish persons and the frequent fires' in London; and five centuries later neither defect had been remedied.

Nor had its susceptibility to the plague. In the three centuries before the Restoration, London suffered seventeen major outbreaks, some of which had lasted for years, all of which had savagely reduced the population. In 1603, 38,000 Londoners had perished, and in 1660 another 30,000. Plague would continue to visit London as late as the reign of Queen Victoria.

The capital, then, was not the safest of places in which a king might live—the more so since it had a reputation for taking violent dislikes to those who ruled there. Both Richard II and Queen Mary I had narrowly escaped death at the hands of an angry London mob, and even the Empress Matilda, the daughter of Henry I as well as wife to the Holy Roman Emperor, had been so hotly rejected when she returned to London to claim the English throne that she had fled the city in terror of her life.

Beloved (as Elizabeth was) or detested (as was James I) the sovereign lived in Whitehall. Until 1512, when it burnt down, the Royal residence was Westminster Palace, adjoining which Cardinal Wolsey had built a vast Thames-side house, extending hundreds of yards towards Charing Cross.

Named York Place the Cardinal's house was a ramshackle edifice of lath and plaster which stretched from the bank of the river (wider then than today) to Horse Guards Parade, but had only one entrance, Holbein Gate. It consisted of a warren of apartments and lent itself perfectly to Wolsey's intrigues. Eventually Henry VIII confiscated it, moved in and renamed it Whitehall Palace.

In 1531, probably because Whitehall was too damp and Hampton Court too distant, he began the construction of another palace (on the site of an ancient leper hospital) which became St. James's Palace. St. James's and Whitehall were to be London's only royal residences for a century and a half.

Upon the death of Elizabeth, the Tudor line came to an end and the English throne was offered to James VI of Scotland, the Stuart son of Mary Queen of Scots whom Elizabeth had had beheaded.

Mary's son came to London as James I, and London swiftly decided that it detested him. Where Elizabeth had bewitched, he repelled, particularly by isolating himself in Whitehall Palace with such gentlemen of his taste as his favourite, 'sweet Steenie'.

Told that Londoners wanted to see his face, he retorted, 'God's wounds, I will pull down my breeches and they shall also see my arse'; and London, though far from puritanical, liked him none the better for it.

It liked him even less for the fact that, to a city that had contained far more Dutchmen, Frenchmen, Italians, Spaniards and Portuguese than ever it did Scots (of whom, when Elizabeth died, there had been only forty) he had brought with him from Edinburgh such a horde of followers that Guy Fawkes was able to plead, in mitigation of his gunpowder plot, 'One of my objects was to blow Scotchmen back to Scotland'.

Though no one can deny that James was loathed by Londoners as a foul-mouthed Scottish recluse and sodomite, it must be admitted that, like Guy Fawkes, he could have made a strong plea of mitigation. His youthful father had been murdered begging those who were about to strangle him, 'Pity me, Kinsmen, for the sake of Jesus Christ, who pitied all the world'; his mother, having married one of the men responsible for his father's death, had been compelled to abdicate; and he, having been crowned King of Scotland when he was thirteen months old, had been brought up by Calvinists who had taught him that his mother was the murderess of his father and a Papist adulteress who had deserted him for the love of her accessory in murder.

He had grown to adolescence (among the ranks of what was arguably the most treacherous nobility in Europe) to be clever, small and unattractive. Emotionally insecure, he had found what he may well have thought was love in the arms of men. He had never seen his mother again, because Elizabeth had kept her captive until her eventual execution; and he had inherited Elizabeth's throne only because his great grandfather, Henry VII, had been her grandfather.

He ascended that throne not unmindful of the fact that princes were little safer in England than in Scotland (Elizabeth's father had put her mother to death) so that he may well have felt both emotionally and physically insecure in Whitehall. He was a wizened king of thirty seven who had sired two sons and a daughter by Anne of Denmark; and in future, whatever Londoners might say of him, he would give most of his time and affection to Steenie.

He died, unlamented, in 1625, his two legacies to posterity being an aviary on the far side of the park from St. James's Palace, and the Board of Trade. He was succeeded by Charles who, unlike his father, ate in public, was devoted to his wife, was a patron of the arts and an habitué of London's flourishing if bawdy theatre. In spite of this, Londoners liked him very little more than they had his father, because he had a Roman Catholic wife and constantly demanded large sums of money.

This Parliament almost invariably declined to give him—one of his few successful demands being, in 1642, for sufficient cash to raise a Royal Regiment of Scots, whose task it would be to suppress the rebels in Ireland. No more successful in his handling of foreign affairs, one of his few popular acts of diplomacy was the marriage of his sister to the Protestant Prince William II of Orange.

Bitterly opposed in all his ambitions by an unsympathetic populace and an obdurate Parliament, he eventually fled London and, raising his standard at Nottingham, precipitated a civil war. After an inconclusive action against the Parliamentary forces at Edgehill, he virtually lost the war when he advanced upon his disobedient capital and was shocked to see its people marching out in superior and defiant numbers to repel him.

Postponing the inevitable, he withdrew and eventually surrendered himself to the Scots—who subsequently abandoned him. Two years later the English beheaded him in Whitehall and the Scots crowned his son at Scone. His Royal Regiment of Scots, (now known as the Lyfe Guard of Foot) was virtually obliterated when Scotland fell into the hands of Cromwell's forces under the command of Monck.

Then followed the ten dreary years of the Protectorate: years during which Cromwell allowed himself to be called Highness, but declined to accept the throne; during which all of London's new and lively theatres were closed and Christmas Day was abolished; during which Cromwell died and his uninspiring son succeeded him; and during which Parliament's powers were, if anything, even less respected than they had been during the arbitrary reign of Charles I.

General Monck's march upon London having precipitated the return to England of Charles II, the capital greeted the King with the ringing of 'bow bells and all the bells in all the churches', not to mention, in a city constantly at risk from conflagration, bonfires by the hundred.

The new king was a witty, pleasure-loving bachelor of thirty, not at all prepared to die on the executioner's block as had his father and great grandmother. Monck's two regiments of Foot and Horse were therefore paraded and informed that, as of that moment, they had ceased to be troops in the country's pay. Then the Regiment of Foot was told that it was immediately to become an 'extraordinary Guard' to His Majesty.

'God save King Charles the Second,' they shouted, throwing their hats in the air, waving their ensigns, beating their drums and discharging their muskets.

Meantime, Monck's disbanded Regiment of Horse had been given to understand that positions as Private Gentlemen in the King's three troops of Horse Guards were available to its members for purchase. 'Most of them,' a journal of the times reported later, were 'well entertained by His Majesty for his Horse Guards'.

Six months later, the King ordered his one time Lyfe Guards of Foot to be re-raised in Scotland, there to garrison Edinburgh and Dunbarton. It would be mainly in London, though, that successive sovereigns would live; it was on Horse Guards Parade that all the Sovereign's Guards, Foot and Horse, would be mounted until 1841; and it is therefore in the London of Charles II that today's Household Division must be said to have been born.

In this London it was possible to hunt deer in Hyde Park (though gangs of footpads made it a dangerous sport), or to look down a grassy field from the Exeter Road (now Piccadilly) to St. James's Palace and beyond it to see nothing in the vista of grass and trees except Westminster Abbey and a glimpse of the Thames.

It was along the banks of the Thames, from Westminster to the Tower, close-packed, that most of London's 200,000 citizens lived, none of them much more than a mile from their king in Whitehall Palace, or from the Duke of York, his brother and heir, in St. James's Palace. From Whitehall the king used to walk through the Holbein Gate, across the parade ground that is used to this day for the Birthday Parade and into St. James's Park. Crossing that parade ground, he would see his grandfather's aviaries—known today as Birdcage walk—on his left, some ponds in the hollow before him, St. James's Palace on his right, and the trees of Hyde Park on the hilltop beyond. Dissatisfied with what he saw, he linked the ponds into a canal, on to which he introduced ducks and water fowl and even a pelican. Eternally energetic, he laid out a long pitch on which to play the fashionable French game of Paelle Maelle, which was a Gallic mixture of hockey and golf; and essentially gregarious, he opened his Royal garden to the pedestrian public.

He also reinstituted Christmas Day, re-opened London's theatres, (which promptly became bawdier than ever, even employing women to play female roles), revived the habits of swearing and gambling, and sired the first of his many bastards. An endearing rake and England's virtual dictator, he transformed society by his royal example and set his Guards a standard of amorality they were to sustain through fourteen consecutive reigns and abandon only in the twentieth century's halcyon days of an affluent London become even more permissive than they were accustomed to be themselves.

Charles II also set the precedent of those great ceremonies in which the sovereign stars while his Household troops play a corporate supporting role. In 1661 he used these troops as his Coronation escort. In 1664 he posted dismounted Life Guards, as they are still posted on Royal occasions, outside his Palace ballroom. In 1671 he used them, as sovereigns have used them ever since, to escort him to his State opening of Parliament.

For this latter piece of apparent ceremonial Parliament was far from grateful. King and Commons were still at loggerheads and 'if it were not for them,' complained Lord Shaftesbury of the escorting troops, 'we would go quickly down to Whitehall and obtain what terms we thought fit'. But Charles could afford to defy Parliament because he not only had his Foot and Horse Guards, he also had almost all the money he needed each year from Louis XIV of France. Since Louis wanted to over-run the States of Holland, and England wanted to steal Holland's American colony, Nieuw Nederland, Charles allowed his goodwill to be bought with Louis' gold.

Such pro-French, pro-Catholic and anti-Dutch diplomacy hardly endeared him to his fiercely protestant nephew, William III of Orange; but Charles, as devious as he was amoral, cared little about that. Let William one day marry his brother's daughter, Mary, and eventually, with her, succeed to the English throne: until then, he, Charles, would rule as a king should rule, and his Guards would keep him as safe in the thousand filthy rooms of Whitehall's spaniel-ridden Palace as a popular king should be.

Not that the king was always at Whitehall; he also liked to play tennis at Hampton Court or to relax either at Windsor Castle or in his squalid little 'palace' at Newbury —to each of which his Horse Guards would escort him, riding the big horses they had imported from Ireland and France, his Foot Guards having marched ahead from London, to protect him on his arrival.

Indeed, for the First Regiment of Foot Guards and the Coldstream, life was an almost endless march. Billeted in inns, taverns and coffee houses all over London, they had daily to march to wherever it was they were needed, be it Southwark, Lincoln's Inn Fields, Hampton Court, Hounslow, Dover or Portsmouth. Yet Charles II's Foot Guards were luckier than those of his successors: at least he spared them the interminable wars of the future, shamelessly appeasing France (by selling her Dunkirk, for example—augmenting the First Foot Guards with the Regiment once stationed there) and sensibly authorising his brother James, with Pepys, to re-build the Navy so that he could at least hold off, if not defeat, the aggressive Dutch.

Rather, he used his 'Household' troops (if one may so describe them in the absence of any other generic term) for a variety of non-belligerent purposes, moulding them, in the process, into a compact, professional, non-political army.

'You are to be careful,' he admonished his colonels in 1671, 'that your soldiers carry themselves civilly and duly pay for what they shall receive at their quarters.' To this end—and to cover every other of their expenses—his Foot Guards were paid ten pence a day, which was just fourpence more than Richard II had paid his archers three centuries earlier.

He was careful himself to appease popular opinion. Though he rarely ceased taking Louis XIV's gold and seriously contemplated becoming a Roman Catholic like his brother, James, he had no qualms about despatching James away from London whenever public feeling demanded it, and he positively fostered the popularity of his bastard son, the Duke of Monmouth, and his nephew, Prince William, both of whom were Protestants.

At the same time, he remained so convinced of the divine right of kings that he consistently refused to contemplate the possibility of William succeeding him to the throne instead of James, or of his bastard, whom he loved, ever coming to the throne at all; and, fond though he was of William, he did not hesitate to wage intermittent naval war against Holland in order to appease France.

Throughout all the years of these wheelings and dealings the king kept his Foot and Horse Guards close and assigned to them all those duties which today would be performed by the police and the fire brigade.

In 1674 the colonel of the Coldstream was ordered to send an officer and sufficient men to the theatre in Dorset Gardens 'whenever you shall think reasonable', so that 'no offence may be given to the spectators nor no affront to the actors'.

In those days of the new, covered, candle-lit theatres both audiences and actors behaved with great abandon. The king himself was said to have sired several of his bastards there. The celebrated Mrs. Davenport allegedly refused even to accompany the Earl of Oxford there unless first he married her—and only later learnt that she had not become a countess as she had thought because the noble Earl had used a kettle-drummer and a trumpeter from the Blues to play parson and clerk at his 'wedding'.

Presumably it was to ensure that the rest of the audience behaved better in the theatre than their king and their nobility that Charles ordered his Coldstream Guards to Dorset Gardens.

As well as being its vice squad, the Foot Guards of Stuart London were its firemen. During the Great Fire of 1666 they battled against what Pepys described as 'a most horrible malicious bloody flame' visible 'above forty miles roundabout' for days and nights under the brave direction of the King's brother, James. In 1676 £25 was distributed, as his Majesty's bounty, between 191 officers and men who fought a blaze at Southwark.

Elsewhere, much of the London destroyed ten years earlier had already been rebuilt, the genius of Christopher Wren shining bright among the speculators' shoddy houses and festering alleys. From Charing Cross a network of new roads provided the skeleton upon which would soon be overlaid the flesh of the West End. And everywhere were coaches—private coaches, hackney coaches and stage coaches.

London had thus become a bustling, boisterous city in which the great event of 1677 was the marriage of William of Orange—five foot six and a half inches tall, twenty-six years old, stooped, sickly and unfashionably dressed—to Princess Mary, five feet eleven inches tall, fifteen years old, statuesquely beautiful and heir to the throne that her father, James Duke of York, would one day inherit from his brother Charles II.

After contemplating her husband-to-be for the first time, the youthful Mary had promptly written to her closest friend, Frances Apsley, begging her to come to her so that 'I may have my bellyful of discourse with you'. And on the wedding day things had so little improved that Charles had attempted to enliven the occasion by urging William, bedded at last with his tearful bride, 'Now, nephew, to your work! Hey, St. George for England!'

Louis XIV was less cordial. Writing to James, he complained, 'You have given your daughter to my mortal enemy'—as, twelve years later (when daughter and husband ascended the throne from which they had driven King James) England was herself to discover.

Only one year later the English were shaken out of any complacency that they may have felt about Roman Catholicism when a Popish plot against the king was allegedly discovered and, in the ensuing hysteria, it was even claimed that either his Catholic brother or his Catholic wife had tried to poison him. For the next few weeks London lived in terror of a Papist coup and hundreds of innocent Catholics were flung into gaol. The king, it was then decided, from his rising to his going-to-bed, must never again be left unprotected; and, assigned this task, his Horse Guard Colonels were given the title of Gold and Silver Stick respectively. They retain it to this day.

Fresh problems now beset the king. Parliament sought to exclude Roman Catholics from ascending the throne, which would have deprived James of the right to succeed, and Charles defeated the Exclusionists only by 'banishing' his Papist brother yet again—this time to represent him in Scotland. Next the Whigs sought so to legislate that Charles's delightful but foolish bastard, Monmouth, would succeed to the throne rather than the Roman Catholic James or the Dutch Protestant

William. Charles ensured that the bill was defeated, promised Louis XIV that he would make England a Roman Catholic nation in return for three years' supply of gold, dissolved Parliament, recalled it to sit in Royalist Oxford, married off his Catholic brother's Protestant daughter, Anne, to the Protestant Prince George of Denmark, and finally—after the discovery of a plot by Monmouth to assassinate both himself and his brother—banished his bastard son to Europe, where he was amiably received by William of Orange.

It was the following February, as William taught Mary to ice skate in Holland, that Charles—after an evening spent 'gossiping' with three of his mistresses—suffered a stroke. Four days later, having secretly received the last rites of the Roman Catholic faith, he died. Devious to the end, he bequeathed to his brother James a race of subjects accustomed, as Evelyn recorded, to 'wanton peace, minding nothing but luxury, ambition, and to procure money for (their) vices'.

'I have only time to tell you,' James wrote immediately to William and Mary in Holland, 'that it has pleased God Almighty to take out of this world the king, my brother'. And advising that he had granted fresh commissions to every officer in the Army, he concluded, 'All the usual ceremonies were performed this day in proclaiming me king in the City and other parts'.

6 James II–William III and Mary

JAMES II's impact on London and the Guards was almost entirely negative. His religious inclinations were unpopular, his Tory supporters were disliked, his decision to reform the Court of 'swearing, drinking and wenching' was loathed, his renunciation of his own Protestant mistress was distrusted, and his surreptitious return to the arms of that same mistress, whom he promptly created a countess, was despised.

Not even his early brilliance as a moderate administrator, nor his undeniable patriotism, could blind his subjects to his bigoted Catholicism; and his later measures to ensure that his troops were housed and paid at anyone's expense but his own were positively detested. His swift suppression of Monmouth's impetuous revolt added nothing to his personal authority; and his desire for popularity lasted little longer than his Coronation. That, however, was undoubtedly splendid, each of the Foot Guard Regiments being richly but differently uniformed, their officers clothed in tunics of cloth of gold, or of crimson velvet embroidered with gold or silver, or of scarlet cloth buttoned down the breast. Their cuffs were heavy with silver plate and all of them wore the fashionable wide brimmed hat adorned with a flourish of white feathers.

The privates wore breeches of red broad cloth, stockings of red worsted and black hats whose brims were upturned and laced with gold galoons; and, as they marched, each regiment carried its colours, which were made of blue, white and crimson taffeta. From Covent Garden they proceeded down the Strand to Whitehall, and thence to Westminster, St. Margaret's and the Abbey, where the new king—escorted by his Horse Guards—was solemnly crowned.

In spite of this the exiled and youthful Duke of Monmouth almost immediately invaded England to challenge the right to the throne of the 'Popish usurper'; and James responded by sending against him two battalions of the First Guards, one battalion of the Coldstream Guards, a small number of mixed troops, seven hundred horse (which included detachments from the Horse and Horse Grenadier Guards, and all the Blues) and sixteen pieces of artillery.

Cautiously commanded by Lord Feversham, this disciplined force met Monmouth's untrained mob at Sedgmoor and, due largely to the verve of a First Guards officer called John Churchill, routed them. Monmouth was discovered hiding in a ditch, and was later slowly beheaded by a sadistic axeman on Tower Hill.

At the King's order, twenty-seven pounds was paid to five Foot Guards (two sergeants and three privates) in total discharge of any liability for the disabling wounds they suffered at Sedgmoor; but elsewhere James proved less generous. As if the macabre example of Monmouth's protracted beheading were not enough, he ordered all who had succumbed to Monmouth's charm to be hunted down. Three hundred peasant supporters at least were subsequently to be seen hanging from roadside gallows and market gibbets. Almost a thousand were deported to the West Indies. And 'Bloody Jeffreys' became so hated a household name that the king was suspected of having inspired him to a covert form of religious persecution.

This suspicion was in no way allayed by the king's reaction to Louis XIV's sudden decision to annihilate those Huguenots who were resident in France. As the slaughter started, Mary wrote from Holland, imploring her father's support for the principality of Orange, into which Huguenots by the thousand were fleeing, and into which Louis had already despatched his pitiless dragoons.

James intervened only briefly and unconvincingly; and when Louis wrote to him that he regarded Orange as his 'incontestably', James abandoned his daughter and son-in-law entirely, refusing, as he wrote, to declare war on Louis 'for a thing of such small importance'.

Worse—having provoked his army by appointing Catholic officers to it, and his Parliament by proroguing it—he now provoked his people by rejecting the Huguenot cause and ostentatiously espousing that of their persecutor. 'My resolution is taken,' he told them. 'It has become the fashion to treat kings disrespect-fully, and they must stand by each other.' The better to stand by Louis, James agreed to exclude Mary from succession to the English throne, allowed it to be rumoured that her sister Anne had promised to become a Roman Catholic, con-sidered the possibility of separating Ireland from England, suggested making his bastard son its Catholic king, and, throwing seven of his Protestant Bishops into the Tower, charged them all with sedition.

Perhaps alarmed by the hostility he had aroused, James had by now summoned half the Regiment of Scottish Foot Guards to London—where the two older English Regiments of Foot Guards had at once dubbed them 'The Kiddies'; issued all his Foot Guards with the bayonet that previously had been used only by their grenadier companies; and brought the Scottish Foot Guards onto the estab-lishment of the English Army—most of which he had scattered round billets at Devon, Windsor, Hampton Court, Deptford, Hounslow Heath, Holborn, Alders-gate Street, Fleet Street, the Savoy, Greenwich, Woolwich, and churches like St. Ann's, Westminster, St. Clement Dane's, St. Mary's, Savoy, St. Giles in the Field and St. Andrew's, Holborn.

Unfortunately for himself he had meantime decreed that all those upon whom his soldiers were billeted must not only feed them but also pay them; and day by day his unpopularity grew. Most of all, though, it was his devotion to Rome that his subjects detested.

As Count Gramont reported to Louis XIV, 'Among the many acts of folly he committed, not least was his going publicly to Papistical Ceremonials, by which he created universal alarm among his Protestant subjects.'

The Count further advised Louis that he had not thought James 'such a fool as to lose three kingdoms for *religion*'—for which heresy he was summarily com-mitted to the Bastille, where he was still languishing when the English king's second wife at last produced a son, so that the throne—long destined to pass to James's Protestant daughter, Mary—seemed suddenly to have become the chattel of a new Catholic dynasty.

William of Orange, however, was as unwilling to be denied his wife's expectations as he was terrified of the prospect of a Catholic England joining forces with a Catholic France against his own tiny Principality and the remaining states of Holland. He therefore decided to invade his father-in-law's triple kingdom, evict him from the throne and 'rescue the nation and the religion'.

No sooner had this invasion taken place (three hundred ships delivering his army of mercenaries to Torbay) than the Scottish Foot Guards (of whom those who were not Protestant were Presbyterians, which, from the king's Catholic point of view, was worse) defected to the cause of Orange. For the First and Second Regiments of Foot Guards, the Horse Guards, the Horse Grenadier Guards and the Blues in Oxford, the choice was not so instinctive. On the one hand, all of them owed their existence to the king's late brother, who had laid upon them a specific obligation to 'resist and withstand all invasions'. On the other hand, Charles had been restored to the throne on two conditions—that England remain a Protestant nation and that Parliament should never again be defied—and James had dishonoured both.

Apparently in a dilemma, the King's Horse and Foot Guards now proved themselves as skilled in the arts of opportunism as General Monck himself, neither of them evincing any passionate desire to support either their king or Prince William until John Churchill had plumped for William, and Princess Anne had abandoned the cause of her father in favour of that of her sister.

'God help me,' James then cried, 'my own children have forsaken me,' and, reluctant to make a fight of it, ordered his army to disband and his navy to sail to Ireland, while he himself quit London.

Meanwhile William, resplendent in armour, rode triumphantly at the head of his army from Torbay toward London. To which, after a series of undignified adventures, King James abruptly returned, to dine in public for the last time. Retiring to bed with a guard of Coldstreamers, he awoke to find William's Blue Guards arriving to take their place. Aware that resistance was futile, he ordered Lord Craven, Colonel of the Coldstream, and one of the few Guards officers anxious to fight for him, to surrender the palace to his son-in-law's men. Then, with William's permission, he descended Whitehall's steps to the Royal barge and sailed down the Thames, in pouring rain, to Rochester—whence William allowed him to 'escape' to France, as the Queen and the infant Prince of Wales had done before him.

William himself chose to elude the thousands who waited to welcome him in Piccadilly by slipping through the park to St. James's Palace and installing himself in the bedchamber of the ex-Queen. Several months later (Mary having declined to rule alone, and William having flatly refused to stay in England as anything but king) Parliament declared the throne vacant and offered it to the couple jointly. They were crowned on 4 April, 1689, each accepting that they would reign with Parliament and that they had no power either to suspend the law of the land or to raise an army in time of peace.

For the Regiments of Foot and Horse Guards they thereby inherited, they thus created a new context. Previously these regiments had guarded a king either so popular as to need no protection or so unpopular as to be beyond redemption. Previously the sovereigns they protected had believed in their own divine right to rule and had preferred to appease rather than do battle with Louis XIV. But now they were the Household troops—albeit Foot and Horse Guards were separate entities—of a King and Queen who had known war with either France or England, or both, for almost all their married life, who had accepted that their role was complementary to that of Parliament, whose dedication to the concept of a Protestant throne in a Protestant England was unshakeable, and whose determination to protect England and Europe from the Popish hands of His Most Christian Majesty, King Louis XIV of France, was implacable.

In short, the Guards—Foot and Horse—who had known who they were for twenty-nine years, were about to find out what they were as well. For them the capering, roistering, posturing days of Restoration London were over: henceforth, for generations, their sovereigns would require protection from Jacobite plots at home and service on one battlefield after another against their enemies abroad.

★   ★   ★

Wasting no time, William relieved householders of the hated duty James had imposed upon them to quarter, feed and pay troops, recalled the army James had disbanded and despatched all the Foot Guards—of whose total loyalty he was not yet sure—to Flanders.

For her part, Mary put Christopher Wren to work modernising Hampton Court and converting a house on the edge of Kensington Park into another palace. Whitehall's fog and mist had made William ill with bronchitis and asthma, and because the air at Hampton Court and rural Kensington was clear, she nagged Wren to finish his task more quickly. Trying to oblige the impatient queen, the architect cut so many corners that the roof of the new Kensington Palace collapsed —to the fury of the king.

William meanwhile had led a force to Ireland which James, with Louis' help, had just invaded. The two armies finally confronted one another from opposite banks of the River Boyne, not far from the town of Drogheda.

Observing William, mounted on a black horse and conspicuous in his armour, James ordered two cannon to advance and fire upon his small party. The first shot killed the horse of Prince George of Hesse; the second ripped open William's sleeve, grazed his shoulder and knocked him forward on to his horse's neck.

A shout went up from James's French and Irish troops, who believed the Dutchman dead. 'Just as well it wasn't closer,' William remarked in his accented English as his wound was dressed, and then ordered those who clustered round him to get back to their posts.

News that William was dead was despatched to Paris, where, for forty-eight hours, it was celebrated with feasts, drunkenness, a mock funeral and the night-long 'execution' of his effigy. In Rome the Pope expressed himself similarly delighted, and by the banks of the Boyne, William had to ride among his troops, waving his

James II at the Battle of the Boyne. Having lost it, he fled

injured arm, to prove himself alive.

The next morning he attacked, fording the river, leading the fight, putting to flight the French and Irish opposition (whom James had commanded from the rear) and ordering his cavalry (which included Horse Guards, Horse Grenadier Guards, and Blues) to the pursuit.

Waiting no longer, James fled all the way back to Dublin Castle and the hospitality of Lady Tyrconnel. 'Madam,' he told her, 'your countrymen have run away.'

'If they have, sire,' she retorted, 'Your Majesty seems to have won the race.'

Properly abashed, James was more tactful, but no less dejected, when he addressed the Mayor and Council of Dublin. 'Though the Army did not desert me here as they did in England,' he told them, 'yet, when it came to a trial, they hastily fled the field.' He left them in no doubt as to his Royal displeasure. 'Henceforward I never more determine to lead an Irish army, and so now resolve to shift for myself.' Boarding a French frigate, he abandoned Ireland to William.

Before, during and after the battle, William had been appalled by the atrocious behaviour of the Irish troops and the cruelty and looting of his English battalions. For this he had summarily hanged a number of his own men and had personally whipped others; but a great victory had been marred by that spirit of almost inhuman vengefulness which seems endemic to the soil of Ireland. The Battle of the Boyne may have ended the first of James's challenges to William and Mary, but it also initiated an apparently timeless era of sullen Irish hatred and wilful Protestant spite. Nearly three centuries later, the main preoccupation of Queen Elizabeth II's Household Division would become and remain the ungrateful task of keeping the bloody hands of each from the murderous throats of the other.

★   ★   ★

For the moment, though, the Guards were busy not in Ireland, which William proceeded to subjugate almost entirely, but in Flanders, where they came to be highly regarded. The Allies, however, were not successful in that summer of 1689 and when winter came, and the fighting was suspended, as was the custom (for lack of fodder among other reasons) the Guards returned to a crude encampment in Ghent. It was a station with which they were to become as familiar (until Waterloo put an end to England's incessant wars with France) as today they are with their barracks at either Chelsea or Knightsbridge.

When spring came in 1690, and the fighting was resumed, the Foot Guards won for themselves a reputation for steadiness. Winter again and Ghent; then another year. Followed by a third winter at Ghent, and a third summer of bloodshed during which William led his army personally and narrowly escaped death time after time. A bullet passed through his periwig and deafened him for days;

his sleeve was torn; his cravat was severed; his chest was bruised . . . and his Foot Guards responded, creating terror by their disciplined volleys of fire, delayed till they stood almost muzzle to muzzle with the enemy. Paradoxically, as well as a disciplined steadiness that was total, they were capable of inspired acts of spontaneous audacity—as when the First Troop of the Horse Guards lost their standard and a private of the Coldstream instantly seized it up and rallied the cavalry to it; or as when the Scottish Foot Guards were commended for the way they had rushed 'furiously forward', and were referred to, for the first time since the days of Charles I, as 'the Scotch Guards'.

Mary ruled in England while William was abroad, her main problem being to make the Fleet fight *for* her and to stop Scotland plotting *against* her—at least until the Campbells slaughtered most of their Macdonald (and Jacobite) hosts. But then the plotting moved south to the capital, where Sarah Countess of Marlborough so successfully intrigued against her that her sister, Princess Anne, no longer talked to her, while the Earl of Marlborough (frustrated by William's refusal to give him a military command) first became her enemy in Parliament and then went farther and made his peace with her father, the exiled King James.

Between times Mary attempted to reform the morals of the Court (and failed, as her father had failed before her), and eventually caught smallpox, of which she died. She had been a loving wife to a congenitally aloof husband, and a cheerful, talkative, devout and courageous queen. 'Everyone,' she remarked calmly as she lay dying, 'needs to be reminded of death, princes as much as anyone.'

London, reminded of death by the Queen's protracted agony, had closed its theatres and coffee shops to wait for the final news. When it came, and was carried across the land by the tolling of bells, the capital and the nation grieved—and William (who had hastened home) seemed likely to fall into a decline. 'Tomorrow I go back to Kensington,' he confessed in a letter, 'but I fear the walls will crush me.'

He was, however, too tough a character to allow that—and was anyway too aware, if he was to rule England without Mary, of the immediate need to bring about a reconciliation with both Princess Anne and the Earl of Marlborough. This done, he left England's administration to a Council of Seven and returned to his wars, where, the following year, he recaptured Namur from Louis XIV and was once, during that famous siege, even heard to exclaim 'Look at my brave English.' Of those brave English, the First Regiment of Foot Guards lost 105 killed and 179 wounded, and the Coldstream Regiment lost 53 killed and 112 wounded. To help recruit trained replacements, William contributed the sums of £494 to the First Regiment of Foot Guards and £271 to the Coldstream Regiment —or £3 for each man killed and £1 for each man wounded.

Unfortunately such trained replacements cost £5 each; which is one of the

Negro Trumpeter, 1st Troop of Horse Guards *c.* 1750 (Painting by David Morier)

The Household Cavalry: the Mall

Coldstream Guards defending the Château of Hougoumont 1815 (Painting by Denis Dighton)

Coldstream Guards 1821 (Painting by Denis Dighton)

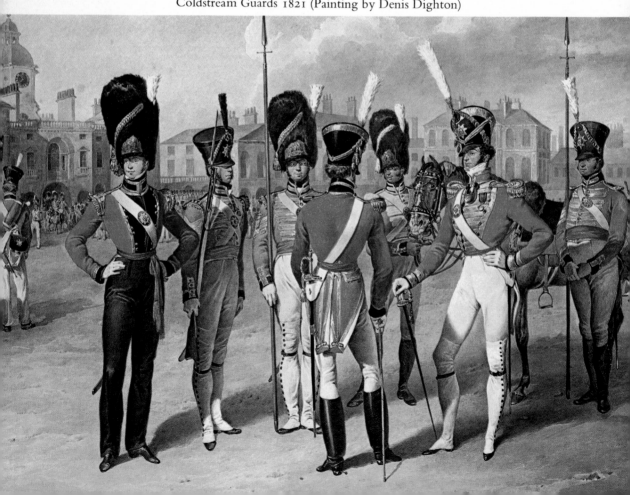

reasons why captains of companies and colonels of regiments so ruthlessly fleeced their men of their pay, making deductions for shoes, stockings, garters, medicines, shaving, food, lodging and even 'losses by exchange'.

Admittedly the King paid his colonels for 5,000 more private soldiers than existed in all their regiments put together, but from that clear profit each colonel had to maintain his regimental band and dress his drummers—and that was ruinously expensive. Two pieces of scarlet ribbon cost him twelve weeks of a private's pay; and a drummer's uniform of scarlet and blue silk cuffed with velvet and lace and adorned with gilt buttons and embroidery cost him £54/3/–, or nearly four years of a private's pay. So he deducted almost every penny of the pay due to each of his soldiers and thereby contrived not only to meet all his expenses but to provide himself and his officers with a reasonable income as well.

At home or abroad, in fact, a soldier was still provided only with bread, cheese and fuel—for which, of course, deductions were made. Anything else that he wanted, like meat or ale, he had to buy from a sutler. Wherever the army halted, the Provost Marshal appointed a market place, fixed the prices, erected a gallows (as the endearing symbol of his office) and claimed from the sutlers a fee on every beast slaughtered and cask broached. That fee the sutler added to the price of the food and drink he sold to the soldiers.

Exploited at every turn, the Guards somehow remained good soldiers. On either flank were respectively their light companies and their tall grenadier companies, and between these marched the bulk of the battalion. In defence, they were taught to fire low, the front rank kneeling. In attack, to the accompaniment of drum-beat and fife, they would advance remorselessly upon their enemy, ignoring his fire and their own casualties. And after a battle any wives who had been allowed to accompany them overseas—six at most from each company of eighty or more men—would search out the dead and wounded.

Yet it was upon these terms that the Foot Guards had so valiantly stormed Namur that William had involuntarily exclaimed, 'Look at my brave English'; and it was following this rare victory over Louis at Namur that William was accorded so triumphant a progress through England that he was even able to ignore the damaging findings of a commission into the massacre of the MacDonalds. But a warning that he was to be assassinated by Jacobites while out hunting was not to be ignored.

So (with honours won not only at Namur but at Lièges and Mons as well) the Brigade of Guards, as the Foot Guards were known, was brought home to England, where the would-be assassins were arrested and executed, whilst, from France, Louis let it be known that he had never approved any assassination attempt and that he was forthwith washing his hands of King James.

The following year peace was declared and William—who had negotiated favourable terms for England and Holland—was received back in London as joyously as King Charles had been after the hated years of the Protectorate.

Unfortunately his popularity did not last. Not unnaturally he preferred the friendship of Dutchmen to Englishmen, and England resented it. Even less unnaturally he was frequently homesick for Holland; but whenever he visited it—without the excuse of war—England regarded him almost as a traitor. Worse, at the very beginning of 1695, it was a *Dutch* maid who lit a charcoal fire to dry some laundry in Whitehall Palace, with the result that minutes later not only the chamber in which the fire had been lit but the entire palace as well was ablaze. In a matter of hours much of the history of England, from the time of Henry VIII, was turned to ashes; and even William, who had hated Whitehall, could appreciate how bitterly Londoners deplored its destruction.

From the Guard's point of view, the focal point of Royal London ceased to be Whitehall as of that moment and moved steadily deeper into St. James's Park, re-orientating as it did so all their ceremonial duties.

Now only one step remained to set both Foot and Horse Guards upon the path they have trod ever since. Under William, England had finally rejected the possibility of a Roman Catholic monarchy, of any kind of submission to a foreign power, and of any other form of government than that of the King in Parliament.

Under William, Foot and Horse Guards had fought the sovereign's wars; but they had never actually been entrusted with the protection of his person, for which William had always preferred to rely upon his Dutch Blue Guards. In February 1699, however, William submitted to Parliament's constant pressure and advised that 'the necessary preparations are made for transporting the [Blue] Guards who came with his Majesty to England ... unless ... the House is disposed to find a way for continuing them longer in his service, which His Majesty would take very kindly.'

But the House of Commons insisted that the happiness and welfare of England depended entirely upon the King entrusting his 'sacred person' to Englishmen; so back to Holland the Blue Guards went, and off to the various palaces, to guard their king at last, marched or rode his indigenous Household troops—as is confirmed by a bill, at the end of that year, for £289.6.8 for lighting (with fires and candles, as was the custom) the various new posts of the Coldstream Guards at Kensington, Hyde Park, Arlington Gate, St. James, Whitehall, Somerset House, the Savoy, Hampton Court and Windsor.

For the rest of his reign, William was a sick man, neither popular nor unpopular, but on civil terms at least with Anne who was to succeed him. When at last he expired, England mourned him perfunctorily and then gave herself over with unrestrained joy to the delights—unknown since Elizabeth's death a century earlier—of an *English* sovereign.

7   Anne–George III

QUEEN ANNE was neither brilliant, beautiful nor flexible; but she had lived through and in the courts of Charles, James and William, and she knew what her people wanted. 'As I know my own heart to be English,' she told them as soon as she was crowned, 'I can very sincerely assure you there is not anything you can expect or desire from me which I shall not be ready to do for the happiness and prosperity of England.'

Well aware that part of William's legacy to her subjects had been a pride in their island independence, and an insatiable greed for overseas possessions, she did not hesitate to send an even larger army than usual to Holland and a substantial force to Cadiz as England's opening gambit against France's new ally, Spain.

'So silent that she rarely spoke more than was necessary to answer a question,' was Sarah Churchill's description of her; and no one knew her better than Sarah, for love of whom she had even defied her sister when Mary was queen.

'You know what I required of you,' Mary had written to her then, making reference to her long-standing demand that Anne see no more of Sarah, 'and I now tell you, if you doubted it before, that I cannot change my mind, but expect to be complied with.'

Required to choose between her sister the Queen and Sarah her life-long friend, Anne (not without Sarah's encouragement) had chosen Sarah. Queen now herself, she seemed more anxious than ever to please her friend, building Marlborough House for her and giving her husband command of the English army—in which capacity Marlborough inspired some remarkable victories and repaid the men who won them for him by stopping the cheese from their ration and taking from the contractors who supplied their daily bread a succession of backhanders totalling annually more than £6,000.

Everything other than bread his soldiers had to purchase from the sutler—including their twice weekly compulsory ration of bacon which made them so thirsty that the sutler also did a roaring trade in ale each evening until 'tap to'—now 'tattoo'—signalled that no more drink was to be sold.

More sutlers than ever now followed each regiment with herds of cattle and wagon loads of ale. Many of them were old soldiers—than whom no one exploits the serving soldier more pitilessly—and some were even soldiers' wives. Of these, Kit Ross was the best known. The widow of a man killed at Malplaquet, and a virago more terrifying than any French cuirassier, she was as celebrated in the Army as Marlborough himself.

For all that they were good soldiers in battle, the Foot Guards were disliked at home as drunken brawlers and bad lodgers. From this public dislike and the continuing demands of the War of Spanish Succession they frequently took refuge in desertion; and from this their Regiments sought assiduously to retrieve them by the use of notices in the *London Gazette*.

In February 1709 one such notice declared: '*Edward Evans, a black (haired) man, wears a black wig, about five foot ten inches high, aged about 34, a pavier by trade.*

'*Thomas Turnell, commonly called Islington Tom, about five feet eight inches high, wears a bushy light brown wig, full face with some small moles on his cheek. He was a labourer to the said Edward Evans, lived at Islington and formally drove hogs.*

'*John Keymoure, a dark brown man, his own lank brown hair, a full nose, thin face, a tinman by trade, supposed to be going to work at his trade in Bristol.*

'*Edward Lovelace, about five foot ten inches high, a lusty well set man, wears a brown wig, very full of pock holes in his face, born at Frome in Somersetshire, a clothier by trade, lately used the Sheers Alehouse in Bell Alley in Coleman Street London and wrought thereabouts.*

'*Whoever secures any of them ... shall have twenty shillings reward for each; but if they will return to their colours in fourteen days time after the date hereof, they shall be pardoned.*'

Clearly Privates Evans, Turnell, Keymoure and Lovelace were wanted by their colonel—and not just because deserters in war-time had to be punished. The offer of a pardon illustrates how valuable fully trained men were to a regiment, how costly they were to replace and how difficult it had become—after twenty years of almost continuous war—either to find recruits or to prevent desertions.

As to the latter, the *Gazette* listed two more Coldstream deserters the following week and three more in June—and the reward for securing any of them went up from twenty shillings to two guineas. This was obviously enough to enlist the aid of most civilians in the apprehension of the unpopular Redcoat because every Regiment's archive is full of the brief orders that despatched an N.C.O. and several men to march to Bristol, or Darlington, or Manchester, or wherever, to collect a deserter and march back to London with him: whereupon a second entry refers succinctly to the facts of his desertion, the futility of his excuses and the savagery of his punishment.

While Whig fought Tory as bitterly as Marlborough made brilliant war upon France, and while the Brigade of Guards distinguished itself by helping reduce one Spanish fortress after another, Sarah Churchill lost no opportunity to exploit her position of favour; but then she overstepped herself—and her Queen became as implacably hostile to both Marlboroughs as once she had been incorrigibly loyal.

The surprising thing is not that her affection for Sarah waned but that it lasted so long. During James II's reign both Churchills had manipulated her so ruthlessly that it was John Churchill, not Princess Anne herself, who wrote to William and Mary in Holland assuring them that she was 'resolved, by the assistance of God, to

John Churchill, 1st Duke of Marlborough, one time
Grenadier, and the only general (before Waterloo)
to win great victories over the French

suffer all extremities, even to death itself, rather than to be brought to change her religion' as her father, the King, had desired. And it was Sarah, not Anne, who wrote to say that 'the Princess of Denmark is safe in the trusting of me, I being resolved, although I cannot live the life of a saint . . . to show the resolution of a martyr.'

Yet no sooner had William and Mary come to the throne than it had been the recently ennobled Marlborough who became one of William's chief opponents in Parliament and his wife Sarah the most persistent intriguer in the whole of Mary's domain at Whitehall.

Then Marlborough had espoused the Jacobite cause and Sarah had driven a wedge between Queen and Princess. All of which the reticent, dark skinned Princess had not only endured but positively welcomed, and always without a word of criticism from her husband, who summed up his own Royal aspirations when he wrote to a friend, 'Talk here of going to tea, of going to Winchester, and of doing everything else except sitting still all summer, which is the height of my ambition. God send me a quiet life somewhere.'

Charles II had early assessed the worth of his niece's husband. 'I have tried him drunk and I have tried him sober,' he declared, 'and drunk or sober there is nothing in him.'

'He is fat, loves news, his bottle and the Queen,' a gossip said of him after his wife ascended the throne, 'and hath neither friends nor enemies.'

From him, then, the Marlboroughs had never feared opposition; but they had been foolish to misjudge his wife, who had had the courage in the past to defy the will of a king, her father, and a queen, her sister. In the event, Queen Anne ordered Sarah out of Marlborough House, allowed rumours of Marlborough's corruption as commander-in-chief to be investigated and as often as possible removed herself from Kensington Palace to Windsor Castle—where, riding in a gig, sharing a bottle with her husband and, like him, grossly over-eating, she could forget affairs of state.

The investigation into his conduct having established that Marlborough had illicitly profited from the contract to supply his armies with bread, the Queen at once dismissed him from all his employments and, as quickly as possible, brought to an end the war that had been his passion.

A year later she died; and because none of her thirteen children had survived her, her throne passed, with Parliament's approval, to the grandson of James I's daughter, Prince George of Hanover, who thereby became England's most foreign and least loved king since William the Conqueror.

★   ★   ★

George I was not popular with his new subjects on any score. He was German and unprepossessing; spoke no English; lived austerely in only one room of St. James's Palace; did not, like Dutch William III, have a beloved English Queen by his side; had imprisoned his adulterous German wife for life in a German castle; had German rather than English mistresses; employed as his official hostess his son's unpopular wife; and could only communicate with his ministers in French or Latin.

These were not the qualities required in a king whose first task should have been to put England's domestic affairs in order. Since the Puritan days that had ended in 1660, English society had become violent and contemptuous of authority.

Though respected as a military, naval and colonial power, the country had become almost anarchic. Its theatres were disorderly, its poor were tyrannised, its night-time capital was the kingdom of the footpad, its country roads were terrorised by highwaymen, Tyburn gallows was as often as not chopped down the night before a hanging, riots and arson were an everyday occurrence, and the Army—England's only instrument of authority—was loathed.

Overseas, in Spain, the Brigade of Guards may have made a name for itself, but those battalions of Guards who had stayed at home were cordially detested. Badly paid, and fleeced by their officers even of the few pence that should have been theirs, they themselves paid badly at the inns and hostleries where they were billeted. Long disliked by Parliament as a source of expense and a threat to its independence, they were also alleged to be intimidating voters at elections, thereby nullifying the contemporary practice of buying votes. In short, most M.P.'s had long since made it their ambition to rid England of its 'Redcoats'.

Even Fortescue, in his *History of the Army*, denigrated them, insisting that, 'The standard appears to have sunk to the worst days of Elizabeth . . . The ranks were filled with professional criminals who passed from regiment to regiment, spreading everywhere the infection of discontent and insubordination.'

But this was a harsh assessment. If these criminals passed from regiment to regiment, it was less because they deliberately sought to spread the infection of their discontent than because one colonel deliberately got rid of them by selling them to another, and he to a third, and so on through all the battalions of the army.

'Week by week,' the outraged Fortescue continued, 'deserters were brought into Hyde Park, tied up to the halberds, or simply to a tree, and flogged with hundreds of lashes.'

Here Fortescue under-stated: hundreds should read 'as much as seven hundred'. And just as appalling were the alternative punishments of running the gauntlet, a halberd's point at the victim's belly lest he 'should hurry unduly', or of being shot by a firing squad of fellow deserters.

Though not all Redcoats were Foot Guards, Boswell made it clear that there were no exceptions. Having a Private of the Guards billeted on one, he asserted, was the equivalent of sharing one's house with 'the greatest scoundrel you can find'. Magistrates meanwhile were so anxious to see the entire Army disbanded that they openly condoned desertion; and George I was angered to discover that many of his officers were no less dishonest and unprincipled than the bulk of his soldiery.

Being angry at what he saw was one thing, being able to change it another. Walpole, an outstanding linguist, had quickly made himself indispensable to the King by his mastery of Latin, and then by learning German, but Walpole sought less to implement the King's wishes than to become the most powerful of the King's ministers—as which he was to create fifty new capital offences and become the scourge of those rural Englishmen uprooted by his Black Acts.

George, unable indefinitely to tolerate the English political habit of conniving with Princes to subvert the authority of the King, had been obliged to expel the Prince and Princess of Wales from St. James's and the Court; and, denied any other instrument of law and order, had employed the Guards to maintain decency in theatres, break-up strikes and supervise so many executions that finally they were dubbed 'the hangman's friends'.

Nor did the Army's unpleasant duties end in England. Overseas lay an empire, and it, too, had to be policed, lest the black slaves of the West Indies massacred their white masters, lest the white servants of wealthy colonists fled in even larger numbers than usual to become pirates, lest the Red Indians over-ran America's fragile settlements and the French forces from Quebec were tempted to march south. So, at any moment, a Redcoat could be posted to billets without a roof in Gibraltar or Minorca; to a winter without blankets in Newfoundland; or, most dreaded of all, to exile without end in the Leeward Islands.

Needless to say, every warning of such overseas postings was accompanied by mass desertions that left behind only the 'discontented, lazy, cunning and malevolent', in consequence of which soldiers, at home and abroad, became notorious for their brawling, for 'accidentally' using loaded instead of blank cartridges at drill, and for being either mutinous, or drunk, or both.

The Guards did not escape these strictures. On the contrary, because defence cuts and overseas postings meant that they were assigned more domestic duties than ever, they found themselves more than ever in the public eye and therefore more than ever disliked.

They continued to march incessantly: marched to their Royal duties at St. James's Palace, Kensington Palace, Windsor Castle, Hampton Court, Bath and Chatham; marched, if embarking for foreign service, to Portsmouth or Dover; marched to fulfil the most extraordinary duties.

On 10 June, 1715, for example, they were dispatched all over London to prevent

Horse Guards Parade, St. James's Park, 1742

people from wearing white roses in sympathy with the abortive Jacobite uprising in Scotland; and in 1716 they were ordered, 'It is his Majesty's pleasure that when and as often as you shall have due notice of a Ball to be held at the theatre in Haymarket . . . one hundred private men, with a captain and other commissioned and non-commissioned officers proportionable, [shall] march and do duty during the continuance of the said Ball at the said theatre. And they are to take care that His Majesty's peace be preserved and, as far as possible, [they are] to prevent all rudeness and indecencies as well in words as in actions. Nor are they to permit any person to enter . . . in habits that may tend to the drawing down reflections upon religion or in ridicule of the same.'

Only England—whose M.P.s habitually described her soldiers as 'lewd profligate wretches' and her officers as 'giddy and insolent'—would have obliged its king to despatch a hundred privates of the Guards, 'and officers proportionable', to prevent acts or words of 'rudeness and indecency' at a Ball. Only England, whilst detesting her 'lobsters', would have demanded, as soon as a riot broke out (be it in Southampton or Cirencester, Bath or Nottingham) that they come at once and restore order. Only England, once the Foot Guards *had* marched, or the Horse Guards ridden, from London to Southampton—or Cirencester, or Bath, or Nottingham—would invariably have declined even to offer them an Orderly Room, let alone proper accommodation. And only in England, once a riot had been suppressed, would the municipality in question invariably have seized upon any excuse to complain to the Secretary of State at War about the presence of the men who had done the suppressing.

As the Secretary of State at War himself observed, in 1717, 'If I take no notice of such things, I shall be petitioned against by twenty or thirty towns; if I enquire into them, the officers think themselves discouraged; if I neglect them, I shall be speeched every day in the House of Commons; and if I give any countenance to them, I shall disoblige the officers.'

Unlike his Secretary of State at War, the King would have been very happy to disoblige his officers, but 1718 was too early for the reforms he had in mind, so he had to content himself with standardising the army's drill—which previously had varied from regiment to regiment according to the whim of each colonel.

In 1720, however, he made his move against some of the gentlemen who had purchased commissions in his army. Shocked by the knowledge that, to enrich themselves, many officers made constant illegal deductions from the pay of their men, he dismissed no less than seven colonels; and outraged by the officers' habit, when tired of life in the army, of selling their commissions for more than they had paid for them, he instituted a tariff. In the year of the rupture of the speculative South Sea Bubble, George had put an end to speculation in the King's commissions.

Yet, ironically, when the Duke of Marlborough died that same year (he whose brilliant military career Queen Anne had so abruptly terminated because of his dishonesty with Army contracts) he was accorded the greatest state funeral ever seen in England; but that again was very English.

As also was the fact that in Southwark alone there were eight hundred and twenty-three ale houses, inns, coffee houses and brandy shops. Whatever that may have implied about the sobriety of Londoners, it also meant that for each of the five hundred and seventy-one privates in the Coldstream Guards there was a billet in which he could live alone—and, should he be dissatisfied, another two hundred and fifty-two unoccupied houses to which he could thereupon take his unwanted custom.

In the last year of his reign, George I demanded a review of his Foot Guards, and four hundred men from each of the Regiments marched before him in Hyde Park, which now had ceased to be the haunt of deer hunters and become instead a place shared by hutted Foot Guards and marauding footpads.

German to the last, George I died (in a carriage, on his way to visit Hanover) in 1727, to be succeeded by the son he so disliked, who cordially disliked *his* son, both of whom were disliked by the people of England.

Yet George II and his Queen did much for London that was to London's aesthetic advantage. It was Queen Caroline, for example, who dammed the little Westborn River, thereby creating the Serpentine, and it was her husband who ordered the surrounding park at last to be cleared of footpads. He also offered his patronage to a fellow Hanoverian called Handel, whose compositions at the time attracted nothing but derision from the rest of English society; and, determined to emulate the appearance and discipline of the soldiers of his Prussian brother-in-law, King Frederick William, he imposed upon one regiment after the other new standards of dress and smartness.

It was likewise George II—whose mentality was very much that of a drill sergeant—who sought constantly to improve the quality of the army at a time when Parliament's only concern—and England's—was to reduce its quantity. 'No sentinel on any account,' warned the Coldstream Orderly Room in consequence, '[is] to quit his arms, nor suffer any bench, chair, stone or seat whatsoever to be in his sentry box, nor drink or smoke on his post, nor wear a night cap when sentry, but [must keep] his hair under his hat and everything in good order.'

From this order there emerges a clear picture of previous Foot Guard sentries lolling unarmed on chairs, hair straggling wildly beneath their night caps, a pipe in one hand and a bottle of gin in the other. The Palace sentry of today can probably attribute his obligatory immobility to his lackadaisical predecessor of 1735.

The King apart, however, no one in England cared that the growing reluctance of innkeepers even to house soldiers, let alone provide them with scarce forage and expensive food, made barracks a necessity. Everyone was obsessed with the notion that barracks would facilitate some kind of military coup under some new kind of Cromwell. So the standing army was cut to a puny 19,000 men; jobbery as to promotions (of mere corporals and sergeants as well as officers) became rife; and the efficiency of the country's defences became negligible.

Troop ships sailed carrying undrinkable water; infantry was despatched to a new war with France without artillery support; small arms were scarce; seaports were panic stricken either by their complete lack of defences, or, if they had defences, by the knowledge that they were little better off than Pendennis Castle, whose forty-six cannon were in the sole charge of a master gunner aged ninety. Gibraltar's guns were too short and its fortifications too puny. St. Kitts' garrison was sixty per cent sick and one hundred per cent barefooted. Unemployment in England, swollen by demobilized soldiers, and exacerbated by inflation, was causing more unrest than ever; and only the King opposed Parliament's determination to do nothing about any of it.

He was also at war with his son, and had been since 1737. 'It is his Majesty's command,' he had then allowed it to be known, 'that none of the three Regiments of Foot Guards take any notice of the Prince and Princess of Wales or any of their family until further orders.' Those orders had not been forthcoming.

In even more brutal fashion, the public made clear *its* loathing for the Guards, rushing to Hyde Park in such numbers to witness the first of them being 'picketed' that the *Daily Post* reported 'several spectators' as having been 'severely injured'. Picketing involved the suspension of the near naked culprit by one wrist with no other support than a sharply pointed stake beneath his bare feet, and for London the chance to watch it being inflicted on one of the King's hated Foot Guards was not to be missed.

'A burthersome and useless army,' was Parliament's description of the Guards and their brothers-in-arms in 1741: so it was their little drill sergeant of a king who in 1739 had been obliged to purchase for them 10,000 foreign muskets and bayonets with which to fight the latest war—which would continue till 1748.

Unpopularity and regimentation notwithstanding, an element of élitism had already entered the ranks of the Foot Guards. Not only were they much feared by their European enemies but they were proud of the fact. So proud, indeed, that once, when the late George I had been reviewing his Militia, all three Foot Guard Regiments had had to be ordered 'not to laugh or make any game of them'; and it was probably not anti-Jacobitism and anti-Popery alone that induced the Coldstreamers, in 1745, to decline to recruit any more Scotsmen, Irishmen or vagabonds! They had become, as they were to remain, snobs.

But if the Guards were becoming more selective as to their recruits, the quality of the men they sent to garrison the colonies was deteriorating fast. On 22 April 1750, for example, a large detachment of men from all three Regiments of Foot Guards was ordered to escort from London to Plymouth 'twelve deserters in the Savoy whom no merchant ship will take on board as they were so mutinous last year when they embarked that it was necessary to land them at Portsmouth.' Delivered safe and sound by the Guards to H.M.S. *Rainbow*, these twelve worthies were shipped to Nova Scotia to become part of its garrison.

Desertions from England's army at home became so common at this time that the punishment for it ceased to be running the gauntlet, or facing a firing squad, and became instead deportation to Carolina as a Redcoat—where such offenders soon earned for all Redcoats the nickname *Bloodybacks*.

Crime became equally as common in the gin-sodden ranks of England's civilians and mass executions in London were commonplace.

'Sixteen criminals being ordered for execution tomorrow,' ran a laconic order of the day, 'and it being apprehended that it may not be safe to conduct them to the place of execution without a guard, a sufficient detachment is to be made from the three regiments of Foot Guards to assist in the safe conducting of the said malefactors to Tyburn, and [is to] remain till they shall have suffered according to their respective sentences.'

Now more than ever 'the executioner's friends', the Guards were also required to nobble society's pleasure-lovers. On 23 October 1749 a hundred Foot Guards were despatched, for the hundredth time, to the King's Theatre Haymarket, there, as usual, to deter the indecent 'and oblige the musicians and butlers to retire in good time'.

Meantime a new Guard House was being built to replace the Holbein Gate that had been destroyed when Whitehall Palace went up in flames, and in 1751 George opened it by driving through its archway in his carriage. The archway led out of Horse Guards Parade and St. James's Park and into the new street of Whitehall. Topped by a suite of offices, above which was a small tower and a clock with a sweetly silver chime (from which Londoners subsequently took their time) it was flanked by barrack accommodation for a hundred mounted men.

It was, in short, the Horse Guards building of today. Now all that remained to complete the Royal London of today was the purchase and modification of Buckingham Palace, the construction of Trafalgar Square, the linking of Trafalgar Square to the Mall, and the linking of the Mall to Hyde Park Corner.

For all of that another ninety years would be required, and George II was to rule for only eight of them; but those eight were years of dramatic change for the Household Cavalry and society alike, the catalyst being the king, who was motivated by a quite appalling snobbery.

Trade and gentlemen, George II decided, were irreconcilable. Gentlemen were those who at best did nothing, at worst practised law or politics, preached in pulpits or purchased commissions. The rest were non-gentlemen, to be avoided at all costs.

Unfortunately a number of the latter category, employing their fathers' un-gentlemanly money, had bought themselves for a hundred guineas the rank of 'private gentleman' in the Horse Guards. As such, in the absence of any good wars, and billeted in London, they had taken to getting drunk, fighting duels and even going into business as the proprietors of coffee houses and taverns. Abruptly the King ordered them either to improve their manners and give up their businesses or to get out of his Horse Guards by selling their rank to someone else.

Then started the Seven Years' War and the older Pitt's era of political domination. George II died in the middle of that war and his grandson, the ill-fated George III, aged twenty-two, succeeded him in 1760.

'Born and educated in England, I glory in the name of Briton,' he pronounced, taking a leaf out of Queen Anne's book; but it won him little popularity among a race who, despising the Scots and insensitive about the Welsh, still called themselves English. Anxious to be known by his subjects as the Patriot King, he found himself instead so little regarded that Boswell could summarily dismiss him as one of 'a shabby family'.

Poor George could do nothing right. It was not his leadership but Pitt's strategy that thwarted France's ambitions in Europe. Nor had he been allowed to marry the English woman of his choice, Lady Sarah Lennox, which might have been well received by his unpredictable subjects; but instead had been required to wed Charlotte of Mecklenburg-Strelitz. And finally—at a time of approaching and unprecedented revolutions in both France and America, a time that would have

A Horse Guard, 1755

taxed the cunning of Richelieu and Machiavelli combined—honest, tactless George was carrying in his body the seeds of an agonising illness that would soon unhinge his mind.

Until the Regency, then, his long reign did nothing to enhance the reputation of his dynasty, his Guards, his army or his country; but it did, in a way, enhance London's reputation (though footpads, pickpockets and whores continued to infest it) because this was the time when most of the aristocracy built their town houses, whose elegantly proportioned rooms, lit by splendid chandeliers, looked out, through windows of the new plate-glass, upon footpaths recently paved with flagstones.

Older than most but not the least of these magnificent residences was Arlington House, which stood at the far end of St. James's Park from Whitehall and was noted for its mulberry gardens, whose leaves had once been much in demand as food for silk worms. When St. James's Palace was partially destroyed by fire in 1761, Queen Charlotte purchased Arlington House. It eventually became Buckingham Palace.

Observing such magnificent houses, it was easy to forget the criminals who prowled the streets. Watching Garrick's performance of King Lear at the theatre in Drury Lane, it was possible to forget the Thames's fearful weekly toll of suicides. Watching Queen Charlotte take snuff from a golden box in such prodigious quantities that the Royal nose was often as dusty without as it was within, it was natural to be frivolous, to leave to Pitt the hiring of German allies to curb France's ambitions, and to ignore the implications of growing Prussian power in Europe and increasing colonial unrest in America.

Ten years of rule by George saw London's population reach a million, most of whom, each night, seemed to be blind drunk, though not a few of the apparently insensible were in fact dead—a world wide slump, aggravated by rocketing food prices, having brought starvation to the capital. On the other hand, a degree of street cleaning and lighting had just been introduced—each household contributing its own burning street lamp each night—so that the city was at least considerably less sordid for the Guards to police than it had been under George I.

George III's main problem, however, was money. The recent war—seven years of subsidising both Prussia and Brunswick—had been ruinously expensive; and the King's constant use of Treasury funds to buy control of Parliament, though supremely effective, had left the Civil List with debts of more than £1,000,000. More taxes had to be imposed upon someone, somewhere. Upon the colonists in America, George thereupon decided; and was shocked when the colonists decided otherwise.

Those Foot Guards not thereafter at war in America were not much more comfortably employed in England, policing the capital, curbing civilian unrest, escorting consignments of gunpowder from Portsmouth to the arsenal at Woolwich and being reviewed at regular intervals by the King. They were, by now, smartly uniformed, uniformly drilled, of more or less uniform height and would soon be at war again with France, which this time would be led by Napoleon. They would remain at war almost continuously from 1792 to 1815.

Spared the discomfort and humiliation of war in the American Colonies, the Life Guards and Blues had spent much of the intervening time escorting the King wherever the Royal whim took him and controlling England's disgruntled populace. There had, of course, been odd forays into battle in Europe, but none had been conspicuously successful. More significant was the transformation of the three troops of Horse Guards into a Regiment of Life Guards, whose privates enlisted, and the construction of Regimental barracks.

As to the Knightsbridge barracks in which—sixty or more to a room—these new Life Guards now lived and cooked, the architect who designed them had clearly understood the needs neither of men nor of horses. Bug-ridden in the summer and freezing in the winter, they had dozens of windows facing the Park, which attracted the King's new tax, and urinals in the attic because no one had thought to instal them anywhere else.

It is said that the architect committed suicide by flinging himself from the highest barrack pinnacle; it is certain that half the taxable windows were bricked in to save money—and only unbricked in time to create a blacking out problem during World War II.

For the moment, though, it was the war against France that preoccupied the English, and in 1794 it went appallingly. The winter was so severe that the Rhine froze over, enabling French cavalrymen to charge Dutch warships; most of the English infantry died of cold as they withdrew to North German ports for evacuation; and such cavalry as survived were left behind to help protect Hanover from the wrath of Napoleon.

The Guards private was still paid five shillings and tenpence a week, from which was deducted three shillings for food and the usual amount for board, clothing, medicine and other 'off reckonings', which left him—as ever—with just enough money to get regularly drunk. He was given two meals a day—at 7.30 a.m. and 12.30 p.m.—and thus remained foodless for nineteen consecutive hours in every twenty four. Until 'tap to' he drank heavily, a habit made all the more inevitable by the cheapness of his liquor and the monotony of his diet of boiled meat and potatoes, or boiled meat and bread, or salted meat and potatoes. Whether serving on the frozen Rhine, in Arctic Nova Scotia or the tropical West Indies, his uniform was the same. And his wife (if he was one of the few so fortunate as to be allowed both to marry and to have his wife follow him overseas) endured the same discipline, punishments and hardships as he, besides having to help forage for his food, share the men's tents and cook their meals.

The defeat of his army in America, the subsequent trauma of the French Revolution, the Corn Law riots and the domination of Europe by Napoleon combined to drive George III out of London. Taking up virtual siege quarters in the fortress of Windsor, he built barracks there for his Foot Guards and the Blues.

The Cavalry he accommodated in what had once been the grounds of a leper hospital; the Foot Guards he housed on the site of an old plague pit; his wife and himself he installed in the grey looming castle that had once been the citadel of Saxon Harold.

He virtually ruled England from Windsor from 1804 to 1810, during which time his patent decency, devotion to his wife and loyalty to England at last won him the affection of his people who now called him Farmer George. But in 1810 the agonies of his illness rendered him apparently insane and he was confined to the castle until he died in 1820.

In those last ten years England was to defeat France in Spain and Napoleon at Waterloo, emerge from the smoke of war as the world's dominant power, and accord to her three Regiments of Foot Guards the title of the world's finest soldiers.

8 George III–Victoria

As his country's chief administrator for much of his reign, and the architect of her worst misfortunes, George III had had courage and magnanimity. Obliged at last to accept Fox into the Cabinet, he had told him, 'I have no desire to look back on old grievances, and you may rest assured that I never shall remind you of them'.

Greeting the first United States' ambassador to the Court of St. James's, he had said, 'I will be very frank with you. I was the last to consent to the separation; but the separation having been made, and having become inevitable, I have always said, as I say now, that I would be the first to meet the friendship of the United States as an independent power'.

Faced with the continued unpopularity of his family, he had neither attempted to shift any of the blame for the War of Independence—although his people had wanted it as much as he—nor ever to curry favour with expedient reforms. 'I will have no

Foot Guards, St. James's Palace, c. 1830

innovations in my time,' he had declared robustly, and accepted sole responsibility for everything done during his reign—which happened to include the building of London's docks, the transformation by Nash of the farmland beyond Marylebone Road into Regents Park and the creation of the nucleus of the library of the British Museum.

He had also lived an exemplary private life, avoiding extravagance and remaining faithful to his Queen in a most un-Hanoverian fashion. Indeed, his fidelity to Charlotte had provided, for his middle-class subjects at least, an example of marital life that was so novel as to lay the foundations of Victorian respectability. Socially, while adhering to the snobbish tenets of his grandfather, he had always been at ease in any company and his manner with his subjects, when he met them, which he went out of his way to do, had been unselfconsciously amiable. Militarily, however, his Hanoverian snobbery had one considerable consequence. When his son, the Duke of York, had suggested that the three Troops of Horse Guards should once and for all be rid of the distasteful nonsense of pretentious Private Gentlemen, he had promptly concurred. The defeat of his army at Yorktown had brought it into great disrespect: the time had come for reforms.

So all the Private Gentlemen were summarily dismissed from his service, compensated for their loss of the rank they had purchased for a hundred guineas, and replaced by any of their number willing to be engaged as regular soldiers, and by the no-nonsense, non-gentlemanly privates of the Horse Grenadier Guards. There were thus created two new regiments, which became the 1st and 2nd Regiments of Life Guards; but they were never to endear themselves to their king as much as his Blues had done.

Even during the sad years of his madness at Windsor, George III remained gregarious and—dressed in a Blues' jacket, an old cocked hat, a sword and a captain's coat—would wander round the town or amble down to Combermere Barracks. Browsing through Knight's bookshop, he once took down a volume of Shakespeare and remarked, 'Sad stuff, sad stuff.' Arriving at Combermere Barracks, he would as often as not demand that he be allowed to inspect it, particularly if there had recently been an influx of recruits. Sighting a tall recruit, he would insist, 'Put him in my troop. Put him in my troop'. Unless, of course, the recruit came from Nottingham, in which case he would have none of him, declaring, 'Disaffected lot, what? What?'

Meantime his son ruled in his stead, and was a very different sort of man. Where the king was thrifty, the Prince Regent was extravagant. Where the king dressed simply, the Prince Regent was flamboyant. Where the King had resisted any relaxation of the laws against Roman Catholics, the Prince Regent had secretly married one, Mrs. Fitzherbert. Where the king lived an exemplary married life, the Prince abandoned his official wife, Princess Caroline of Brunswick, after the birth of their

Horse Guards Riding School, *c.* 1830

daughter Charlotte, and thereafter lived in the carefree style of a bachelor at Carlton House.

Both, however, had inherited George II's dislike of trade, so that, by the time of the Regency, perfect gentlemen worked at nothing, not even one of the professions. On the other hand, talent was instantly acknowledged, and there was a considerable flourishing of the arts and architecture, the latter being not infrequently associated with a sycophantic desire to please the king's self-indulgent son—as when Regent Street was designed and built by Nash to provide His Royal Highness with elegant access from Carlton House to Regent's Park.

The wives of Regency gentlemen other than the King were shamelessly neglected in favour of hunting, gambling, clubbing and politicking. Entrée to Almack's Club meant more to the average upper-class husband than the feelings of his wife, membership to it being so restricted that only six Foot Guards' officers out of three hundred had been honoured with vouchers enabling the holder to go there and dance Scottish reels and the quadrille. Later, when the waltz became not so much the fashion as a mania, wives of Almack members saw less of their husbands—and Foot Guard Regiments less of their officers—than ever.

When not dancing, gambling, hunting or drinking, gentlemen spent much of their time eating. Lord Westmoreland, for example, 'made nothing of a respectable joint or a couple of fowls', and none of his contemporaries ate moderately, potatoes being served with everything and obesity being rife.

These then were the main pursuits of those who had recently officered the Brigade of Guards in Spain and Portugal and were about to lead Wellington's regiments at Waterloo; but there was one other pursuit just as important—the daily five o'clock parade of gentlemen on horseback and ladies in carriages through Hyde Park.

Which was positively rural, cows and deer grazing under its trees, no houses visible, only a few paths to disturb the sylvan illusion and absolutely none 'of the lower or middle classes', as an ex-Grenadier called Gronow put it, 'intruding themselves'.

Of those permitted to intrude themselves, Beau Brummel was the most extravagantly elegant. Invariably immaculate, and fastidious to a degree about the line of his clothes, he was constantly imitated but somehow never rivalled.

'Where do you get your blacking?' he was asked.

'Ah,' he sighed, gazing at his exquisitely polished boots, 'my blacking positively ruins me. But I will tell you in confidence, it is made with the finest champagne'.

None of this finery, nor even the euphoria that followed Waterloo, managed to endear the Prince Regent to those middle and lower classes excluded from Hyde

Members of 2nd Battalion, Grenadier Guards, 1860

A group of recruiting Sergeants in the London of 1875.
Behind them two shoe shine boys look apprehensive

Officers of the Blues who served in Egypt in 1882

Park's five o'clock perambulations. Rather, they stoned him when he opened Parliament in 1817, allowed no opportunity to pass of showing sympathy to his abandoned wife, the Princess of Wales, and when she died, as Queen, in 1821, turned her funeral into a violent demonstration against him by defeating his plan to send her cortège inconspicuously through the northern suburbs to the docks (so that she could be buried in Germany). Lying in wait for the cortège at Kensington Gate, Hyde Park Corner, Cumberland and Tyburn Gates, thousands of Londoners did battle with the escorting Life Guards and diverted the procession right through the centre of the capital.

It was a bad beginning to the reign of George IV, whose father had died at Windsor the year before. Died white-haired, blind as well as deranged, and totally alone, because Charlotte had pre-deceased him by two years, leaving him no consolation in life at all but the presence of his beloved Blues — whom the new king had promptly incorporated into the Household Cavalry and ordered up to London, to take their turn with the Life Guards doing sentry duty at Horse Guards and providing him with his constant escorts.

To his father's memory, George IV erected only one statue, and that in the grounds of Windsor Castle, where it was seldom seen and was anyway unrecognizable because it looked, with its Roman uniform, more like Julius Caesar. But if the new reign was unnaturally swift to bury Caesar, at least it continued the dead king's habit of cultivating talent in the arts and architecture, industry and transport, and even in political philosophy.

George IV was undeniably the leader of an immoral and self-indulgent upper class, yet beneath this veneer of prancing dandies, bewigged footmen, chinoiserie and Ruritanian uniforms was a ruggedly inventive society that produced the first passenger-carrying steamship in 1811, the first passenger-carrying train in 1825, the first of industry's iron machines that knew 'no suffering and no weariness', and the first aristocracy in Europe to experience an uneasy concern for those in its employ.

As to London, George IV's reign transformed it. Great stores like Swan and Edgar, Fortnum and Mason and Hatchards were built in Piccadilly. Everywhere houses were springing up, and everywhere more were needed. Madame Tussaud opened her waxworks. Clubs mushroomed in St. James's and Pall Mall. And, declaring Carlton House 'no better than a slum', the king moved into what had once been known as Arlington House, instructing Nash to convert it into a palace fit for a king and St. James's Park into grounds fit for a palace.

Thus the original Arlington House became Buckingham House and St. James's Park, which had degenerated from seventeenth-century French formalism into an English meadow bisected by a nondescript canal, became a small but agreeable lake surrounded by lawns, trees and gardens.

Today most of what Nash did to transform Arlington House is invisible to the onlooker from the Mall, but its grandiose entrance can still be seen—a mile away at Marble Arch. To which it was removed, twenty years after its erection, because, for all its grandeur, it was too narrow to accommodate the Royal coaches.

By 1830, then, the King was living in Buckingham House, his surviving brother and heir, Prince William, Duke of Clarence, lived a few hundred yards down the Mall at Clarence House, and his niece, Princess Victoria, lived a mile or so away, with her mother, the Duchess of Kent, at Kensington Palace.

All the Guards lived in barracks not too distant from the posts they were daily required to mount, and their duties in London had been substantially reduced by the recent though belated creation of a police force. Their interminable marches to duties outside London had virtually ceased, because of the construction of a network of railways; and their reputation had been vastly enhanced by their achievements at Waterloo and by such subsequent prestigious additions to their uniform as bearskins for the Foot Guards and cuirasses for the Household Cavalry. Which is not to say that any of them were yet comfortable while they served or secure upon their discharge from service.

In 1797 the Coldstream N.C.O.'s had started a Pension Fund for themselves on discharge, or for their widows and children on their decease. Sergeants paid in fourpence a week and corporals twopence; but the system broke down in 1824— when claimants' dues exceeded payments in.

Because soldiers smuggled liquor into their barrack rooms whenever it was not otherwise available, contractors were allowed to rent canteens from which they sold the worst kind of liquor at the highest possible price. Because their rent provided Parliament with some £50,000 a year, no-one in authority bothered to ensure that the contractors provided the soldier with a decent service.

Nor, once men were installed in barracks, did anyone in authority, or in the Regiment, bother to ensure that their accommodation was hygenic. In fact, a convict in his cell was allotted two and a half times the space allotted to a soldier; no space at all was allotted to the soldiers' wives, who lived in a corner of the barrack room behind a blanket; and the mortality rate of soldiers in London barracks was two and a half times that of London's civilians.

In spite of which, though always amoral, and drunk whenever they could afford it, the men of the Foot and Horse Guards had become so much better behaved in the 1820's that they were almost popular.

Summoned to London by George IV, the Blues received a letter from the Mayor of Windsor which would have been inconceivable twenty years earlier.

'*When we recollect the uniform politeness and liberality of the officers,*' the letter ran, '*and when we look back to the remarkable integrity, the undeviating regularity and the genuine respectability of the N.C.O.'s and Privates, we feel called upon for the warmest expression of our gratitude and our respectful esteem.*'

This was a far cry from the days when all soldiers were deemed 'lewd and profligate wretches', and, just as popular opinion had changed, so also did the attitude toward their men first of their officers and then of Parliament itself. If anything, however, the morals of both Foot Guards and Household Cavalry were now looser than ever, but no one minded that because society, from the King down, was also immoral. What mattered was that the Guards had at last been relieved of the odious title 'The executioner's friend', and had ceased their endless public brawling. London had become a vast and rapidly expanding metropolis and the Guards, at its centre, had effortlessly adjusted to the vices and double standards of metropolitan life.

The King's use of snuff was a perfect example of those double standards. Because it was fashionable, he carried a snuff box from which he regularly took a pinch between thumb and forefinger. Because he disliked snuff, he just as regularly allowed all of it to escape as he raised his hand to his nose and sniffed. But because the King apparently took snuff, every officers' mess passed round its own large snuff box after the port that followed its regimental dinners. In Regency London what mattered

Non-Commissioned Officers of the Blues who served in Egypt in 1882

was not what one did but how one did it—and how one looked. Thanks to George IV, the Guards looked handsome, and sinned with style.

Little changed for the Household troops when the Duke of Clarence succeeded his brother and moved into Buckingham Palace. Like George IV he had contracted a longstanding liaison with a commoner—the actress Mrs. Jordan—before his marriage to a German Princess: unlike George, he had little influence on anyone, including his Foot and Horse Guards; and of the great social, industrial and scientific changes that took place during his short reign none was to emanate from the Palace.

Those changes were, however, not to be ignored. The abolition, in 1831, of labour for children under the age of nine was the first sign anywhere of a conscience being transplanted from the heart of society into the soul of the body politic, and once the process had begun, it became and has remained a regular feature of Parliamentary surgery. It should not be forgotten that society's conscience began, most improbably, to stir during the reign of George IV and that today's British child may owe the fact that he is educated until he is sixteen to legislation conceived during George IV's reign and delivered during that of his liberal, popular but ineffectual brother, William IV.

Similarly, in an army where there were no rewards, only punishments, and no recreations, only duties, Guards officers began to provide libraries for the literate, gardens for the illiterate and savings banks for any with cash to spare. And fifteen years after the people of Windsor had expressed 'their gratitude and respectful esteem', Parliament set up a commission to enquire into military punishments.

And so, in 1836, very belatedly, there were instituted good conduct pay and medals, three meals a day, an adequate ration of fresh meat in the tropics, regimental banks and regimental schools for soldiers (sixty per cent of whom were illiterate) and their children.

Admittedly the Army's conscience remained *otherwise* impervious to the dictates of society's conscience till about 1915; but had society not made its conscience felt until 1915, the Guardsman and the Trooper of today would quite conceivably be no better looked after by his officers than was the Private of the Foot Guards and Household Cavalry in 1830.

★   ★   ★

Veterans of 3rd Battalion Grenadier Guards, Tower of
London 1894 (Sergeant Cooke pouring)

In 1834, the Palace of Westminster was burnt to the ground—to the relief no doubt of its M.P.'s, for whom the stink of the Thames (into which London's novel sewage system now ingeniously spilled all of its unwholesome effluent) had become intolerable. A new Palace of Westminster was designed, work on it was begun and its opening was celebrated in 1859. The sonorous chimes of Big Ben then usurped the role of the old, silver-throated Horse Guards clock as London's acknowledged time-keeper.

Meanwhile, William had died and young Victoria, who had never approved of his long and faithful relationship with Mrs. Jordan, came to Buckingham Palace. There she despatched her domineering mother to a separate apartment and overnight became, to the surprise of all, very much a queen. 'I delight in this work,' she wrote, and even in the stubborn years of her widowhood took pleasure from the fact that, during her long reign, Britain had become Great, her kingdom had become an Empire and London's population had quintupled to a total of six million.

For much of that time, the Thames stank so intolerably that its pleasure craft had been laid up and the Law Courts had even contemplated moving clean out of the capital. During that time, as well as the new Houses of Parliament, the Embankment, the great railway termini, the great hotels and all of the middle classes' new semi-detached suburbs (not to mention Westminster and Belgravia) were built.

Quite early in Victoria's reign Landseer's lions were added to Nelson's Column to complete Trafalgar Square, the Spring Gardens at the Whitehall end of the closed Mall were removed and Trafalgar Square was linked to the Mall—which, at its Buckingham Palace end, was linked to Hyde Park Corner by Constitution Hill.

It thus became possible for the Queen to leave the Palace by three routes instead of one. Ignoring entirely the new routes of Constitution Hill and Trafalgar Square, she invariably had her coach, or carriage, driven down the Mall, on to Horse Guards, through the arch and into Whitehall; and to this day Horse Guards Arch remains the one formal entrance to St. James's Park and Buckingham Palace—one of the main duties of the sentries posted there being to prevent any vehicle, other than those whose passengers bear an ivory pass, from driving through it.

1841 thus saw the advent of a London with which today's Guardsman, or Trooper, would be instantly familiar, even if the presence of Marble Arch in front of Buckingham Palace momentarily bothered him. But he would soon remember (from his Guardsman's repertoire of mainly false historical facts) that Nash's entrance only became Marble Arch when it was removed to the top of Oxford Street in 1851, and then would feel almost completely at home in the St. James's Park of Queen Victoria. Who, for all her autocratic manner toward Prime Ministers, had a marked sensibility toward her soldiers and servants.

At Windsor she visited the Guards' barracks and was so shocked by their bad

Changing Guard at the Horse Guards, 1880 (from *The Graphic*)

ventilation that she ordered them rebuilt.

At Balmoral she invariably attended the Gillies' Ball, enjoyed the energetic Scottish dances, and was not at all put out by their hard drinking.

At Balmoral, on the contrary—following the guns of her beloved Albert's shooting parties—she would ride side-saddle on her pony until she grew weary, then would dismount at a convenient cottage and accept from the crofter's wife, with whom she would chat, a refreshing cup of Usquebaugh or Mountain Dew. This she found so beneficial that eventually she took a stock of it back to London where it was unknown—until some anonymous lady in waiting gossiped that there was always a bottle of Usquebaugh at the Royal bedside, and Society began to follow the Queen's example, thus creating a world market for Scotch Whisky.

Perhaps likewise following Victoria's example of interest in her soldiers, officers of the Household Brigade raised £9,000 in 1852 to create a hostel for fifty-six soldiers' families just off London's Vauxhall Bridge Road. These were the first Married Quarters in London. Queen Victoria herself demanded the building of the first Married Quarters in Windsor.

Victoria made travelling by rail as fashionable as whisky, using the train to visit Balmoral, Osborne and Windsor, not in the least displeased that the railway was as popular with the poorer of her subjects as it was convenient for Albert and herself. In fact it provided for the poorer of her subjects a freedom to travel—to take holidays—to escape—never known before. It was for them as marvellous a passport to new frontiers as the chartered jet was to become for the working classes of her great, great grand-daughter, Elizabeth II; and for the Queen herself it was a means of escaping from London to the fresh air which she loved without losing touch with her ministers.

When the Crimean War loomed on the horizon, Victoria and Albert experienced at first hand London's traditional capacity for sudden hostility. Lord Palmerston had just resigned from his post as Home Secretary and London had decided (quite wrongly) that he had been forced out of office by the combined machinations of Albert and the Russians. 'Thousands of people surrounded the Tower to see the Queen and me brought to it,' (to be committed), Albert wrote to Stockmar. Then the war with Russia ceased merely to loom and became a shamefully ill-organised, protracted fact; and suddenly no-one any longer doubted the loyalty of the Queen and her Consort.

Not even the fact that she flatly forbade the use in the Crimea of her Household Cavalry made them doubt her patriotism (and had it done so, the fate of the Light Brigade would soon have changed their minds) because the Crimean War was known to be a Government rather than a Royal War, whereas the Household Cavalry were acknowledged to be Royal rather than Army troops—the latter being a distinction maintained to this day by the Life Guards.

After the war, suddenly aware of the capital to be gained by supporting the army, many M.P.'s joined a sympathetic public in belated demands for healthier barracks, cricket grounds, fives courts, gymnasia and even recreation rooms.

Life service was abolished; free education for soldiers was made compulsory; a brand-new barrack was built at Windsor (on the foundations of a railway station designed by a protege of Ruskin; and naturally abandoned when Ruskin himself was involved in a domestic scandal); and regiments ceased being the property of their colonels and became instead the responsibility of the War Department. The Queen's men had become almost human.

Upon Albert's death Victoria refused any longer to attend to the ceremonial aspects of her sovereignty. Pleading ill health, exhaustion, grief—anything—she declined to participate; but behind the scenes she continued to exert every ounce of her not inconsiderable energy, intelligence and will to the influencing of her Government and ministers at home and her Royal relatives abroad.

No one, however, least of all the Queen or her Prime Ministers, even considered the inadvisability of leaving London-based soldiers, after deductions, with no more to spend than two pence a day—which was insufficient even for an evening's drinking. The young men of the Foot and Horse Guards therefore transformed into an enterprise what had long prevailed as a free-lance occupation—the sale of their services to homosexuals.

'When a young fellow joins,' wrote one, 'some one of us breaks him in and teaches him the tricks . . . We then have no difficulty in passing him on to some gentleman, who always pays us liberally for getting a fresh young thing for him.'

Phrases like 'We all do it for money' . . . 'All the best gentlemen in London like running after soldiers' . . . 'There are lots of houses in London for it, where only soldiers are received and gentlemen sleep with them', leave no room for doubting that theirs was a well organised business. One of its several headquarters was a tobacconist's shop next door to a barracks, where a foreign lady would 'receive orders from gentlemen and then let us know'.

These soldier prostitutes were not innocents and their trade continued until the unprecedented pay rises of the 1960's made it superfluous—though operations were resumed when inflation left the London based Guardsman and Trooper as short of cash as anyone else in the early 1970's. Then, availing themselves once again of their traditional source of extra cash, and using a tailor's shop as their agency, some hundreds of them went back into business. It was as inevitable among the ranks of an underpaid Household Division as is an occasional susceptibility to bribery among the ranks of an underpaid Police force.

In the last decades of the nineteenth century, however, Victoria had more important matters upon which to expend her energies than prostitution. Instead she managed to restrain Palmerston and Russell from encouraging Denmark to go to war with Prussia; spoke forcefully in favour of slum clearance; signed the Royal Warrant that at last abolished the two hundred year-old practice of officers purchasing their commissions; and insisted upon the erection of a memorial to her beloved Albert which—sited where it was—considerably hastened the development of the market gardens south of Kensington Park into great houses for the rich, great centres of education like the Imperial College of Science and two of the capital's greatest museums—as a consequence of which, Hogmire Lane, which ran down the middle of this newly elegant area, was re-christened Gloucester Road.

Abroad, she had some slight influence on the young man who became Kaiser Wilhelm II, approved the purchase of England's Suez Canal shares, resented Gladstone's failures in the Sudan and visited Dublin for three weeks in 1900 as a gesture of her appreciation of the gallantry of her Irish troops in South Africa.

In appreciation of them, in fact, not only had she come out of retirement but, aged eighty-one, and the worst of sailors, had also crossed the Irish Sea. She was soon, as well, to approve the establishment of a Regiment of Irish Guards. She may not have understood the Irish problem—on the contrary, she regarded it as positively disloyal of the Irish even to claim that they had a problem—but she knew enough about human nature to appreciate that Queens (like music) can be used to soothe the savage breast, and she was sufficient of a Queen not to be deterred from appearing publicly in Dublin by the possibility of assassination.

She died in 1901, having rarely been seen by the majority of her subjects for almost forty years, yet revered as the Empress of what had indisputably become

Albert, Prince of Wales, in Blues Uniform

the greatest Empire the world had ever known, served by an army which the Boer War had transformed into the most efficient on the face of the earth, and known best to her servants and her Household troops—among whom it was common knowledge, for example, that she had always eaten so fast that others at her table had frequently had their plates snatched away only half-empty.

By their very infrequency the ceremonial events of her reign—the opening of the Great Exhibition in Hyde Park, Albert's funeral, her Jubilee, her own funeral—made an extraordinary impact; and when Edward VII succeeded her, and George V succeeded him, it became clear that the old Queen's obdurate withdrawal from public life had, in fact, enhanced rather than deprived London of the ritual splendours it associated with a monarch who lived in St. James's Park protected by four Regiments of Foot Guards and three of Household Cavalry.

Pioneers, 2nd Battalion Grenadier Guards, c. 1860

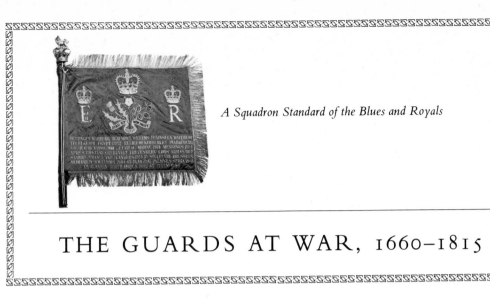

A Squadron Standard of the Blues and Royals

THE GUARDS AT WAR, 1660–1815

9 *The Guards at War in Europe 1660–1763*

FROM 1660 until today, the Guards and Household Cavalry have spent most of their time fighting one kind of war or another. Even Charles II—who was reluctant to provoke or defy anyone—made calls upon them from time to time.

In May 1664, he despatched 50 Coldstreamers to Guinea; and in 1665, he ordered 300 Foot Guards to embark on the Fleet (along with the bulk of the Household Cavalry) because Holland had insisted upon a war between herself and England. Her Fleet being superior to England's, she had unfairly decided to fight it at sea; and unable to ride down the Channel, or march across it, the King's Guards had perforce fought on it as embryonic Marines.

From 1672 to 1674 there was a second bout with Holland, during which Charles —putting expedience before integrity—allowed Louis XIV of France to become his ally and gave orders that 'Eighteen soldiers of each of the twelve companies of the Coldstream here in town [are] to embark on board such ships as the Duke of York shall appoint.' Four days later a Company of Coldstreamers was instructed 'to march to Canterbury and go for France with the battalion formed for the service of the King of France.'

Thus were they and their colleagues from the First Regiment of Foot Guards 'blooded' in Europe; and since then their blood has rarely been given time to dry before fresh wounds were inflicted upon them.

Not that the nation ever showed them the slightest gratitude for the blood they shed during Charles' reign. On the contrary, through its Members of Parliament, it drew up a list of eight reasons, entitled a Quest of Grievances, for reducing the Household troops, chief among which were that they were illegal, expensive, a refuge for Papists and superfluous to 'His Majesty's most happy and peaceable reign.'

Mindful of his father's fate at the hands of an earlier Parliament, Charles chose to ignore the Quest of Grievances but did make a few anti-French noises to convince England of his dedication to the Protestant cause.

To this end John Churchill, now a colonel, was sent to Flanders to take command of a brigade that included two battalions of Foot Guards; but before he could strike a blow against France, Charles—who needed money, which Parliament refused to vote him—accepted a massive bribe in gold from Louis and, pulling his army back to England, abandoned his allies, Holland, Germany and Spain.

Of these, Holland was the least pleased. As if nothing untoward had happened, however, Charles quartered his Guards at Somerset House—from which, as the *Protestant Intelligence* reported, his mother 'the Queen had already retired, according to His Majesty's order, to St. James'—and thereby, at a stroke, made himself independent of Parliament while committing his two most likely enemies— Holland and France—to war with one another.

He then married Portugal's Catherine of Braganza and, having received Tangier as part of her dowry, recommended that Parliament take measures for its protection; but Parliament declined to grant him the necessary supplies. Charles thereupon insisted that England's rich trade with the Levant would be lost if Tangier fell; and eventually 240 men of the First Foot Guards, and 120 Coldstreamers, were ordered to sail, with 240 other troops, from Portsmouth to Tangier.

They stayed there for four years, after which Charles decided that the Levant trade was either less valuable or less vulnerable than he had at first thought and— abandoning this portion of his dowry—recalled his Guards to London.

Charles died the following year, 1685, and was succeeded by his brother James, who inherited not only a throne but the best appointed and best disciplined army in Europe. As a practising Roman Catholic he had no need to fear Louis XIV and as Louis' friend he felt sufficiently secure to ignore the Protestant clamourings of his son-in-law, William of Orange.

In the event, he grew so over confident that he not only brought Irish Catholic officers into his army but even proposed raising a fourth wholly Catholic troop of Horse Guards. At which England grew alarmed; and when his second Catholic wife produced at last a Catholic son, William of Orange decided to depose him.

William's invasion succeeded largely because James lacked determination. In the absence of his decisive orders, Major General Churchill and other senior officers abandoned James to join the Protestant cause, and Parliament offered England's

An Officer of the Royal
Regiment of Horse Guards, 1742

throne to the deposed king's handsome daughter and her small, ugly, sickly but indomitable husband. Who, for the next thirteen years, led his suddenly acquired English army in endless wars against Louis XIV, James II and Roman Catholicism.

James, for his part, fled to France where he was received with the utmost courtesy by Louis XIV, and treated with the utmost chivalry by William III. From England the latter sent him his coaches, horses and pistols; from France the former despatched him to Ireland with ships, troops, officers and—lest he miss the trappings of majesty —a dinner service of gold and silver.

Having been received in Dublin with full honours, James set off for Londonderry, hoping there to receive the loyalty a Stuart king could surely expect from Scottish settlers.

Unfortunately Londonerry's Scottish settlers were Protestants and in no mood to welcome a Catholic king. Warned of James's approach by a group of apprentices, the fortified city slammed its gate against his army. James returned to Dublin— where the Irish Parliament had already obeyed his order to assemble but, having assembled, had naughtily proceeded to abolish the supremacy of the English Parliament (which was not what he had had in mind, since he planned soon to be *its* master as well).

It had also confiscated the property of Protestant churches and absentee landlords, annulled grants of land made to Protestant immigrants and proscribed no less than 3,000 Protestant land owners and aristocrats. Infuriated by this insolence, England demanded that Ireland be crushed—and William promptly took measures to oblige his new subjects. Sailing to Belfast with an army of 35,000, which he led south through a June heat-wave, he overtook James's force camped by the River Boyne.

Gazing down upon the enemy's tents, he murmured, 'I am glad to see you, gentlemen. If you escape me now the fault will be mine'; and if, in fact, some of his enemies did escape, it was only because they fled faster than his units of Household and other cavalry could pursue them.

William then marched upon Dublin and, having captured it, laid seige to Limerick—where the Irish (men, women and children) fought with such vicious determination that he raised the siege and returned to England.

His Irish flank secure, William took his English army to Flanders where, for the next seven years, he waged valiant but inconclusive war against France. At least, though, it was a less hideous kind of war than more civilized Europeans have developed since. It began each year in May, when the rains had stopped, and it ended each year in October, when the rank and file went into makeshift winter quarters, and their officers went home to their estates.

For almost another century this season for war was scrupulously observed; and during that century the utmost ingenuity was exercised in creating excuses for setting one army against another.

By the time Queen Mary died, her husband William had achieved little more than a stalemate in his epic struggle against France. When William himself died, nothing remotely resembling a victory had been won. When Anne became Queen, she lost no time in espousing the claim to the Spanish throne of an Austrian Prince and going to war with the French, who had espoused the conflicting claim of Philip v. The season of 1704 thus saw her instructing Marlborough—whom she had made Lord General of her army and a Duke as well—to 'cause 600 private soldiers, with a competent number of commissioned and non-commissioned officers . . . of our First and Coldstream Regiments . . . to embark [for] Portugal to be employed in Our service there.'

So they marched to Portsmouth (with thirteen wagons to carry the arms, tents, kettles, field cookers and extra clothing of the men; and ten wagons to carry the impedimenta of their thirty-odd officers) and embarked for Portugal.

In Holland, meantime, another twenty-five Companies of Foot Guards had been assembled, while a third force of six hundred had been dispatched to Spain.

The latter were besieged by the French in Barcelona for what was left of the 1705 season, during which 'never any soldiers behaved better', some of them even throwing back the enemy's grenades upon them. Discouraged by such unorthodox tactics, the French celebrated the opening of the 1706 season by raising their siege, the more superstitious among them taking note of the fact that the occasion was marked by a total eclipse of the sun.

Peace came in 1713, but Parliament's hopes that it could at last reduce the strength of the Army were dashed when the Jacobites staged their Scottish insurrection in 1715. Instead of reductions, each Regiment of the Guards was at once increased by a battalion, bringing their combined strength to almost a third of the total strength of England's standing army.

A short two year war against Spain was followed by an unprecedented twenty years of peace, during which George I managed to keep the hands of the politicians off the Army and George II to modernise it.

Trade with South America was to England in those days what North Sea oil has become today—an imagined source of limitless wealth—and when Spain suddenly insisted that England seek less rather than more of this golden trade, England went joyously back to war. 'They may ring their bells now,' growled Walpole then. 'They will be wringing their hands before long.'

England required her colonists in America to contribute 4,000 of the 12,000 men whose task it became to reduce Spain's South American garrisons. Denied proper pay, clothing, food and medicine, afflicted with yellow fever, misinformed about the Spanish defences by their guides and led by an incompetent general, the expedition was doomed from the start. Eventually, therefore, at the siege of Carthaghena, the American colonists threw down their ladders and fled. 'The general,' raged a dying colonel, 'ought to hang the guides, and the King ought to hang the general.'

In the end, yellow fever won the war as it palsied the English, deterred the French and decimated one Spanish garrison after the other. Worse, those American colonists who had survived England's leadership returned to their settlements full of hatred for all Redcoats. The Guards had taken no part in this futile little war; but they were to pay some of the price for it between 1776 and 1781.

The fact that the fighting had stopped in the New World in no way precluded the continuation of hostilities in the Old World. On the contrary, throughout each of the seasons of 1739 to 1763 the soldiers of England and Europe were constantly required to march, fight, kill, disengage and march again.

England's allies were at first Holland, Hanover and Austria, her enemies Prussia, Saxony, Bavaria, France and Spain. Initially they fought over who should rule Austria: later, the Allied cause was greatly enhanced when Austria bought off mighty Prussia with the bribe of Silesia. Thereafter Frederick the Great fought against the French—a tradition his people were to sustain without interruption until 1945.

The great characteristics of the English soldier in this war were his irresponsibility on guard, his arrogance toward foreigners, his outrages upon civilians, his excellent discipline in battle and his deadly fire power in both attack and defence.

He carried a pack weighing sixty-three pounds three ounces, was familiar with the intricacies of Prussian and English drill and was sustained by an unexpected regimental pride. He was just as shockingly led as his French counterpart, but not so well cared for when wounded, and brutally disciplined.

His cause was little advanced by the confusion that reigned among those who planned for him. The first English transports to dock at Ostend had brought not soldiers but all the Army's women; only twenty cannon had been found to support him and his 16,000 colleagues; and his commander's plan to march on Paris while France's army was contained by Austria and Prussia had been vetoed by George II on the grounds that it was Austria who was at war with Bavaria, not England with France.

Nor, in the event, was the foot soldier's cause enhanced by the fact that his mounted colleagues never bothered to train their horses to steadiness in the face of gunfire. In those days, cavalry played the role in battle that tanks and armoured cars perform today; and today's infantry would not be pleased were their tanks and armoured cars to become uncontrollable at the first sound of gunfire.

Having assumed personal command of the army in 1743, George II at last allowed his forces to clash with the French—although it was more a case of the French having trapped his Allied force at Dettingen than of the Allies having sought out their enemy.

Shouting guttural words of encouragement, George capered about on a restive horse as the English soldiers faced France's famed Household Cavalry. As the first shots were fired those closest to the King urged him to take care. 'Don't talk to me of danger,' he roared. 'I'll be even with them.' At which moment, with women shrieking and children crying, the full din of battle erupted—and the King's horse bolted.

As George careered helplessly through shot and shell, the youthful Duke of Cumberland's horse likewise bolted and the Blues' chargers became almost unmanageable.

Finally regaining control of his mount, the King leapt from the saddle announcing, 'I can trust my own legs better,' and walked back to his own lines—where Lord Stair had meantime assumed command. At his order the English began a steady, deadly fire by the platoon; stood rock-like in the face of every French onslaught; and then, uttering a fearful roar, charged.

Thus challenged, the French infantry fell back while their Household Cavalry charged. To be met, head on, by the English light cavalry, who sliced clean through them, slashed a way back into their midst and finally broke them.

Re-forming, the French returned to the attack, not once but time after time until—to the order, 'Britons strike home. This is a fine diversion'—the Horse Guards and the entire cavalry strength of the Allies were flung into the battle against them and they were routed. It then needed only a swift pursuit to annihilate them as they fled across the River Main; but King George, once again proclaiming that England was merely Austria's auxiliary, not France's enemy, called off his army, sat under an old oak tree and ate a large lunch of cold mutton. It was the last occasion upon which an English king led his men in battle.

George was succeeded as Commander by his second son, the twenty-three year old Duke of Cumberland, who was popular and brave but no military genius. War with France having at last been declared, the young Duke decided to lead a Brigade of Guards, a Brigade of Household Cavalry and his assorted allies into battle against Marshal Saxe at Fontenoy.

The Marshal awaited the young Duke's arrival with justifiable confidence, having so positioned his French Army that it was protected on the right by the River Scheldt and on the left by the Forest of Barri while, in front of him, lay an open slope up which Cumberland's forces would have to march to meet him. Saxe's cannon commanded this approach.

Ignoring the cannon shot which enfiladed their massed ranks, keeping step to the implacable beat of drums and the cheerful shrill of fifes, the Brigade of Guards marched up the half mile slope as majestically as if it were Horse Guards Parade, 'their perfect order never lost, the stately step never hurried'. Reaching the crest they halted, and Lord Charles Hay not only doffed his hat to the enemy but also, raising his flask, toasted them.

'I hope, gentlemen,' he then shouted at the French, 'that you are going to wait for us today and not swim the Scheldt as you swam the Main at Dettingen?'

Turning then to his own line, he continued, 'Men, these are the *French* Guards and I hope you are going to beat them today.'

'For what we are about to receive,' intoned a gloomy English private, evoking a roar of laughter from his comrades.

'Messieurs les Gardes français,' Hay finally suggested, 'Tirez les premiers.'

'Non, monsieur,' the French allegedly declined. 'Nous ne tirons jamais les premiers'—but promptly did so, more than a little rattled and firing high. To which the Brigade of Guards replied, from thirty paces, with regulated and murderous volleys that decimated the French, killing 19 of their officers and 600 men.

At that moment a great victory could have been Cumberland's; but his Dutch allies failed to turn the enemy's flank, and his Brigade of Household Cavalry sat curiously inert, giving the French time to launch their own cavalry in a counter-attack that forced the Allies into a savagely contested withdrawal. In spite of the generous support then offered by the Household Cavalry, almost half the Allied infantrymen were killed, two-thirds of the dead being English.

The Redcoat's reputation—high enough since Dettingen—was greatly enhanced by Fontenoy; but the battle itself, because it was not only costly but encouraged the final Jacobite uprising in Scotland as well, was counter-productive.

Cumberland's army was hurriedly recalled to England to resist the Pretender's advance. A bounty of £6 was offered to any recruit enlisting in the Guards before 24 September (of £4 to those enlisting after the 24 but before 1 October) and the Brigade of Guards was assigned the defence of London.

The Scots having already won two victories on behalf of the Catholic Pretender, England's anti-Papist prejudice—fanned by the Methodists—became so vehement that even the Quakers approved of armed resistance to Prince Charles, whose revolt began to lose impetus when he advanced into England and hundreds of his Highland supporters declined to follow him. It went into reverse when, upon the advice of some of his Scottish chieftains, he withdrew from Derby towards Montrose, in order to link up with a French invasion force.

Pursued all the way to Glasgow, he eventually joined hands with the French and laid siege to Stirling Castle. But his siege was ineptly mounted and anyway the English were approaching; so he led his 9,000 men to Bannockburn where he won a brief victory.

Ignoring the rules of the game, Cumberland now advanced from London and, in a relentless winter pursuit, harried the rebels far into the barren highlands and then, at Culloden Moor, inflicted a bloody defeat on the Pretender's army.

The epilogue to this drama was staged on 11 June, 1746, when 'a sufficient detachment from the three Regiments of Foot Guards' was ordered 'to be at Southwark on Saturday the 14th to receive 400 French prisoners into Porchester Castle'; and on 26 November when a detachment from the Foot Guards was instructed to 'be at the new gaol in Southwark on Friday next the 28th to assist in guarding the condemned rebel prisoners to Kennington Common and likewise to assisting in their execution.'

Provoked by France's support of this the last of the Jacobite rebellions, George II's armies returned to Europe for another indecisive year. Occasionally there were clashes; more often there were endless marches and mere threats of clashes. 'I do not like all this moving about,' an English officer jeered. 'I shouldn't wonder if one day or another we were to fall in with the enemy.'

It was forty years now since the Allies, under Marlborough, had won any great victories, but they seemed content to wage a war of disciplined movement, avoiding any form of conclusive contact. When peace came, they even seemed undismayed that decades of conflict had won them nothing.

Maria Theresa, upon whose behalf the Allies had last gone to war, now provoked them into declaring war upon herself by plotting with France to retrieve Silesia from Prussia.

Observing that the Austrians and French were blatantly massing on his frontiers, Frederick the Great sent a note to Maria Theresa asking if these manoeuvres portended war and begging her to reply straightforwardly.

Her reply being utterly evasive, Frederick next contacted his wife. *Madame*, ran his dutiful letter to her, '*a rush of business has prevented me from writing until now. This letter is to take my leave of you, wishing you health and contentment during the troubled times ahead.*' And that was the last she saw of him for seven years, during which he and his Prussians, aided by Hanover and England, fought off most of the rest of Europe.

The so-called Seven Years War was the first occasion upon which Britain entered a conflict at the behest of a politician rather than a king. It was the precedent for innumerable political rather than royal wars to come; and even though George III was to claw back the prerogative George II had so tamely surrendered, his own reign would see that prerogative revert forever to Parliament.

Having declared war on France and her allies at the behest of Pitt in 1756, Britain did not, however, rush precipitately into action. In the event, it was 1758 before a British force, commanded by Lord George Sackville and incorporating all the Foot Guards, the Horse Guards and the Blues, joined the Hanoverians—and found itself opposed by forty battalions and sixty squadrons of Frenchmen at Minden.

'Advance,' the Foot Guards were ordered, 'at the sound of the drum' . . . but orders in those days were as difficult to promulgate as often they were to hear, and the Foot Guards advanced *not* when the order was sounded but to the sound of the drums that were already beating.

If the Allied commander, Prince Ferdinand, was thereby disconcerted, the French were first astounded and then appalled. More remorselessly even than at Dettingen, and more terribly even than at Fontenoy, the Guards advanced upon them, delivered their scything volleys of fire, swept their infantry aside and punched a hole through three lines of their cavalry.

Ferdinand then requested Lord Sackville to order his cavalry to attack. Lord Sackville apparently did not hear, and the cavalry did not attack.

Had they done so, the war would probably have ended then and there; but not only did Lord Sackville ignore Ferdinand's first request, he ignored the second, third, fourth and fifth requests—and though victory of a sort went to the Allies that day at Minden, the war itself dragged on for four more years.

For his misconduct, Lord Sackville was court martialled and adjudged 'unfit to serve His Majesty in any military capacity whatsoever'. For their failure to charge, the Horse Guards and Blues were dismissed by the Foot Guards as 'Hyde Park soldiers . . . big men on big horses . . . useless in battle.' And to prove how lunatic politics can be, Lord Sackville subsequently became Britain's War Minister, thereby enormously assisting the American colonists in their revolt against the English King.

For all that, 1759 was a year of colossal success for Britain, with victories in Canada, India, Germany, and off the coast of Portugal. By 1760 she had an unprecedented 190,000 men under arms; and when next her army clashed with that of France— at Warburg—her cavalry was determined to make amends.

Led by the Marquis of Granby, who was Colonel of the Blues, twenty-two squadrons of horse pushed ahead of the infantry and broke into a gallop. First Granby's hat blew off, and then his wig; but Granby galloped on, and his squadrons followed his bald and gleaming head.

Momentarily flung into disarray, the French eventually counter-attacked and the King's Dragoons seemed likely to be overwhelmed. At once the Blues rallied to the support of the Dragoons, and drove off the French. Up then galloped Granby's three batteries of guns, to be followed, as their fire began to shatter the French counter-attack, by the Allied infantry. At which the French broke, with Granby's cavalry in ruthless pursuit, and the battle was won. Reporting this victory to his commander, Granby saluted, though both hatless and wigless! Since when, in his honour, the phrase 'to go at it baldheaded' has been part of the English language, and the Blues have continued to salute their officers even when hatless or capless.

For the rest of the war Ferdinand continued to dash hither and thither, making one army do the work of two as he held two enemies to a stalemate. In England George III had become King and was virtually buying control of Parliament while his soldiers continued to shed their blood in Europe but won no further victories. When peace came in 1763 Pitt's strategy had succeeded in containing France at the unconsidered but far from inconsiderable cost of making Prussia a new major power.

Having waged war almost non-stop for twenty-four years, the British soldier had achieved an unrivalled reputation for steadiness under attack and for his capacity to kill with the musket. Off the battlefield, however, he was adjudged to be 'of inferior character to the Germans', his 'loose behaviour' coming 'ill from men that looked down on all the rest of the [Allied] army'.

At least, though, he was never anything less than competent in battle. His officers, on the other hand, 'from the general to the ensign . . . though brave enough, knew nothing of their duty'. Such ignorance did not bode well for the clash that was coming in America.

10 The Guards at War in America

FOLLOWING the voyages of discovery to the North American continent, and their early exploitation by English traders and French Jesuits, London's merchants had organised an expedition which virtually evicted the French from Canada by the beginning of the seventeenth century. But, needing money, Charles I sold Canada back to France for £50,000, and Charles II ceded to France his various settlements on the Hudson.

Meanwhile, and farther south, New England had virtually smothered New France under a blanket of settlements that stretched from Virginia to Massachusets, and from Connecticut to Rhode Island. As Charles I fought to retain his throne, these four federated colonies had become cussedly independent, and had remained so until 1684, when Whitehall brought them to heel (along with such more recent settlements as Pennsylvania and the port of Nieuw Amsterdam, which had been siezed from the Dutch and renamed New York).

Three nations thus occupied North America—the English, who farmed and fished; the French, who traded far inland for furs; and the Indians, whom the French sought sedulously to convert to their faith and their imperialist cause.

Though English settlers outnumbered French traders by 90,000 to 12,000, they were riven with squabbles about boundaries and religion, ill-led and without friends. When William III declared war on France, war also broke out in America. It lasted a desultory seventy years and was indecisive because the numerically superior English settler was a less skilled woodsman than the French trader of furs, and was anyway incapable of collaborating with his neighbours.

While France made no attempt to help her colonists, New England's settlers resented such aid as Parliament elected to send them. The Redcoat, they virtuously maintained, did nothing but teach them to 'drab, drink, blaspheme, curse and damn'. They preferred the risk of being defenceless, they maintained, to the certainty of being corrupted by English defenders.

But then, in 1689, the Indians, prompted by the French, swept down from Canada and wrought bloody havoc upon their hopelessly disorganised settlements. So, in 1690, the colonists decided to retaliate and thereafter, year after year, raid and counter-raid became the pattern.

Peace in Europe did not bring peace in America; and in 1709—fearful of further massacres—the settlers finally petitioned Queen Anne to help them conquer Canada and Nova Scotia.

For once a joint effort was made not only between Redcoat and settler, but also between the Army and the Navy. Nova Scotia fell in 1710 and much of Canada was ceded to England in 1713. Raids and counter raids persisted however.

The Death of General Wolfe after his victory over the
French at Quebec, 1759 (Engraved by Thomas Brown
from a painting by Benjamin West)

Then, as the English settlers attacked in strength once again, the French—based
now upon Quebec—began to build riverside forts in unoccupied English territory.

Virginia sent a young officer called George Washington to order the French to
withdraw. Though politely received, Washington was told that such a withdrawal
would be carried out on the orders of Quebec, not of Virginia.

The following year, 1754, frequent skirmishes took place between French tres-
passers and English settlers, who, despite the exhortations of Benjamin Franklin,
remained so disunited that the French usually emerged the victors.

So Virginia sought England's help, as a result of which two regiments of five
hundred reluctant men were sent to North America under the command of General
Edward Braddock—a rough, brutal and insolent man of great courage and no
tactical flexibility whatsoever. A sometime Coldstreamer, historians assert that
he had learnt his few military skills in Flanders and that of tact he had never learnt
anything at all: his Regiment today insist that he has been much maligned.

Be that as it may, it was only Benjamin Franklin's soothing intercessions, in fact,
that eventually persuaded the colonists to provide him with some at least of the

wagons, horses and militiamen he demanded for his advance upon the French fortresses along the Ohio River. The advance itself was an unnecessarily tedious affair
wherein every molehill was levelled and every creek bridged; and as Braddock's
force crashed and stumbled into mountain and forest, Colonel George Washington,
who was on his staff, must have realised that the English had no idea how either to
attack or to defend themselves against irregulars.

Eventually Braddock's force came under heavy fire from an enemy it could not
even see. Five horses were shot from under Braddock himself and his two conspicuous regiments were cut to ribbons before finally he was mortally wounded.

'Who'd have thought it?' he groaned as, some days later, he died. Not Whitehall,
certainly, which first proceeded to import Hanoverians and Hessians to defend
England so that it could send more reluctant, conspicuous and unpopular Redcoats
to defend America; and then, when Minorca fell to the French, shot Admiral Byng
for defending it with too little conviction, introduced conscription for home service
and reinforced America with an even heavier infusion of British Regulars.

In 1758 the first fruits of this policy were born as Wolfe and Amhurst, having
reduced the French fortress of Louisburg, advanced lake by lake, swamp by swamp,
and blockhouse by blockhouse across Canada.

Wolfe was red haired, singularly ugly, a martyr to rheumatism and the stone,
and a general at the age of thirty-two—having been an officer since he was fourteen.
More importantly, he had discovered the secret of waging war in North America.

A large British fleet navigated the supposedly unnavigable (for strangers) St.
Lawrence and anchored a few miles from Quebec. The French loosed fire ships upon
it: English sailors in rowing boats towed them aside. Wolfe probed; and one
night, as the fleet sailed unseen past Quebec's guns, even risked a frontal attack.
But this having been repelled, he settled for a siege.

Only then, searching with his telescope, did he perceive the narrow path that
scaled the precipice beyond the city. Feinting for weeks, he deceived Montcalm so
that twenty-four volunteers could scale the cliff, kill its guards and enable 4,500
Redcoats to reach the heights.

Upon them Montcalm launched an immediate attack. Though shot through the
wrist, Wolfe urged his men to remain calm, and only when the French had advanced
to within thirty-five yards did he give the order to fire. From one end of the line
to the other, two perfect volleys were then delivered; and when the smoke had
cleared the French line was seen to be shattered. Wolfe's order to advance with the
bayonet completed its rout.

But Wolfe himself had been shot through the groin and the lung. 'There is no
need,' he dismissed the surgeon who came to assist him. 'It is all over with me.'

'How they run,' someone remarked.

'Who run?' asked Wolfe.

'The enemy, Sir. They give way everywhere.'

Issuing orders to cut off this retreat, Wolfe turned on his side and uttered his last words. 'Now, God be praised, I will die in peace.'

Montcalm died fighting in the city; Amhurst cleaned up the remaining pockets of French resistance and pacified the Indians and North America was made safe from the French; but there was no-one flexible enough to save it from England's cussed colonists sixteen years later, because Wolfe was dead.

★   ★   ★

From the earliest days, America's settlers had drawn little distinction between Redcoats and negroes, while the Redcoat, so cheerless was service in America, had drawn little distinction between soldiering and slavery. There were no sutlers from whom he might obtain a few extra supplies; there were no opportunities for plunder; the settlers loathed him; the Quakers despised him; many of his comrades were there only because (as criminals, Papists or deserters) their regiments at home had got rid of them; desertions were frequent; and once the French had been routed the settlers saw no need for their continued presence.

'If the French colonies should fall,' a perceptive French officer had years earlier foretold, 'Old England will not imagine that these various provinces will then unite, shake off the yoke of the English monarchy and erect themselves a democracy.'

The French officer was right. From the very beginning England had never understood, nor even attempted to understand, the mentality and aspirations of those who had emigrated to America. In 1677 she had sent a mixed battalion of First Foot Guards and Coldstreamers to suppress their abortive revolt. In 1686 she had sent more of them to Boston, which loathed them. In 1713 there had only been 900 Redcoats available to defend all the settlements in America, and those settlements had been under consistent attack by Indians. By 1775 the King had so alienated his freedom-seeking emigrants that they were prepared to fight rather than pay the taxes demanded of them. And then too few troops were sent against them too late, under generals too hide-bound to achieve anything but eventual defeat at their hands.

It was in the spring of 1775 that a British force, having destroyed a rebel magazine at Concord, was attacked as it was marching back to Lexington. A British detachment came out to rescue it and saw its survivors collapsing to the ground within the square they formed, 'their tongues hanging out of their mouths like those of dogs after a chase'.

Having killed three hundred Redcoats for the loss of ninety of their own men, the Provincials elected delegates to a Congress which voted to raise its own army, print its own currency, reject Lord North's Conciliatory Proposition and appoint

The Surrender of Lord Cornwallis after his defeat by the
Americans and the French at Yorktown, 1781 (Painting
by John Trumbull)

George Washington its Commander in Chief.

In February 1776 a detachment of the Foot Guards, 1,100 strong, was ordered to
hold itself in readiness for embarkation from England. The King gave permission
for officers 'to make up an uniform with white lace . . . the sergeants to have their
coats laced with white instead of gold, and the coats of all . . . to be modelled on
that currently worn by the Coldstreamers'.

In other words, everyone was to be as visible as possible to the colonists' militiamen
who (during the Canadian campaign) had at last learnt to harness their independence
of spirit to the demands of irregular warfare in forests and mountains.

The Guards detachment, along with 86 women and 17 children, embarked at
Portsmouth on 29 April, 1776. Almost a year had elapsed since the crisis erupted
and, during that year, Washington had scraped together an army.

At first the King's troops were successful; but the Navy seldom co-operated with
the Anglo-Hessian Army and the Army never pressed home its attacks. In the best
tradition of today's guerrillas, the colonists simply fled when in danger and returned
to the fray when their composure was restored.

Winter of course put an end to all activity as far as the British were concerned; and

June of 1777 seemed early enough to resume hostilities. Winter again won the race in 1777, and a new British commander restarted the war just as late in 1778 as his predecessor had started it the year before.

Another detachment of Guards had been sent across the Atlantic in March 1777 and further detachments were to be embarked in March 1779 and January 1781. They fought bravely, marched interminably and occupied towns, churches, fortresses and farmhouses; but they could not remain in occupation of all that they captured, nor could they seize every wood, and guard every bridge, and make impassible every stream: so the locals, when too hard pressed, continued simply to disperse and reassemble another day.

Nor did the settler risk attacking the Army's defensive squares. Instead, skilled in camouflage and sharpshooting, at home in his own woods, he picked off individual Redcoats and bided his time.

In 1778 the British withdrew from Pennsylvania to consolidate at New York— only to find that the French Fleet was outgunning their own and that the tide of war had begun to turn against them.

Though Cornwallis led an Anglo-Hessian force of about 7,000, including nearly 600 Guards, to a splendid victory in 1781, his casualties were so great that he was obliged to withdraw to the coast of Virginia where, holing up in Yorktown (to await the arrival of 5,000 promised reinforcements and 23 ships from New York), he was at once besieged by Washington's vastly superior force of 18,000, more than half of whom were French.

This mixed force of French and Provincial troops, having occupied the outworks that Cornwallis had abandoned, broke through his first line of defence on 6 October, 1782. From 9 October to 11 October they bombarded Yorktown and advanced to within three hundred yards of the main defence works. On 14 October the French took the first of two vital British redoubts and the Provincials, 'in the true spirit of emulation', took the second.

On 16 October, the Guards and their supporting grenadiers counter-attacked the French guns; but more than a hundred cannon survived this sortie to resume bombarding them. Desperate now, Cornwallis attempted to ship his men across the river to Gloucester Point under cover of darkness; but a midnight storm frustrated the attempt and he decided instead to capitulate.

From his Guards Brigade he had lost only one major, one sergeant and three soldiers killed. In view of the fact that no less than three lieutenant colonels, twelve captains, one ensign, two adjutants, one Quartermaster, one surgeon, twenty-five sergeants, twelve drummers and 465 rank and file were thus tamely surrendered, along with some 6,000 others, Yorktown cannot be regarded as a gallant Guard's failure.

For the Americans, on the other hand, it was a great victory that won them the war. For six years Washington had kept his nerve, maintained the pressure and used exactly the right tactics. He had forgotten nothing of the lessons he had learnt under Braddock, and the British had remembered nothing of the lessons taught them by Amhurst and Wolfe.

A bleak order, dated July 7th, 1783 concluded the doleful chapter of England's rule in America. 'The detachment of the Brigade of Guards lately arrived at Spithead from North America on *H.M.S. Jason*,' it said, '(are) to be disembarked at Portsmouth and march to London and join their respective regiments.'

Thus did some 360 Foot Guard prisoners of war come inconspicuously home.

11   *The Guards at War in Europe 1793–1814*

THE FRENCH Revolution caused little revulsion and even less apprehension in England until it guillotined Louis XVI and its infant Republic began to deny English ships access to European ports. Then England formed the anti-Republican confederacy of monarchies. Even so, it was France who declared war in 1793.

Thereupon George III's second son, the young Duke of York, led an army to Flanders, and the old pattern of war was resumed. The Duke led boldly, his Cavalry (including the Blues) attacked frequently, the Brigade of Guards maintained its reputation for steadiness and the spring's successes promised a summer of brilliant victories.

'The French, who had been accustomed to the cold, lifeless attacks of the Dutch, were amazed at the spirit and intrepidity of the British, and not much relishing the manner of our salute immediately gave way,' wrote a Guards Corporal.

'The Brigade of Guards,' the Adjutant General confirmed, 'advanced under a heavy fire with an order and intrepidity for which no praise can be too high. After firing three or four rounds, they rushed on with their bayonets.'

After the disagreeable events of the War of American Independence, the Brigade of Guards, it seemed, was back in business. Back with its old dash: back also with the innovation of Light Companies which carried shorter muskets and less kit, were more mobile and could be swiftly deployed. But just as the Americans had shocked the Guards by using unorthodox tactics so now did the Republican French—by fighting straight through the winter. All the successes of spring forgotten, Britain's army—destitute of supplies, munitions and fodder—crawled through the snow to ports of embarkation in Northern Germany, while the Duke of York returned home to become a mere Commander in Chief, and the repatriated Blues were despatched to Nottingham to act as mere industrial policemen.

1794 saw the emergence of a new kind of war—the kind to which the world has become accustomed ever since—a war of ideologies and propaganda. On the one side was Republican France, on the other the Royalist Allies. Chief of the Allies was England, and England was led by William Pitt.

So France declared Pitt 'an enemy of the human race' and ordered no quarter for any Englishman or Hanoverian, nor even for England itself, which the French National Convention charged with being 'capable of every outrage on humanity and every crime toward the Republic. She attacks the rights of nations and threatens to annihilate liberty'.

Thus did Robespierre abandon the rules of chivalry and preach instead the doctrine of total war. Responding, the Duke of York expressed his abhorrence of such a philosophy, but promised 'tenfold' vengeance upon French soldiers, their wives and children should Robespierre's 'atrocious' order be obeyed. Hitler and Churchill could have been using the same script in 1940; and what Rommel became to the Allies in 1942 the young Bonaparte was fast becoming to the Allies of the late eighteenth century.

Faced with a long war, and even the prospect of defeat, the British did what they could whenever they could. 1,200 men, including eight light Companies of Foot Guards, were sent on an expedition 'to blow and destroy the basin, gates and sluices of the Bruges Canal'. They failed; but the Guards fought viciously in the sand dunes before dying, escaping or being taken prisoner.

When disturbances broke out in Ireland, a Brigade of Guards was despatched to restore peace and protect Britain's rear.

When the Dutch became Britain's enemies once again, the Guards invaded Holland and fought a series of inconclusive battles.

When Napoleon occupied Egypt, the Guards—specifically those stationed in Ireland—were shipped to the Middle East, to train as the spearhead of an invasion force.

In March 1801 they and the rest of the English force rowed and waded ashore against a confident, desert-conditioned French army—and defeated it. Though Napoleon himself was not in command, this Egyptian surrender was regarded by the rest of the world as his first failure; but the peace that followed was illusory.

As First Consul, Napoleon was soon making no secret of his intention to invade England; and England made no secret of her intention to resist. The King took up quarters at Windsor Castle; Martello Towers were built all over the country; and the N.C.O.'s and Corps of Drums of the Guards Brigade in Egypt contributed £111.5.7 to a Patriotic Fund 'for the relief of any who might suffer should the implacable enemy of our country invade her shores'.

Crowned Emperor at the end of 1804, Napoleon abandoned his plan to cross the channel and set about crushing all of Europe instead.

Life Guardsman, *c.* 1790

In June 1806 he intervened in a squabble as to which of the claimants to the Spanish throne should sit upon it and, deciding that none of them should, made his brother the new King. Ten days later a revolt broke out in Portugal. It quickly spread to Spain and eventually led to Sir Arthur Wellesley being sent from Cork to co-ordinate this unlikely challenge to the Emperor's authority.

In 1807 the Danes succumbed to Napoleon's demands that they abandon their neutral stance and cease all trade and commerce with Britain. On 9 August, a detachment of Coldstream and Scots Guards landed in hapless Denmark and invested Copenhagen while the Royal Navy bombarded it. The Danish fleet surrendered, intact, and the Guards entered Copenhagen on 7 September.

In 1809 the Guards landed in Portugal, to join Wellesley's army of 25,000 (which included 3,000 Germans and 9,000 Portugese). Wellesley initiated a series of minor but effective battles quite unlike anything the French had encountered since Marlborough's day. The Grenadiers distinguished themselves at Corunna, the River Douro was crossed, Oporto was taken and the enemy was constantly harried. The Guards—in Wellesley's own words—'set a laudable example'.

At Talavera they did more. At Talavera, in fact, the whole army did more, so that the French were obliged to withdraw, giving the Allies their first victory in Spain.

Flushed with victories of his own over the Austrians, a vengeful Napoleon now promised Wellesley—whom he dismissed as a mere general of Sepoys—'shame, defeat and death'. George III, on the other hand, made Wellesley a viscount and, adopting the name of Wellington, the new viscount withdrew his army back into Portugal, where, on behalf of Napoleon, Marshal Massena at once invited the Portugese to surrender.

'Can the feeble army of the British general expect to oppose the victorious legions of the Emperor?' he demanded. 'Already a force is collected sufficient to overwhelm your country. Snatch the moment that mercy and generosity offer. As friends you may respect us, and be respected in return. As foes you must dread us and, in the conflict, must be subdued. The choice is your own—either to meet the horrors of a bloody war and see your country desolated, your villages in flames, your cities plundered, or to accept an honourable peace which will obtain for you such blessings as a vain resistance would deny you forever.'

The Portugese having rejected 'the moment that mercy and generosity' offered, Massena had to admit that the Allied lines—guarded as they were by the sea, the Tagus and the fortifications long since erected upon Wellington's far-seeing orders—were unassailable. Though his army numbered 300,000 to Wellington's 48,857, Lisbon was so obviously secure that he declined to attack.

For the next nine months, moreover, Wellington so consistently outmarched and outfought him that by the beginning of 1811 the French were on the retreat and by 3 April Portugal itself had been liberated.

Now the Life Guards and Blues arrived, most of their horses, after a bad voyage, palpably unfit. 'The strictest attention must be paid to the rubbing of horses' nostrils with vinegar at the first sight of any indisposition', the order was therefore given. 'On most occasions of this sort they ought to be bled in the mouth until the arrival of the veterinary surgeon.'

As to those who rode the horses, most of the soldiers had cut off their pig tails and dispensed with powdering their hair while at sea, and when ashore had found that the shoes issued to save their jackboots did not fit, that their pay had not arrived, and that their officers knew so little of drill that Wellington described one of their early charges as 'the undisciplined stampede of a rabble'.

But they trained, and improved—the Life Guards picturesque in leg hugging trousers, tight high-collared tunics and elaborately plumed helmets with a metal coxcomb—and as they crossed the frontier into Spain, Wellington first raised his hat to them and then declared, 'Farewell, Portugal. I shall never see you again'.

While the Allies invested one Spanish fortress after another, Napoleon started his march on Moscow. As his 475,000 men advanced across Russia, the Allies entered Madrid. Winter came, and Napoleon's advance froze to a halt. Prussia abandoned him, and Bavaria and Austria sprang to Russia's support. Napoleon reinforced his army in Germany at the expense of his army in Spain, where Wellington forced the French backwards. When Spain was cleared of the Emperor's legions, Wellington decided to take the battle to France itself.

On 14 April, 1814, his army captured Toulouse. The French made a desperate counter-attack from nearby Bayonne and briefly recaptured St. Étienne. The Guards evicted the French from St. Étienne. And only then did both sides learn that they had fought in vain because Napoleon had abdicated on 11 April. Elba, in future, was to be, it seemed, his sole domain.

12   The Guards at War in Europe: Waterloo

DUE LARGELY to the carelessness of his British Commissioner, and prompted by rumours that the Allied monarchs wanted him confined on remote St. Helena, Napoleon soon escaped from Elba, crossed to the French coast near Cannes and there rallied a vast army to his Eagles. Louis XVIII, his successor on the French throne, lost no time in fleeing to England and the Allies were equally swift to offer the Duke of Wellington the command of a defensive line that extended from Switzerland to the North Sea.

While Napoleon marched to Paris, which he entered in triumph, Austria, Russia, Prussia and England came to an agreement never to lay down their arms until he was defeated once and for all.

To that end England was to spend £116 million in what remained of 1815 and forthwith to send all the troops and cavalry she could muster to Belgium. From Prussia, General Blucher began a march to Belgium and from Paris Napoleon set forth with 150,000 men and 296 pieces of artillery, confident that he could destroy Wellington's 64,000 men and 160 guns.

'The worst army I ever commanded,' was Wellington's description of the force at his disposal. Sailing from Ramsgate to Ostend to join him, General Sir Robert Picton was equally critical.

'If I had 50,000 such men as I commanded in *Spain*, with *French* officers at their head,' he grumbled, 'I'm damned if I wouldn't march from one end of Europe to the other.'

Piqued, his A.D.C. replied, 'This is the first time we have heard, Sir Thomas, that French officers are better than ours.'

'What?', roared Sir Thomas. 'Never heard they were superior to ours? Why, damn it, where is our military education? Where are our military schools and colleges? We have none. Absolutely none. Our greatest generals, Marlborough and Wellington, both learnt the art of war in France. Nine French officers out of ten can command an army, while our fellows—though as brave as lions—are totally and utterly ignorant of their profession. Damn it, Sir, they know nothing. We are saved by our non-commissioned officers, who are the best in the world.'

And not even the officers he so scorned seem to have been disposed to rebut him. 'After leaving Eton,' wrote Captain Gronow of the First Regiment of Guards, 'I received an ensign's commission during the month of December 1812 . . . and cannot but recollect with astonishment how limited and imperfect was the training which an officer received at that time. He absolutely entered the army without any military education whatever . . . The excellence of our non-commissioned officers alone prevented us from meeting with the most fatal disasters in the face of the enemy.'

With some officers, indeed, not even the excellent non-commissioned officer was able to cope. Ensign Dawson was discovered by Gronow far from his men and 'surrounded by muleteers with whom he was bargaining to provide carriage for his innumerable hampers of wine, hams, potted meat and other good things which he had brought from England. He was a particularly gentlemanly and amiable man, much beloved by the regiment. No one was so hospitable, or lived so magnificently. His cooks were the best in the army and he had besides a host of servants, of all nations—Spaniards, Frenchmen, Portuguese, Italians—who were employed in scouring the country for provisions.'

Very sensibly, Lord Wellington had sought out Ensign Dawson and found him in his tent, 'alone at a table with a dinner fit for a king, his plate and linen in good keeping, and his wines perfect'. But before the year was out, the gentlemanly and amiable ensign had dissipated his entire fortune and been obliged to leave the Guards.

Of his brother officers, many, due to a similar self-indulgence, had been captured in the Peninsular War simply because they were so grossly overweight that when ambushed they were unable to flee. The most abstinent of them was accustomed to several bottles of port per dinner: the more highly regarded of them consumed four or five: and the most admired put away no less than six.

Of the latter, none was more admired than Lord Saye and Sele, who served omelettes made entirely of the eggs of golden pheasants and drank 'absynthe and caracoa in quantities which were perfectly awful to behold'. There were even times—presumably when he could not face another omelette or drink another glass of caracoa—when he would simply order his manservant, 'Place two bottles of sherry by my bedside and call me the day after tomorrow!'

Finally, these flabby and semi-sodden officers wore tunics and breeches so tight that any kind of exertion was difficult. 'Nobody,' complained Gronow, 'can conceive the inconvenience of our military costumes . . . or the annoyance of needing a constant coiffeur to powder hair'—about which the Duke of Cambridge, the Army's Commander in Chief, was most punctilious. Nothing so put him out as officers with unevenly powdered hair. Yet the coiffeur of the day, to whom everyone went, charged five shillings simply to *cut* hair. It was enough to make many a young officer long for the renewal of war—of which, for all their incompetence, they had no fear at all.

'Now I had barrack duty in town,' one of them complained during the month before Napoleon escaped Elba. 'Walking up and down St. James Street and such like [is an] expensive and not amusing duty to do after active service abroad.' Presumably the middle days of June 1815 found him less disconsolate as he prepared to face the Emperor's enormous army in Belgium.

Which army had divided, part of it, under Marshal Ney, to capture Quatre Bras, the other part, under Napoleon, to head off the Prussians, under Blucher, at St. Armand and Ligny.

In spite of Blucher's gallant attempts to join hands with Wellington's left flank (and perhaps because Blucher laboured occasionally under the delusion that he was pregnant by an elephant) Napoleon flung the Prussians back and might well have won the battle for Europe then and there had not Marshal Ney, for his part, failed to dislodge the Guards from Quatre Bras, in spite of the fact that they had marched twenty-six miles in a day to resist him.

'*All the world's in Paris*', was a popular song at the time, and the Guards had sung it lustily as they marched; but when they sighted the enemy the singing stopped, their officers dismounted, the senior subalterns took the King's Colours and the junior ensign the Regimental Colours from the sergeants carrying them, and, taking up their defensive positions, they all prepared to receive a vastly superior force of Frenchmen.

'I shouldn't give sixpence for *your* chances,' a friend encouraged one of the senior subalterns who laboured under the weight of the King's Colour. Events were to prove his prophecy as accurate as it was tactless: by nightfall the senior subaltern and five hundred others of the First Regiment had fallen.

Quatre Bras, on the other hand, had not. Even so, advised of Blucher's defeat, Wellington was obliged to pull back his army so that its left flank would become accessible to the re-grouping Prussians. Though he had ridden forty-three miles the previous day, and escaped capture at Quatre Bras only by putting his horse to the gallop and jumping a ditchful of startled Highlanders, he seemed tireless as he trotted from one vantage point to the next, and no one was left in any doubt that he knew exactly the line he now wanted.

In fact, he had known it for days, having not only reconnoitred the area himself, but having also studied a report of a long ago reconnaissance by the Duke of Marlborough. Thus, when the belated news of Napoleon's advance into Belgium interrupted the Duchess of Richmond's ball in Brussels (a cavalry brigade stationed at Mons had inexplicably failed to report the Emperor's earlier movements) Wellington was able to take the Duke into a study and—drawing his thumb nail down a map—explain, 'I shall fight him here.' *Here* being a ridge just south of Mont St. Jean.

'If only,' the Prussian General, Baron Muffling, later remarked to Wellington, to whose staff he was attached, 'there were an apparently weak point in the *right* flank of your position, so that Bonaparte might assail it and neglect his own right wing to such an extent that he should fail to discover the march of the Prussians.'

Wellington took the point, and chose Hougoumont's small château as that apparently weak point. It was a risk, because his right wing guarded his line of communications to England. Should Hougoumont fall, his army would be cut off from home, supplies and reinforcements.

'It all depends,' Wellington remarked to the visiting and apparently ubiquitous M.P., Mr. Creevey, pointing at a British infantryman, 'on that article there! Give me enough of him, and I am sure.'

His right flank, then, by night-fall, was the Chateau Hougoumont; his main force held the central ridge of Mont St. Jean with his heavy cavalry standing to arms just below its skyline; his left flank was optimistically deployed to meet the Prussians; and his advance outpost was La Haye Sainte. The next move, when morning came, would be Napoleon's.

First, though, a miserable night was spent by both armies. Rain lashed them as they prepared for battle, and froze them as they attempted to sleep; and nowhere were conditions worse than at Hougoumont, whose château walls had to be loop-holed, gates reinforced, outbuildings fortified and orchard occupied.

'The field where we were,' wrote one of its defenders, 'was half way up our legs in mud' and 'nobody, of course, could lie down.'

Elsewhere in the grounds there was less mud and many men shared sodden blankets. General Byng, whose rank precluded the sharing of a blanket, covered himself with straw and 'bellowed lustily when trodden on'. Almost none slept, if only because of the thunder which, 'like heaven's artillery, accompanied by vivid flashes of lightning, peeled in solemn and awful grandeur'.

At dawn, all stood to at Hougoumont—on the château walls and in the out-buildings, and in the grounds, in hollow squares, awaiting the inevitable cavalry charge. There were Hanoverians and Nassauers, First Guardsmen, Coldstreamers and Scots Guardsmen, the Light Companies of the First Division and artillerymen; and they all waited.

Wellington rode up and moved the Scots Guard out of the orchard to a position between a haystack and the main gate that led into the château. He ordered the Light Companies, 'Defend your post to the last extremity.' He despatched the Hanoverians and Nassauers to the orchard to replace the Scots Guards. And the waiting continued, both armies firing a veritable *feu de joie* at dawn as they sought to dry out their flint lock muskets.

Nothing, though, could hasten the drying out of the soggy fields that separated the two armies, so Napoleon delayed his cavalry onslaught while Wellington's men refreshed themselves with gin and wet bread, sitting round laboriously constructed fires.

The sun rose and the day became fine and clear. From its position along the ridge of Mont St. Jean, the British Army looked down upon the long French lines, from which came the glitter of thousands of cuirasses, and tantalising glimpses of the Emperor on his white charger.

'Je les tiens donc, ces Anglais,' Napoleon gloated, staring uphill at Wellington's waiting army.

'If well placed,' one of his generals felt constrained to warn, 'and attacked from the front, the English infantry is invincible by reason of its calm tenacity and the superiority of its rifle fire.'

'Sire,' General Foy confirmed, 'Wellington never shows his troops, but if he *is* yonder, I must warn your Majesty that the English infantry in close combat is the very devil.'

Unpersuaded, ignoring the streak of swift, unpremeditated daring his adversary had displayed at Vitoria, the Emperor remained convinced that he could out-

The Captured Eagle, by J. P. Beadle. Taken by the Royal
Dragoons from the 105 5th French Regiment

general Wellington and then defeat the Allies piecemeal. Wellington meantime—
the better to see what Napoleon might be doing—had climbed a tree.

There his colleague General Alava found him.

'How are you, Alava?' greeted His Grace, quite unperturbed. 'Bonaparte shall
see today how a general of sepoys can defend a position.'

That defence began at about 11.30 in the morning when suddenly the bands of
several French regiments began to play, then the French artillery opened fire and
finally the ominous rhythms of the *pas de charge* were beat on enemy drums. As
the *cuirassiers* galloped forward, bellowing 'Vive L'Empereur', a profound silence
fell upon the whole of Wellington's line.

Unaware of Wellington's tactics (which remained to lure him on to the Allied right wing, so that he would not observe the approach of the Prussians toward its left), Napoleon opened the battle with an attack all along the line from the outpost at La Haye Sainte to the right wing at Hougoumont. From whose orchard, upon the third onslaught, the Hanoverians and Nassauers were evicted; but the Scots Guards, First Guards and Coldstream Light Companies promptly counter-attacked and ejected the French.

'Hard pounding,' a wry Wellington was soon to comment. 'We shall see who can pound the hardest.'

At La Haye Sainte, General Sir Thomas Picton's force survived Marshal Ney's massive attack, even though Picton himself was killed and his Dutch contingent had fled. Wellington sent a brigade forward in support and Lord Uxbridge—who commanded the heavy cavalry—not only took it upon himself to order a charge but impetuously put himself at its head.

Drawing their swords, adjusting the 'scales' of their metal chin-straps, the brigade walked its horses up on to the skyline of the ridge of Mont St. Jean.

'Now, gentlemen,' Wellington exhorted as they trotted past him, 'for the honour of the Household Brigade!' He had given Uxbridge carte blanche, and was about to regret it, but apparently had no qualms about the 'heavies' at that moment.

They cantered until their sixteen-year-old trumpeter (who had done seven years service already) sounded the charge, at which they galloped—the Blues, the First Life Guards and the Second Life Guards—two thousand huge men on two thousand huge horses—all thundering toward the French, swords flashing—with Uxbridge (the man who should have been observing, co-ordinating and controlling their attack) recklessly at their head, one horse after the other being shot from under him.

English cavalry met French cavalry and the French, overwhelmed by the Household's dash and resolution, not to mention its bigger and fresher horses, broke and fled.

Elated, the First Life Guards, supported by the Scots Greys, careered onwards and into the ranks of French infantry, all cohesion lost, but sheer momentum and daring transforming a hundred little duels into a corporate victory from which, by sheer good luck, they were able to withdraw.

The Second Life Guards, meantime, found themselves clear through the enemy's infantry and among the limbers of his artillery. Having destroyed fifteen cannon and wrought as much damage as possible, it was clearly time to go home; but the French had other ideas.

Fresh French cavalry fell upon the exhausted Second Life Guards. The improvident Uxbridge galloped back to bring up his reserves, and found that he had none. All had joined the fray. All, except for the steadier supporting Blues, with their steadier Cromwellian traditions, were scattered everywhere and suffering fearfully for their temerity.

French guns, infantry, cuirassiers and lancers had joined forces to hunt down the Second Life Guardsmen, while the Blues did their utmost to retrieve them. A startling impromptu victory (by a mere eighteen squadrons of horse against a corps of infantry, a brigade of cavalry and a mass of artillery) had degenerated into an unco-ordinated mêlée.

Admittedly there were heroic episodes. Captain Kelly and the prize-fighter Corporal Shaw, for example, hacked their way through a host of the enemy until Shaw—flailing with his helmet—was fatally pierced and then shot dead by a French drummer boy. Kelly promptly despatched Shaw's assailant and then managed to fight his way through to safety because, as he later explained, his charger 'was well bred, very well broke and of immense power'.

Courageous riders and well bred chargers notwithstanding, only 250 men and horses returned from the charge to muster behind Wellington's lines. 'Thank you, Life Guards,' he said; but Gronow, in his memoirs, writes that the Duke was furious and the survivors dejected, 'their horses blowing sorely' and their contribution to the battle virtually at an end.

'Where are *our* fellows?' the hard pressed infantrymen kept demanding as, time upon time, the French cavalry descended upon their squares, first upon the front, then upon the sides, searching for the vulnerable spot, the one way in.

'Courage mes enfants,' exhorted La Bédoyère, 'the English waver and will soon give way. Charge those squares and the day will be ours.'

All day long every square had been bombarded, its defenders adopting the unprecedented expedient of lying flat as the shot fell and the grape flew. Even so, their losses were appalling to witness, every yard a corpse or a man shockingly wounded, the air so acrid that it was almost impossible to breathe and the smoke of gunpowder so dense that it was almost impossible to see. The mutilations— particularly of the face, where it was common to see entire jaws sliced off by grape shot—were so ghastly that cavalry attacks came as a positive relief, accompanied as they were, by silence from the French artillery.

Even so, the earth would shake under hooves 'advancing like a tidal wave'. 'Vive l'Empereur,' the French cavalry shouted. 'Prepare to receive cavalry,' the squares were ordered. And, having admitted the artillery's guns within their four human walls, the infantrymen rose to their knees, bristling steel, and awaited the riders who had conquered the whole of Europe.

Because the squares fired low, to dismount the enemy cavalrymen, then picked them off as they lurched through the mud in their cumbersome jackboots and cuirasses, none of the squares was ever penetrated; but the impudence of the

French and the carnage they inflicted enraged the British. 'Why don't our fellows come and pitch into theirs?' they shouted—and Wellington, who was everywhere on his favourite horse, pale under his enormous cocked hat, did not explain.

But Napoleon, too, was having cavalry problems as Soult protested the futility of further charges. Not that the cuirassiers had lost their nerve but that their horses—foam flecked and trembling at the sight and smell of so much carnage, at the din of bullets striking breast plates—had begun to pull up at least twenty yards short of the terrible English squares, obliging the officers who rode them to dismount and—brandishing their useless swords, crying a last 'Vive l'Empereur'—be mown down.

'Vous croyez Wellington un grand homme, General, parce qu'il vous a battu,' Napoleon sneered, and insisted that Soult resume the charges.

Then Ney attacked the outpost at La Haye Sainte a second time, and took it at about 4 p.m.; but he had no reserves with which to exploit his success, and the opportunity passed as Wellington's battered heavy cavalry hurriedly plugged this gap in the Allied line.

At Hougoumont, meantime, the orchard had been captured, the hay-stack and outbuildings set on fire and the main gate valiantly attacked by Frenchmen bearing rifles and axes; but the resistance continued.

'If Grouchy does not come up,' Napoleon now confessed to Jerome, 'or if you do not carry Hougoumont, the battle is decidedly lost. So go. Go and carry Hougoumont, coûte que coûte!'

Wellington likewise issued further orders for Hougoumont. Acknowledging that the château was ablaze, he instructed: 'You must however keep your men in those parts to which the fire does not reach. Take care that no men are lost by the falling in of the roof and floors'; but, 'after they will have fallen in, occupy the ruined walls inside the garden . . .'

It was the Coldstream and Scots Guards who took the brunt of the endless attacks on Hougoumont, and at no time did they yield. Through hedges, around the burning hay-stack, in and out of outbuildings and by the crucial main gate man fought man with bayonet, sword, bullet, axe and sheer brute force.

No less than three French divisions having been committed in vain to the attack on Hougoumont, Napoleon decided to bombard it. The ensuing conflagrations drove the Scots Guards snipers out of the haystack and gardens and back to the château wall, where the Coldstreamers gave them cover.

There the French pursued them, undeterred by the withering Coldstream fire. Led by an axe-brandishing sous-lieutenant, nicknamed L'Enforceur, they hurled themselves upon the main gate which was barred with a length of heavy timber. L'Enforceur hacked through the gate and those supporting him battered it open. Two lieutenant colonels, two ensigns, two non-commissioned officers (brothers

Up Guards and at 'em—the order that destroyed Napoleon's
final onslaught of the Imperial Guards

called Graham) and a handful of ardent privates (all of them Guards) killed the
French intruders and closed the gate again. The battle for Hougoumont, though
far from over, had been won.

'It was touch and go,' Lord Saltoun later declared. 'A matter of life and death,
for all within the walls had sworn they would never surrender.'

An adjutant confirmed Saltoun's sombre words. 'Our officers,' he said, 'were
determined never to yield; and the men were resolved to stand by them to the
last.'

Thus, when the remnants of the First Guards Light Companies left Hougoumont
and joined the First Regiment in the centre of the line, General Maitland publicly
congratulated them. 'Your defence saved the army,' he declared. 'Nothing could
be more gallant. Every man of you deserves promotion.'

To this day, the Scots Guards who stood firm among burning outbuildings
and repelled wave after wave of Frenchmen regard Hougoumont as their finest
hour. Forced to yield from time to time, they had withdrawn only so far as a

hollow beneath the château walls; and as soon as the Coldstream's fire through the loopholes in those walls had given them a respite, they had counter-attacked. They had had no idea what was happening elsewhere in the battle; and even when the battle was won, their struggle had continued as bitterly as ever.

One example tells the story of them all. A private regained consciousness in the arms of his colonel. 'I was shot a wee bit about the temple,' he felt obliged to explain, and struggled to his feet, only to faint again and be carried to the chateau kitchen where he lay with the rest of the wounded. Minutes later every officer in his company was dead and its command had passed to the senior sergeant.

'What o'clock is it?' Wellington asked one of his staff, back at Mont St. Jean.

'Twenty minutes past four,' a colonel told him.

'The battle is mine,' the Duke then observed, 'and if the Prussians arrive soon there will be an end of the war.'

Yet still the French cavalry—cuirassiers, heavy dragoons, lancers, hussars and carabiniers—attacked the fatal, chequered squares.

'Many a time,' confessed Gronow, 'the heart sickened at the moaning which came from man and scarcely less intelligent horse as they lay in fearful agony upon the field of battle.'

'Their fire was dreadful,' Napoleon himself lamented, 'and as to charging, one might as well have charged stone walls.'

Not that it was the French alone who suffered. 'For God's sake,' implored the English wounded—laid out in wagons and left to swelter on that hot June day—'for God's sake, give us water.' But no one had time to water most of them; and those few for whom an officer filled his shako from a nearby muddy pool were the fortunate exceptions.

By early afternoon, though the surgeon's knives were already blunted from so many amputations, many more remained to be performed.

'Take your time, Mr. Carver,' muttered a sardonic officer whose leg had been nearly severed at the thigh. He died soon after the surgeon, a Mr. Gilder, had attended to his stump.

An ensign had the remnants of his leg amputated and then hopped, declining all assistance, to the wagon that would bear him out of battle.

And scores of Life Guards—striped naked by the enemy within whose lines they lay—died totally neglected.

Between and behind the lines the few soldiers' wives allowed to accompany their husbands to Belgium did their best. Mrs. Osborne, the wife of a Private in the Scots Guards, was busy tending the wounded when she was shot in the arm and breast. Being a soldier's wife in the nineteenth century was no better than it had been a hundred years before.

At five o'clock Napoleon advanced his artillery to within a quarter of a mile of the frustrating English squares. Wellington countered by withdrawing his infantry just over the crest of the ridge and ordering them to lie down. Stunned with fatigue, most of them fell instantly asleep.

But not for long, because up the slope toward them Napoleon now despatched three fresh regiments of the Grenadiers of his Imperial Guard. In a solid, tramping, roaring phalanx of thousands upon thousands of bobbing bearskins and out-thrust bayonets, France's all-conquering veterans were executing their terrifying Grande Advance.

'*Now*, Maitland,' shouted Wellington, 'Now's your time!' And (raising his voice so that it could be heard even above the enemy's roar of 'Vive l'Empereur. En avant, en avant,') called, 'Stand up, Guards.'

Firing as they topped the crest and knelt, the two battalions of the First Guards hit the Imperial Guard with deadly, disciplined volleys. Hit its massed phalanx with bullets that could not miss, that plucked from the flower of France's army 'a bouquet to all slaughter'.

Then, clashing head-on, British Guardsmen fought French Guardsmen, hand-to-hand. Assisted by gravity and their fellow countrymen, and inspired by their insular contempt for 'Boney and his Froggies', the First Regiment stopped the Imperial Guard dead in its tracks and inflicted upon it a kind of butchery it had never before endured.

'I observed a big Welshman of the name of Hughes, who was six foot seven inches in height,' Gronow records, 'run through with his bayonet and knock down with the butt end of his flint lock I should think a dozen at least of his opponents.'

Ten minutes of it was enough. All momentum lost, assailed from the rear by English sabres and from the front by English bayonets, the Imperial Guard turned and fled; and from the incredulous ranks of the French Army below there arose the unprecedented cry, 'La Garde recule. Sauve qui peut.'

At Hougoumont, also, the slaughter subsided; but elsewhere, even as the Prussians arrived in force, French cannon continued to belch defiance, one of their last shots striking the hapless Lord Uxbridge, who sat on horseback beside Wellington. Flung to the ground, he cried, 'By God, I've lost a leg.'

'By God,' acknowledged Wellington, looking down, 'so you have.'

Later, riding with Baron Muffling, Wellington passed Hougoumont, its main gate covered in bloody hand-prints, its orchard of shattered apple trees littered with red, blue and green-clad corpses, its charred haystack surrounded by scores of shrivelled and dehydrated dead.

'You see,' he said simply, 'the Guards held Hougoumont'—2,000 of them, he might have added, against 18,000 French veterans and so many French reserves that there had been none left to exploit Ney's break through at La Haye Sainte.

Of the battle as a whole, Wellington confessed that it had been 'a damned nice

A Life Guardsman Charging the Enemy at Waterloo

thing. The nearest run thing you ever saw in your life'. But he was in no mood to rejoice. After eighteen hours in the saddle, he was doubtless tired and perhaps a little despondent. 'I am quite heartbroken by the loss I have sustained,' he lamented. 'My friends . . . How many of them I have to regret.'

Later that night, though, back in Brussels, and suitably refreshed, he spoke more like the victor he was.

'Well,' he declared, 'thank God I don't know what it is to lose a battle; but certainly nothing can be more painful than to win one with the loss of so many of one's friends.'

Mr. Creevey, of course, sought him out and as they shook hands Wellington told him, 'I have won the greatest battle of modern times with 12,000 of my old Peninsular troops'.

'What sir?' queried Creevey, 'With 12,000 only?'—because Wellington had commanded 65,000 at Waterloo, among whom, as well as Englishmen, were Hanoverians, Nassauers, Dutchmen and Belgians.

'Yes, Creevey,' Wellington insisted, as much presumably for Parliament's ears as for those of an individual M.P., 'with 12,000 of my old Spanish infantry. I knew I could depend on them. They fought the battle without flinching, against immense odds. But nearly all my staff and some of my best friends were killed'. And then, before Mr. Creevey could outstay his welcome, 'Goodnight. I want rest and must go to bed.'

For him it was the end of his finest day. For Napoleon it was the end of an awesome career. For England it was the beginning of forty years of unprecedented glory. For the wounded it was the middle of a long, untended night of thirst and torment. But for the Guards—Foot and Horse—it was the culmination of a hundred and fifty years of regimental history.

Lord Uxbridge acknowledged the fact with a gesture typical, in its eccentricity, of a Household Cavalry officer who had had nine horses shot from under him during the day and had himself been shot off the tenth. After an operation by candle light, he ordered that his amputated leg be buried in the battlefield of Waterloo.

Just as effectively buried was the Guards' rankling humiliation of defeat in America. Thirty-four years old that defeat might have been, but the Brigade never forgets; and it needed Waterloo to expunge the shame of Yorktown.

The better to sustain its extraordinary memory, the Household Division cherishes the weirdest relics, of which inevitably, Waterloo has provided its share. One of the hooves of Napoleon's charger, Marengo, is now a snuff box on the dining table of the officers' Guard Room at St. James's Palace. Officers entertaining there are inclined to laugh it off, describing it as Marengo's 'thirteenth authentic hoof' and explaining that 'English gentlemen don't put snuff in their *own* horse's hooves'; but so long as there is a sovereign to guard at Buckingham Palace, that awful snuff box will remain on that splendid table.

In the Household Cavalry Museum at Windsor, on the other hand, one of the honoured exhibits will always be a cast of the skull of the pugilist Corporal Shaw. This was disinterred from Waterloo at the suggestion of Sir Walter Scott, who had met him modelling at the studio of the artist Haydon—and who should have known better. Just as proudly displayed is Lord Uxbridge's artificial leg. Fortunately it has not yet occurred to the Household Cavalry to replace it with the original amputated limb, but that time will inevitably come.

As well as relics, of course, Waterloo was to yield a rich harvest of honours, controversy and personal tragedy.

His Royal Highness, stated the London Gazette of 29 July, 1815, *has been pleased to approve of the First Regiment of Foot Guards being made a Regiment of Grenadiers and styled 'The First or Grenadier Regiment' in commemoration of their having defeated the*

Grenadiers of the French Imperial Guards . . . As a further token of his Royal pleasure, the Regent ordered that the First Regiment should assume not only the French Imperial Guards' title of Grenadiers but also their head-dress, the bearskin.

Not satisfied with that, the Prince Regent declared himself 'Colonel in Chief of the Household Cavalry as a mark of his august appreciation of their gallantry at the Battle of Waterloo'.

'Ah,' commented the Duke of Wellington, when he received this news in Paris. 'His Royal Highness is our Sovereign and can therefore do whatever he pleases. But this I will say—the cavalry of *other* European armies have usually *won* victories for their generals: mine have invariably got me into scrapes.'

France's General Excelmann was inclined to agree. 'Your horses are the finest in the world,' he said, 'and your men ride better than any continental soldiers. With such material, your English Cavalry ought to have done more than in fact they ever achieved on the field of battle. The great deficiency is in your officers, who have nothing to commend them but their dash and the way they sit in their saddles.

'Indeed, in my experience, your English generals have never understood the use of cavalry. They have constantly misapplied that important drill of a grand army, and have never employed the mounted soldier at the proper time and in the proper place.'

Determined to be fair, Wellington qualified his words of censure. 'They have always fought gallantly and bravely,' he admitted, 'and have generally got themselves out of difficulties by sheer pluck.'

But Excelmann was to have the final and damning word. 'I have seen them so tightly habited that it was impossible for them to use their sabres,' he told Gronow, who was not a cavalryman and whose memory of the words of both the Duke and the General might have been less than perfect when he reported them in his memoirs in 1862.

His recollection of the occupation of Paris, on the other hand, bears all the hall marks of authenticity. He mentions Scottish troops bivouacked on the Champs Élysées causing consternation among the city's ladies by their lack of 'culottes' . . . The Champs Élysées itself being ankle deep in mud, flanked only by an occasional house and lit at night only by the occasional lantern, hanging from a cord . . . The new-styled Grenadiers, camped in the Bois de Boulogne, being openly critical of their Prussian neighbours' vandalism, but not taking into account the ruthlessness of the French occupation of Berlin nine years before . . . The fickle French, who only a month ago had screamed 'Vive l'Empereur' for Napoleon, now screaming 'Vive Le Roi' for Louis XVIII . . . Wellington resisting the French demand that Napoleon be shot, but unable to save Ney, who was convicted by his own country-men of treason and executed . . . The endless duels, for the most trivial of reasons, between English, French, Prussian and Russian officers, who killed one another by the score . . . The Life Guards taking up quarters in Paris instead of returning to their Public Duties in London.

Two years later, in 1817, the Rector of Framlingham died and willed the considerable sum (for those days) of £500 to 'the bravest man in England'. The invidious task of nominating the Rector's beneficiary was alloted to the Duke of Wellington, who declared:

'It is generally thought that the Battle of Waterloo was one of the greatest ever fought. Such is not my opinion, but I say nothing upon that point. The success of the Battle of Waterloo turned upon the closing of the gates of Hougoumont. These gates were closed in the most courageous manner, at the very nick of time, by the efforts of Sir James Macdonnell. I cannot help thinking Sir James is the man to whom you should give the five hundred.'

But Colonel Sir James Macdonnell—of the Coldstream— demurred, saying that he would accept the bequest only if he could share it with one of the two Graham brothers who had assisted him in the courtyard at Hougoumont. Thus £250 went to Sergeant Graham and with it—along with a still widely held and ludicrous belief that he actually barred the gate with his forearm—the title 'the bravest man in England'.

Strangely, Gronow mentions Sergeant Graham nowhere in his account of Waterloo. Strangely, because he was one of the few men of his time to decry the army's habit of nominating on its muster roll of fame no-one beneath the rank of captain. Nothing would have given him more pleasure than to defy official practice by reporting the valour of a lowly sergeant; but, on the morning after Waterloo, mid all the tales of derring-do, he had heard no mention anywhere of Graham— perhaps because he was in a Brigade that fought nowhere near Hougoumont. Sir James may have been right to insist that the title of 'bravest man' should pass from himself to Sergeant Graham: the title of 'most generous man' must assuredly be his.

The title of 'pluckiest', on the other hand, would have been widely shared by those hundreds of wounded survivors, of whom Captain Percival, of the First Regiment of Foot Guards, was typical. At Waterloo, all his teeth and both his jaws were shot away. Though hideously maimed, he rejoined the Grenadiers at the Tower of London in 1818. There he was accepted by his brother officers, respected by his men and fed porridge and broth until, 'his body presenting the appearance of a skeleton,' he died.

Two years later, George III died at Windsor and the Blues were incorporated into the new king's Household Cavalry and granted quarters in London. It was a privilege they had earned by singular steadiness and cohesion at Waterloo: it was a privilege denied them for five years only by a lonely king's need for their company and the reassurance of their presence.

A last and belated consequence of Napoleon's defeat was England's determination to commemorate every aspect of her final victory in appropriate style. The result was Trafalgar Square, which dramatically altered the geography of St. James's Park, Whitehall and London's palaces.

Access into St. James's Park—which for centuries was possible only through Holbein Gate, and then, from George II's time, through Horse Guards Arch—was now also possible from the bottom corner of Trafalgar Square into the recently macadamised Mall, or from Piccadilly, where the Duke of Wellington lived, down a new road called Constitution Hill, to the front of Buckingham Palace itself. With these new entrances to St. James's Park came a new itinerary for the Brigade of Guards and the Household Cavalry as they mounted their daily Guards, provided escorts for their numerous Sovereigns and fulfilled their frequent ceremonial responsibilities. It was Waterloo and final victory over Napoleon, in fact, that produced the ceremonial routes of today's Household Division, the title of 'Grenadier Guards', the bearskins of the Brigade of Guards and the jackboots and cuirasses of the Household Cavalry at Knightsbridge.

*The Queen's Company Colour
Royal Standard of the Grenadier Guards
presented by Her Majesty the Queen
on 14th April 1953*

THE GUARDS AT HOME

13   *The Guards and Discipline*

YESTERDAY,' REPORTED *The Scout*, on 1 August, 1654, 'We had a Court Martial for trying stragglers.' Eleven were tried, eleven were convicted, and their general, one George Monck, decreed that one of them should die for all. They were to cast dice to decide which of them should be hanged.

Yet so harsh was life in Cromwell's Model Army that an innocent soldier said to one of the prisoners, 'If thou wilt give me £5, I will throw for thee, for I have obtained leave.'

The money exchanged, the innocent man stood in for the convicted man; and was lucky when the dice were thrown.

'But suppose,' his officer later rebuked him, 'you had thrown *alms all*, and so lost your life?'

'Sir,' replied the soldier, 'I have hazarded my life many a time before for eight pence a *day*, so might I not as well venture to do it for £5 a minute? 'Tis gallant pay, Captain. Nothing venture, nothing have.'

At the same time as eleven of Monck's soldiers diced for their lives, because they had been guilty of straggling, a group of his officers, who were guilty of planning his assassination (as part of an anti-Commonwealth plot) were, with his approval, merely cashiered. This was hardly equal justice for all, yet the general's soldiers, according to his biographer in 1833, 'with a mixture of familiarity, good nature and affection called him Honest George Monck.'

Be that as it may, it was as Charles II's Lord General, and an Earl, that he imposed upon the whole Army those standards of discipline that he had imposed as a mere Republican regimental commander six years earlier.

Because Charles chose to avoid war on the Continent, not so much was seen, during his reign, of the harsher military punishments—except for desertion. In the records of the Orderly Room of the Coldstream Regiment, a typical entry reveals that on *30th September 1678, John Rymer, now in gaol at Derby, and Richard Carr, in gaol at Stafford, deserters from the Coldstream Regiment and lately apprehended, (were) to be conducted to the guards of the Coldstream Regiment in St. James Park.*

The sparse phraseology gives no hint of what was involved. In order to 'conduct' the two deserters to St. James's Park, an N.C.O. and two men had to march from London to Derby to collect Rymer, then from Derby to Stafford, to collect Carr, and finally back to London, to hand both over for punishment.

With the advent of the eighteenth century, such punishments became more, not less, barbarous. Discipline was enforced with a variety of tortures (ranging from picketing to the wooden horse) as well as the lash. Those responsible for instilling discipline seemed to compete with one another in devising new ways of suspending, trussing, dislocating and degrading their man; and having flogged almost to death those deserters they did not hang, they branded them with an indelible D.

Yet nowhere in the annals of Guards' history is there any record of recruits being press-ganged. However hideous life may have been within the ranks of the First, Coldstream, Horse Guards or Blues, it was for many presumably worse outside.

In 1760, admittedly, there was heard the first whisper of official revulsion against cruelty as an officer's manual exhorted, 'Never beat your soldier, it is unmanly. I have too often seen a brave, honest, old soldier being banged and battered at the caprice of an arrogant officer'. But this did not mean that an officer should never order someone else to bang and batter honest old soldiers. Indeed, should any soldier go absent without leave, or otherwise offend, he could confidently anticipate something much worse than a mere battering—as John Furleigh discovered on 7 August, 1790, when he was *'sentenced and received 150 lashes for missing his guard, spoiling his beste Regimental cloathes and ill treating Corporal Newlin who was sent in search of him'*.

And that very same day (which was typical of every day for a hundred years before and about sixty years thereafter) Thomas Everett did no better—rather worse in fact—when he received *'200 lashes for neglect of duty, laying out of quarters, making away with two shirts, one pair of shoes, two pairs of stockings, a third coat and blue gaiters.'*

Richard Owen, however, received a mere hundred lashes for *'neglect of duty, laying out of barracks and being frequently guilty of the like behaviour.'*

Yet men exactly like these, their native stolidity tempered by constant drilling, had become so steady that advancing columns of them were capable of ignoring the cannon's round shot as it bounced and ricocheted visibly toward them. They ignored it because it was forbidden to step aside.

The late Duke of Gloucester inspects the Scots Guards

This steadiness was to prove as counter-productive in the American War of Independence as it had been rewarding in Europe. Conspicuous in their red tunics, the inflexibly disciplined triple ranks of Guards offered their elusive woodmen enemies a splendidly solid target. Because of which their traditional three rank formation was subsequently, if belatedly, reduced to two; and fighting thus, as proud as ever of their steadiness, they won great victories in the Peninsular War.

They were equally proud of their traditions: one of which was that they only presented arms to Royalty and high-ranking officers in the Guards or Household Cavalry. It was not, for example, until 1812, when he was appointed Colonel of the Blues, that the great Duke of Wellington himself became eligible for such a courtesy. 'Thank God,' he growled then, 'I'll get a "Present" out of the Guards at last!'

However tolerant his attitude toward the paying of compliments by members of the Guards, Wellington was uncompromising when it came to the paying for their crimes. In 1813 an enterprising Foot Guards Private was caught passing Spanish dollars made of pewter rather than silver. He was sentenced to 800 lashes and died before his punishment was done.

'Would it not have been better,' one of his officers protested, 'to have condemned him to be shot? It would have been more humane, certainly more military and far less brutal.' But Wellington was not to be moved. Throughout the Peninsular War, and the brief period of peace that followed it, any soldier caught stealing or committing any act either of 'violence or brigandage' was tried by a drum-head court martial and summarily hanged. And although punishments were very gradually reduced in severity after Waterloo, those less severe punishments were imposed far more frequently and for a multitude of offences visible only to the eye of a Guards non-commissioned officer.

Thus, although Private Joseph Renwick of the Blues was sentenced to two hundred lashes for 'constant irregularity of conduct on all occasions, being dirty and not parading for Kings Guard on Wednesday 1 January 1817', it soon became more common to sentence such offenders as he to solitary confinement on bread and water and by the second half of the century—following the Crimean War, where one had 'to be very careful how one pillages as the general orders are so strong on the subject'—discipline by savagery was modified to discipline by attrition.

That attrition began the day a man enlisted in any of the Regiments of Foot and Horse Guards and ceased only when he was discharged. It began with the mindless, interminable buffing of boots; it continued with the fanatical prosecution of such crimes as doziness, horribleness, lateness, disobedience, impertinence, absence, and even dumb insolence; its exponents were stentorian N.C.O.'s; and its sanctions were prolonged confinement to barracks and ruinous loss of pay.

Well into the twentieth century men could still be accused of such a peculiarly military offence as dirty flesh and inspections were still almost synonymous with persecution—and, at times, victimisation. Non-commissioned officers still revelled less in the power they wielded than in the terror they inspired. Regimental and Company Sergeant Majors (and their Household Cavalry equivalents) were still shrieking, petty tyrants for whom, in the absence of an army, society would have been hard put to find employment, and officers (except when awarding punishments) still gazed indifferently down upon the ranks of tyranised regimental ants swarming beneath them.

'In my day,' confesses a Regimental Quarter Master Sergeant of the 1970's, 'back in the 1950's that was, you *dreaded* losing pay. Get charged and lose the equivalent of forty pence today and you'd think, "What'll I *do*? How'll I *manage*?"'

Even in the sixties, when army life had become so much more civilised—if only because it would otherwise have attracted no volunteers from the ranks of Britain's suddenly affluent young civilians—Guards and Household training came as a profound shock to the recruit.

'I was shattered,' a Scots Guard sergeant freely confesses of his days at the Depot in 1962. 'I didna know there were people like that. Hundreds of them—screaming at

A kit inspection, Irish Guards at Caterham Barracks in
1935, at the height of the days of spit and polish

Because Corporals and Lance-Sergeants are not entitled to use the Warrant Officer's prestigious pace-stick, they carry a smaller cane instead—but no less proudly

you and shouting. It was like being in a different world. Ma two mates, the ones I joined up with, they both said to hell with it and bought themselves oot. But me, well ma father had always told me the Guards were *the* Regiment; and once I'd joined he kept telling everyone *his* son would never buy himself oot, so I had to decide I wouldna let them beat me.

'Actually, I kept m'sel going by telling m'sel, "Life in the battalion, once you get oot of this hell hole, will be better." That was the great thing, that life in the battalion would be better.

'So finally I got sent to the battalion. And straight-away I'm thrown a buff belt and this sergeant is SCREAMING at me, 'CLEAN IT'— and I think to m'sel, this is just like the depot. It was three weeks before anyone spoke a civil word to me; and if you were to ask me what good those months of screaming and shouting did me, either as a person or as a Guardsman, I'd have to say none at all.'

'It's all different today,' admits a Warrant Officer at Pirbright. 'You can't swear at 'em any longer. And even if you threaten to dock their pay by a *tenner*, it doesn't terrify them. Today's guardsman doesn't acquaint discipline with terror. Certainly he'd never acquaint terror with a fine of a tenner. More likely he'd just say, "Shall I write you a cheque?"'

Nevertheless, the system still works. Every time they pass an officer, Guardsmen still fling out their chests, thrust back their shoulders and snap out a clicking salute. Every time an order is given, it is still unhesitatingly obeyed. Every time a State occasion is celebrated, it is still impeccably adorned. And wherever an enemy threatens, the Household Division is still renowned for the steadiness that gave Wellington his victory at Waterloo—although it has also acquired, of late, a degree of cunning and versatility which, had it been present in 1776, might well have denied America's colonists their great victory over Cornwallis at Yorktown.

'It is requisite in a General,' postulated George Monck, 'to mingle love with the severity of his discipline.' On the other hand, he insisted, 'the greatest virtue which is required in a soldier is obedience'.

Though no longer tyrannised or terrified, today's Guardsman or Trooper is no less disciplined than any of his predecessors. Slightly less 'sharp' on the parade ground than the products of 1920–1939, he is nowadays better educated than they were, and the master of more sophisticated weapons than were theirs. The question that nevertheless remains is 'Why have some 6,000 of him, average age twenty-two, chosen to submit themselves to an average period of nine years service in the Household Division where discipline today, relative to the discipline of contemporary civilian life, is as harsh as it has ever been?'

'But suppose,' one could well rebuke the man who volunteers for the dangerous gamble of service with today's Guards or Household Cavalry 'you throw "alms all" and so lose your life?'

He can hardly justify his action by pleading, 'Tis gallant pay'; but, coming from a society whose excitements are mostly vicarious, he may well reply, 'Nothing venture, nothing have'.

14   The Guards and Tumults, Seditions, Conspiracies

To read the Orders of the Day of any of the Regiments of the Guards is to read a great deal of England's social and political, as well as her military history.

Written in clear copperplate, these day-to-day orders, from 1660 onwards, are as objective as historical documents can be and make no attempt either to explain or to justify their content. In the process, they provide a vivid account of those many duties (other than protecting the Sovereign and fighting the Sovereign's wars) that have been performed by the Guards and Household Cavalry for more than three hundred years. Each Regiment has volumes of these orders, but a random selection from any one of them gives an adequate impression of the whole.

In May 1664 fifty Coldstreamers were drafted 'to form the Duke of York's expedition to Guinea and fifty more to help man his ships'—the future King James II being, for the moment, England's Lord High Admiral.

In May 1667 the Coldstreamers took delivery from His Majesty's stores at the Tower of London of '120 firelocks to replace those lost in the Fire of 1666.'

On 8 February 1676 a detachment of Guards was despatched to Lambeth 'to aid in suppressing the great tumults of disorderly persons of the trades of hatters, weavers, etc;' and in November of the same year eighty-four men were ordered to embark for two years service in Virginia.

On 14 December 1678, 'the Battalion of the Coldstream, on arrival from Flanders,' was ordered, 'to disembark at the Tower and quarter in the Hamlets in the Tower'.

On 10 October 1683, ten men and an officer were ordered 'to convey money to Portsmouth'.

The order of 18 October, 1685 gives some idea of the Foot Guards' interminable peregrinations. 'Captain Landy's troop, when relieved, to march from Chichester to relieve Captain Lucy's troop at Portsmouth. Captain Lucy's troop at Portsmouth, when relieved, to march to Barnet' . . . And so it went on, with the unfortunate Foot Guards marching from Lambeth to Reading, Portsmouth to Greenwich, Barnet to Hoddesdon, Chichester to Salisbury, London to Newark (or Mansfield, or Nottingham) Birmingham to Manchester, and Hertford to Huntington.

The Horse Guards were no less busy, an unhappy detachment of the Blues even being despatched to Bristol on Christmas Day of 1666 simply to compel its Quaker shopkeepers to observe the Holy Day and close their shops; but at least the Blues were able to *ride* from Oxford to Bristol.

As also they were able to ride to Chichester in 1682 when the Bishop demanded protection. From whom? The Blues' orders did not bother to specify. It was enough for them to know simply where they had to go and what they had to do when they got there.

Equally cryptic is the Coldstream order of 17 August 1685 which baldly required one officer and sixty men 'to attend Mr. Pepys, Secretary to the Admiralty'. The order of 8 March 1689, however, is self-explanatory, requiring both Coldstream battalions to spend the rest of the winter in Ghent, and subsequently to commute, a battalion at a time, between Flanders and London, fighting Louis XIV on behalf of Dutch King William in Flanders, marching from London to Windsor, Maidenhead, Slough, Datchet, Eton, Bath, Newmarket, Richmond, Hampton Court and Kensington in order to protect English Queen Mary.

At the end of the seventeenth century, highwaymen on country roads and robbers on London's streets were an even worse affliction for England than the Popish threats of Louis XIV. Accordingly, in 1699, the Blues were ordered 'to quarter near to London in order to clear the roads of robbers'; but this task was impossible—the robbers simply taking themselves elsewhere until the Blues moved out again and the ranks of the hunted being constantly reinforced by recruits from the hungry, the dispossessed and those who had deserted from Queen Anne's Army.

Of these, ex-cavalrymen were always the most dangerous, because they usually decamped from their regiment both armed and on horseback, to be transformed into instant highwaymen. But there were also rich pickings available to anyone on foot who had the nerve and the muscle to rob those foolish enough to be abroad at night on the unlit streets of London.

As if swarms of robbers and great tumults of disorderly hatters and weavers were not trouble enough for Queen Anne's unfortunate Foot Guards, there were also the likes of Doctor Sacheverell—who was prosecuted in 1709 for having preached an inflammatory sermon, and upon whose behalf mobs of sympathetic Londoners thereupon began to riot with such determination that six men had to detach from the Whitehall Guard to go and protect the Bank of England. The Gordon Riots of 1780 made these picquets a nightly event continued for almost two hundred years. In appreciation of which long and latterly almost wholly decorative service the Bank of England presented the officers' Guard Room at St. James's Palace with an enormous silver rose bowl, which now stands, devoid of roses, in the corner of the room, on top of the colour television set.

In 1711 came the first of many orders requiring the Foot Guards to act as a combined censor and vice squad, when a lieutenant and fifty men of the First and Coldstream Regiments were required to parade at Covent Garden 'to prevent any mischief that may happen at the Playhouse'.

Some explanation of these cryptic instructions may be found in a pamphlet published by Jeremy Collier and entitled '*A short view of the Immorality and Profaneness of the English Stage*'. In the brave but puritanical manner of John Bunyan (whose incessant pamphlets had so enraged the Courts that he spent much of his life in gaol) Collier deplored the profusion of swear words in stage dialogue; and George I's ministers were as much determined to protect their new Protestant dynasty from accusations of sacrilege in the theatre as they were to purge the theatre itself of seditious Jacobite propaganda.

On Christmas Day of 1713 no less than six hundred of the Foot Guards and a hundred Horse Guards were ordered to proceed to Rochester to suppress a mob of Marines 'assembled in a tumultous manner in contempt of Her Majesty's authority and to the disturbance of the peace of her subjects'. The Marines were to be instructed to 'return to their obedience' and, if they obeyed, the Guards were 'to proceed no further'. Out-numbered and out-gunned, the Marines finally accepted the savage punishments implicit in returning 'to their obedience'.

By 1719 London's weavers were at it again, as an order of 28 July makes clear.

'Guard Your Fuze' from *The Granadiers Exercise of the Granade in His Majesty's First Regiment of Foot-Guards* by Bernard Lens, 1735

'A detachment of 100 men,' it said, 'to march on Thursday next to Spitalfield's market to assist in the preservation of the peace as well as to prevent any disorder that may happen during the time the weavers shall stand in the pillory there.'

And no sooner had they ensured that the weavers of Spitalfields were pilloried in an orderly and peaceful manner than they were called out to attend the King's Theatre in the Haymarket to prevent disorders of a very different kind at its opera rehearsals, masquerades and Balls. Today it is difficult to imagine what exactly those disorders might have been, and every expert on the subject gives a different answer, but the truth lies somewhere embedded in the facts that theatres were dimly lit, society was lusty and crowds were the habitat of whores and pickpockets.

1722 brought another kind of duty—the State funeral of John, Duke of Marlborough, whom his contemporaries had dubbed 'the greatest Englishman of them all'. Two hundred and forty years later his descendant, sometime Grenadier Sir Winston Churchill, would be similarly acknowledged and his body similarly escorted through the streets of a grateful London. Fifty-four years *earlier*, in 1672, John Churchill had himself, as a mere ensign in the First Regiment of Foot Guards, marched behind the coffin of the Duke of Albemarle, whose march on London in 1660 had precipitated the establishment in England of all the Regiments of Guards.

For Albemarle the ceremony had been magnificent; for Winston Churchill it would be superb; for Marlborough it was stupendous. While his body was brought to Marlborough House, to lie in state, the Foot Guards were drilling, day after day, so that every detail would be perfect

After a month's preparation, the funeral was staged, the route—from Marlborough House up Constitution Hill to Piccadilly, along to Charing Cross and down to Westminster Abbey—being lined with privates of the Foot Guards in scarlet coats, each wearing on his breast a small bunch of cypress, each of the Regimental Colours wreathed with cypress, every officer black scarfed, and guns from the Tower booming their mournful salute every sixty seconds.

Bands led the procession, followed by horse-drawn guns, after which came Marlborough's generals accompanied by heralds, officers-at-arms and the chief mourners.

Then, transported in a gorgeously canopied car, came the coffin—topped with a suit of golden armour, surrounded by dozens of military trophies and heraldic devices to signify victories won and towns captured.

As the car passed down the route an order new to Foot Guards rang out and was constantly repeated. 'Reverse your arms', came the order. 'Rest on your arms reversed.' Whereupon every officer slowly lowered his pike, the ensigns concerned slowly dipped the colours and each soldier slowly revolved the muzzle of his rifle forward and downward until it touched the ground—at which moment every head bowed and each man assumed a posture of extreme melancholy.

At the Abbey, which was draped with sable and lit by candles, George I presided, and the anthem '*Cry ye Fir trees, for the cedar is fallen*', especially composed for the occasion, was played on the organ. As the coffin was lowered into its vault—beside the bones of Oliver Cromwell—Garter King at Arms proclaimed, 'Thus has it pleased Almighty God to take out of this transitory world unto His mercy the most high and mighty and noble prince, John, Duke of Marlborough,' and snapped his wand, flinging its fragments into the vault.

Which was the signal for three rockets to soar heavenwards from the Abbey, to be acknowledged by the roll of distant drums, which were the prelude to the thunder of a triple salvo of guns emplaced at Horse Guards.

Then came another roll of the distant drums, prompting a triple salute from the muskets of 2,000 soldiers of the Foot Guards, which was followed by a final roll of the drums. The greatest Englishman of them all was gone, consigned (mid uniquely English ceremonial) to a vault shared (with typical English irony) by Oliver Cromwell and farewelled (with peculiarly English hypocrisy) by the German King who had succeeded the English Queen who had sacked the deceased Duke for his dishonesty.

What mattered, though, was not any element of hypocrisy but rather the form and trappings of the occasion, which had been so supremely effective that almost all of them—for the funerals of later great Englishmen—have been retained.

★   ★   ★

The great Englishman of 1722, when Marlborough was buried, was, of course, Robert Walpole—whose administration was notable for the fact that no man worth robbing could consider himself safe on the streets of London, and that many of those not worth robbing became even less safe in the forests that had always been their home because Walpole's laws obliged them either to quit the forests or to risk being hanged.

In such a pitiless social climate the 'criminal' element in London was inevitably augmented. And not only in London. To enforce Walpole's Black Laws, the Coldstreamers, were ordered, in August 1725, to provide 'a detachment of 64 men, under a lieutenant and an ensign, to march to Barnet and [there] be assisting in seizing and securing the deer stealers who infest His Majesty's chase of Enfield'.

For the same reason, on 26 March, 1726, a detachment of forty Coldstreamers, 'with commissioned and non-commissioned officers proportionable' was ordered 'to march to Kingston on Tuesday morning next and be a guard over the criminals to be charged at the assizes there'.

When forty Foot Guards are required to prevent the escape of criminals from a court of law, those criminals are either very dangerous or very unpopularly held in custody. Since deer stealers (forest dwellers whose staple food was venison) can hardly have been regarded as a danger to society, whatever Walpole's legislation may have implied to the contrary, their persecution—and subsequent execution—was approved only by landowners and was detested by England's numerous poor. As the instruments of Walpole's laws, the Foot Guards, scattered in bunches of half-a-dozen in the tavens and ale houses of London, were detested even more.

The right to hunt deer was not the only Royal one requiring protection. A detachment of Life Guards was despatched to Winchcombe to destroy a crop of tobacco—which had been declared illegal because the colonists of Virginia had the sole right to grow it. To burn a man's crop is little less endearing than to hang him, so the King's Horse Guards were no more popular than his Foot Guards and the King himself no less unpopular than both.

Upon George I's death, England decided that it liked George II no better as King than it had as Prince of Wales, and Londoners seized the first opportunity to demonstrate their disloyalty—which was a Royal Ball at the Haymarket Theatre. There the Third (Scots) Regiment of Foot Guards had to protect the new king's guests as they arrived and later keep the peace in the streets so that they could go home again.

Wars and Jacobite rebellions preoccupied the country for the rest of George II's reign and inevitably, when the rebellion of Jacobite Scots was crushed at Culloden, it was the Guards—a thousand of them—who had to 'attend the execution of the Earl of Kilmarnock and Lord Dalmenno' in August, of some anonymous and untitled rebels in November, and of Lord Lovat the following April.

When the Seven Years War ended, and George III came to the throne, England was in no less of a turmoil. There was considerable unemployment; John Wilkes, the M.P., had denounced the terms of the Peace Treaty; the Blues (reduced from 52 men to 29 a troop) spent all their time preventing unrest at Nottingham and York; and Parliament had axed the army and cut its pay by five per cent.

George III at once rescinded the pay cut as far as the Foot Guards were concerned, but the Navy had already mutinied and sailors were rampaging through London, which made the Guards' task of patrolling the streets more disagreeable than ever.

Indeed, as the Royal need for new sources of taxation impelled George III to one ill-conceived impost after another upon England's colonists in America, it is difficult to see why anyone joined any of the Guards Regiments at all—until one remembers that unemployment has always been good for the recruiting of privates and that Guards officers were in those days afforded the privilege of a vote. Since both the King and his M.P.s sought constantly to woo this vote with bribes, it became profitable, once the War of Independence was out of the way, to be commissioned in the Guards.

1780 saw so much civil disorder that the military were instructed to 'act without waiting for direction from the civil magistrate and to use force for dispersing illegal and tumultous assemblies'. The magistrates themselves had long become reluctant to face any more mobs and read the Riot Act. Thereafter the officer in command of the troops confronting a mob would himself recite the Riot Act, and it was for this reason that Captain Edward Kelly of the Life Guards always kept in his gauntlet a piece of cardboard on which were inscribed the required words.

As the riots grew worse, so the four battalions of Foot Guards, now living in a tented camp in St. James's Park, assumed responsibility not only for the safety of the Crown, the Bank of England and the centre of Government, but also for such unlikely institutions as the British Museum, the Royal Academy of Arts, the Savoy Prison Hulk and the Mint.

The next two years having done nothing to reassure the King that his subjects were growing any less restive, these emergency duties were transformed into regular duties. They remained an additional burden for the Foot Guards until 1821—except for the British Museum, for which sentries were provided till 1865.

As well as being burdensome, these duties were thankless. By day, habitués of the Museum Reading Room never ceased complaining of being 'much disturbed by the military music of the Guards as they exercised in the garden'; and at night the local citizenry protested so volubly about bellowed challenges that the custom developed of challenging with a stamp of the foot.

The Napoleonic wars at least gave the country something else to think about than Corn Law Riots and the threat of machinery; but no sooner had peace been declared than domestic unrest became as widespread as ever, the Blues being frequently despatched from Windsor to Reading and Henley, and the Foot Guards being even more shamefully overworked by George IV (who had added Brighton Pavilion to the list of his official residences requiring sentries) than they had been by George III.

The creation of a Police force in 1829 should have eased their burden, but these were the days of growing mechanisation (which caused frequent demonstrations) and of the birth of a new empire (which had to be defended).

While three-quarters of the army were thus constantly overseas, the Guards at home—Foot and Horse—found themselves busier than ever. They attended William IV's funeral and Queen Victoria's Coronation. They were called out to fight the fire that destroyed the Houses of Parliament; they successfully fought a fire that would have destroyed the Foreign Office: they quelled a London demonstration that earned the Life Guards the title 'The Butchers of Piccadilly': they patrolled nightly from the barracks in Knightsbridge, Horse Guards and Portman Street: they were delighted when Victoria sold to the Brighton Corporation (for £50,000) the Pavilion her uncle had had built for £376,000: but depressed because she acquired two other residences in lieu: and in 1852 they gave Wellington an even greater funeral than Marlborough himself had received in 1722.

As Foot Guards lined the route, a procession that included eight squadrons of cavalry, three thousand soldiers and three batteries of guns moved slowly past them. It took the procession two hours to pass each private of the Foot Guards; and only two minutes of those two hours were spent with arms reversed and head bowed in melancholy tribute to the duke in the black and golden catafalque which —though its design had been personally approved by the Prince Consort—Thomas Carlyle contemptuously dismissed as 'More like one of the street carts that hawk door mats than a bier for a hero.'

'The greatest State funeral ever accorded a commoner' behind them, the Guards reverted to normal, reporting, in 1865, that they needed new sentry boxes at the British Museum, 'the old ones being quite worn out'. Learning that these would cost £90, the Museum trustees decided to do without the protection they had deemed necessary the past seventy-four years and the Secretary of State for the Home Department agreed to discontinue the Foot Guards' service both there and at the National Gallery.

A duty discarded here was counter-balanced by a duty imposed there, however. British privateers had been shipping supplies to the Confederates in the American Civil War, and President Lincoln had sent envoys to the French offering them Canada, if only they would declare war on England. England responded by despatching a Guards Brigade to Canada—where they did nothing but ceremonial duties and a lot of stevedoring.

For most of the rest of Victoria's reign life was rich, prestigious and so peaceful that Government (which invariably shuts the stable door long after the horse has bolted) passed the Riot (Damages) Act of 1886, providing that anyone whose property was damaged by people acting riotously and tumultuously could claim damages from their local police authority.

All over the country the police had become so much more effective and the populace so much better employed that the need for Foot Guards, Blues and Life Guards to intervene had been rendered virtually non-existent. In fact it was not until 1911, in George v's reign, that another exceptional call was made upon them.

In January of that year three anarchists, led by Peter the Painter, holed up in a house in Sidney Street and opened fire on the police who sought to arrest them. The Home Secretary, Winston Churchill, having ordered the 1st Battalion Scots Guards to assist the police, seventy soldiers, under the command of a Captain, came from the Tower of London to Houndsditch and set up their Maxim gun facing the house in Sidney Street. After a desultory siege, the house burst into flames and the three conspirators were presumed to have died in the conflagration.

As if a new pattern had thereby been set, the Guards (as soon as they were free to do so after World War I) embarked on a fresh sequence of freakish duties. In 1922, they were sent to Constantinople to help the Turks restore order after the Chanak crisis. In 1926, they escorted convoys of strike-breaking lorries from the London docks. In 1927, they sailed to China, to protect British interests in Peking, Canton and Shanghai, while the locals fought a ferocious civil war. In 1937 they suppressed disorders in Palestine and re-occupied the Old City of Jerusalem. And in 1939, the 2nd Battalion of both Scots and Coldstream Guards were packed and standing by to supervise the plebiscite in Czechoslovakia that Mr. Chamberlain thought Hitler had promised him. Hitler spared the Guards this degrading task by ordering the Wehrmacht to march on Prague instead.

For the following six years the Guards were too busy displaying their habitual staunchness and versatility in battle to be able to do police work, but no sooner had the Nazis surrendered in Italy than they were ordered into Trieste, to protect Germans from Yugoslavs, Chetniks and Ustashi from Titoists, and neighbouring cities with Italian majorities from annexation by Tito's partisans.

At home in England, in the first years of peace and a new Labour government, there were frequent calls upon Guardsmen to intervene in unofficial strikes in such essential services as the London docks and Smithfield meat market.

And in 1948 came the murderous onslaught of the Chinese Communists in Malaya upon planters and tin miners that initiated twenty years of emergency policing in one colony or ex-colony after another.

Palestine, Cypress, Aden, Kenya, Borneo, Zanzibar, British Honduras and Uganda—all of them, and more, were to demand a Guards presence, and some of them demanded it more than once. British Honduras, which is now Belize, and living in constant fear of greedy Guatemala, demands it to this day; Hong Kong has come to expect it; Ulster cries out for it; and the Guards, in consequence, have become unrivalled in the art of controlling vicious little wars and wet-nursing emergent little nations.

As to the latter, expressionlessly impartial, they would fly in, restore law and order here, quell a mutiny there, root out a rebel lair somewhere else, and then, just as expressionlessly, depart—not to the beat of drums, or the skirl of pipes, nor with colours proudly born, but quietly, like orderly tourists, standing in line to board the planes that would fly them home.

There the madness of Ulster awaited them. Thence they flew to Belfast to fight the Government's impossible war. And returning to London they resumed their role as the Tourist Board's star attraction, obeying to the letter the succinct and comprehensive standing orders that govern the performance of all their duties in the capital, not excluding that of protecting Heathrow Airport from attacks by foreign terrorists.

The mounted sentry at Horse Guards, bleak faced under his plumed helmet, heroic in his sculpted cuirass and martial in his jackboots, knows that he is not there simply to be photographed holding his sword erect before him. On the contary, he is very much aware that he 'should have a good view up and down Whitehall and be on the alert to warn the dismounted sentry of the approach of persons entitled to honour from the Guard, of troops on the march, and of mobs'.

In the event of a mob approaching, he knows that 'the gates will be shut and the Guard will fall in, dismounted.'

In the event of the mob becoming threatening, he knows that 'a sealed box of ammunition is kept locked to the floor under the senior N.C.O.'s bunk'.

And in the event of a mob attempting a coup, it would be he and his colleagues, and *their* colleagues at Knightsbridge, and their friendly rivals, the Foot Guards, at Chelsea, collaborating with Scotland Yard and the Metropolitan Police, who would instantly resist. One sealed box of ammunition under the bunk of the senior N.C.O. at Horse Guards may not seem much with which to resist a coup; but as well there is three centuries of experience of mobs of all kinds, and of warfare of all kinds; and there is more practical knowledge of urban and guerilla warfare than is possessed by any other division of any other army in the whole of the modern world.

15   *The Guards' Bands*

MODERN MAN is so inclined to listen to music on discs, sound tracks, transistors or cassettes that he more often than not forgets the added dimension that watching musicians at work can lend to enjoying the music they play. Concert-goers and pop fans know it; but for those in between (for whom music has always been something either taped or piped, recorded or broadcast) it may take a top class military band to prove it.

Military bands combine almost all the virtues of other music-making combinations with their own peculiar virtues. They can play either classical or popular music; but *they* play *theirs* on the move. They can act as lime-lit principal performers one moment and the unobtrusive source of superb background music the next. They can enliven both marching soldiers and flat footed civilians. They can move a holiday crowd to song or a commemorative assembly to tears. They are the musicians of Britain's monarchs and the moving spirit of every royal occasion. And throughout the world the military bands of the Household Division are probably the best-known of them all.

Of these, the first (in its modern form) was the band of the Coldstream Regiment, which was established in 1785. Before then, although bands had been available for hiring by the month, the Foot Guards, as often as not, had marched—in peace and war—to the piercing rhythms of drums and fifes, and the Household Cavalry to the strident accompaniment of trumpets and kettledrums. But in 1780 the Hanoverian passion for aping the army of Frederick the Great led to the introduction of a Prussian type military band.

For all that George III was apt to boast of his Englishness, he was as partial to Germans as either his grandfather or great-grandfather had been before him, and it was at his instigation that almost all the trumpeters in the various bands formed during his reign came from Hanover.

Regiments used their bands as much to encourage recruiting as to keep their men in step, and it was probably for this reason that in 1807 the Life Guards (whose horses were not required to keep in step) also formed a band, offering its mainly German musicians contracts for three to five years at a daily wage of four shillings and sixpence, rising to six shillings, most of which was paid by officers of the regiments.

Unlike any other regimental band, every member of the Life Guards band was mounted and, whenever the Sovereign was present, wore a State coat, which was a capacious tunic of red velvet massively embroidered with gold. Charles II's trumpeters and kettledrummers had worn it: now, at enormous expense, the entire mounted band was dressed in it. It still is; each State coat (made by Gieves and Hawkes in Savile Row) costing the equivalent of seven return flights from London to New York.

Even though these military bands were originally a Prussian institution, and despite the fact that most of their musicians were originally Germans, and their bandmasters either German or Italian, they soon became anglicised. The musicians adopted English names, and their N.C.O.s not only trained them to march in the English fashion but also evolved for them a sophisticated variation of the 'form' so peculiarly convoluted that only Guards' bandsmen could then, and can now, execute it. Known as the Spin Wheel, its intricacies have never been committed to paper, but were and will continue to be passed on by word of mouth from one generation to the next, so that it has become a peculiarly British tour de force.

When George III took up his siege-quarters at Windsor Castle, to await and resist Napoleon's invasion, he invited the Blues to send their band to the Castle each Sunday evening to play on the East Terrace. Such royal approval was flattering, of course, but it yielded not a penny toward the vast annual sum required to support a military band. The Duke of Northumberland, who was Colonel of the Blues, therefore contributed the then considerable sum of £900 a year merely to help maintain it. Later his successor, the Duke of Wellington, having paid out his first £900 contribution, announced that, excellent though the band was, he preferred no longer to burden his fortune with its upkeep. That entire burden then devolved upon the officers of the regiment.

Needless to say the Life Guards never stinted themselves once their decision to form a band for each of their regiments was taken. Their First Regiment even imported a negro, whom it planned to train as a kettledrummer (but, having failed to do so, was obliged to discharge); and their Second Regiment—when negros had become almost as fashionable as chinoiserie—included in its mounted band no less than four black trombonists. These two bands cost the Life Guards a fortune;

but in those days all officers of the Life Guards had a fortune.

The Foot Guards' officers did not allow themselves to be outshone—the more so since the twenty-odd members of each of their Corps of Drums were now entitled to wear white facings and a pattern of fleur de lys on their red tunics (as a compliment to the drummer who had captured a French colour at Waterloo, many of them believe today; but others insist that the white facings were worn before Waterloo). Marching at the rear of the band, these splendidly tunicked drummers and fifers lent a Foot Guards parade as gallant an air as all the Life Guards' bandsmen together in their sombre cloth of gold.

Unlike the musicians, whose presence was not required at battles, a battalion's Corps of Drums *was* expected to accompany it (musically as well as physically) into battle and once there was required to convey orders by sounding routine calls.

Musicians *were*, however, required to follow their regiment wherever it might be posted in peace-time, and this, when colonial postings became commonplace, tended to discourage foreign recruits and hasten the process of anglicising the army's bands.

That process completed, military bands remained unchanged until recent years when, like the Regiments for which they play, they became vastly more professional. Today's bandsman is a musician of the first quality who has enlisted primarily as a wind instrumentalist. He may well be a splendid violinist; he may even join the Regimental Orchestra and play at Investitures, Banquets and State Dinners; but his main function will always be to perform as a well drilled bandsman with the Guards.

Once enlisted, his life will consist of little else than rehearsals, performances and travelling to and from performances. His repertoire will be vast and he will be capable of playing elaborately arranged compositions while performing complicated drills. More than that, he will perform both the music and the drills with such panache that the spectator will fail even to perceive that on each instrument is perched a small oblong sheet of paper—on which are written the notes that he reads as he plays as he marches.

Whatever the Household Division does in London, its bands accompany and uplift it. Every day of the year the Guard is changed at Buckingham Palace. With each new Guard to the Palace comes its own band. Only rain keeps them away, because it damages their uniforms and instruments; and being human, they frequently pray for rain.

Twenty years ago they needed no more than an official forecast of rain to be excused the march to and from the Palace, and the long performance at it; but meteorology finally proved so inexact a science that the system was changed. Today, if it is actually raining, the Captain of the New Guard declares, 'Wet Mount'—which is an English way of saying 'no mount'—and if it is not raining

Side Drummers of the Scots Guards

regardless of the outlook, the band will set off for the Palace, followed by a lorryful of capes—which can be issued and donned upon the falling of the first damaging droplet.

Apart from accompanying the Guards upon their ceremonial duties, the various Household bands frequently play for the Queen at her more private functions. When she is in residence at Windsor, for example, a band still plays each Sunday on the East Terrace—each programme having first been vetted by the Lord Chamberlain.

At State functions, where foreign dignitaries are present, tact is vital. As one Director of Music explained, 'If the President of Egypt were present, one would naturally avoid playing excerpts from *Fiddler on the Roof*. And one mustn't get national anthems *wrong*. It wasn't a Guards band that did it, but it *was* an army band that played the old Mussolini anthem for the Italian Football team at Wembley in the Fifties—and the Italians weren't pleased'.

In fact gaffes are non-existent, the Household bands being celebrated for their tact, courtesy and wit. Should foreigners be the Queen's guests at Windsor, they will certainly hear some of their national music from the East Terrace on Sunday afternoon. Should a singer be honoured at an Investiture, the band will naturally play his biggest hit.

Behind each small courtesy lies a good deal of work : the thought, the sheet music, the rehearsal. Nor will the eventual performance necessarily be the end of the matter. Should some outlandish melody feature in the Changing of the Guard, because some minor foreign personage has been admitted as a spectator to the Palace forecourt, the Queen is as like as not to send a message to the Director of Music enquiring for whom it was played. She has done so often enough, for the Guards are her Guards, the musicians her musicians and the Palace forecourt part of her home.

Though proud of their role as musicians for the Queen, the Household bands do not forget—or perhaps are not allowed to forget—that originally each of them was the property of a regimental Colonel and his officers. The Household Division has a cricket club at Burtons Court. In the season, matches are played each Wednesday and Saturday. One of the Household bands is required to attend and play throughout each match and, at approximately 5 p.m.—either at the end of an over or the fall of a wicket—to play the National Anthem, during which all the players stand to attention.

Wherever, and for whomever, the Household Division's bands perform, their music is of the highest quality and their showmanship superb. Two hundred years of evolution has produced an entertainment that needs no props, no scenery, no lighting, no stage-manager and no producer—just the bandsmen, their uniforms, their instruments and their music.

For the Massed Bands of the Household Cavalry, of course, there is the added requirement of horses—two to lead and carry the massive double drums, followed by six rows of eight. But the Massed Bands of the Foot Guards, marching twenty abreast and eighteen ranks deep, have no need of horseflesh to make their presence felt. Formidable in breadth and depth they demand attention; and led by their Drum Majors in State Dress they compel it.

Again, however, their effect is achieved only by enormous effort. For every performance there are countless rehearsals, and at each rehearsal a Drum Major can be seen—like a sheep dog working its flock—circling, prowling and snapping at the heels of his marching and sweating musicians.

A tune played, a manoeuvre completed, the Massed Bands will be halted, a step ladder will be brought up at the double, the Musical Director in charge of the

Three Pipers of the Scots Guards

rehearsal will mount it and voice his criticisms through a loud hailer, and the cycle will start again.

Trombones in front, brass solidly behind, drums judiciously spaced and five braided ranks of the Corps of Drums bringing up the rear, five Regimental bands swiftly become one and master the intricacies of both music and drill, so that soon, as mysteriously as a flock of birds in flight, they can, all 360 of them, upon an instant, change the shape, speed, texture and direction of their entire formation— and in the process miss neither a note nor a beat.

Even more than the fighting men of the Foot and Horse Guards, the bands pay fanatical attention to detail—if only because they are to the soldiers what an orchestra is to an opera or a ballet company. From them come at least half the cues in every Household performance; from them could come ill-judged tempi or fortissimi that could wreck the marchers' rhythm or drown the vocal cues.

As a consequence, even the Major General concerns himself with the minutiae of their performances. Observing them at a rehearsal for a concert at the Albert Hall, he sent a note to the Director of Music pointing out that the microphone cable was too visible, that to leave the microphone on the floor meant that the Director of Music had most unbecomingly to bend down and pick it up for each of his announce-ments, and that the cannon shots in the '1812' were far too loud.

That concert was a commercial rather than a military enterprise; and therein lies the most recent development in the long evolution of the Guards' bands. In the eighteenth, nineteenth and first half of the twentieth century they were a costly luxury: today, they are self-supporting.

Almost every year one band or another—including the Scots and Irish Pipe bands —is touring professionally overseas; Household Division bands are always in demand for private functions; their satellite orchestras are equally busy; cabaret engagements are common; and recording sessions are frequent.

For all this extra-curricular work the individual musician receives a share of the engagement fee. In addition, many of them—in what little time they have left— teach music privately. No-one belonging to the Household Division can be said to enjoy an idle life; but none of them is busier than the idlest of their musicians— who understandably, when due to accompany a Changing of the Guard, sometimes pray for rain.

16 Officers

UNTIL 1871, COMMISSIONS were obtained in all the regiments of the Guards and the Household Cavalry—as in the rest of the Army—by purchase. They were never cheap, but the pay they yielded annually was between ten and fifteen per cent of the capital outlay, they could be re-sold, and they provided opportunities for advancement by ensuring proximity to the Sovereign and access to London's Society.

Before 1871, so long as he had money, a young man needed nothing else to become an officer of the Foot or Horse Guards. Admittedly courage, horsemanship and an eye for the lie of the land were valuable, but they were not essential, and anyway came naturally to the sons of a landed gentry which hunted hares till the eighteenth century and foxes thereafter.

Of military skills the would-be officer had no need at all: non-commissioned officers provided them, 'and I am all for it', Wellington approved. If you had gentlemen for officers, Wellington pointed out, you could not 'require them to do many things that should be done. They cannot speak to the men, for instance. We should reprimand them if they did. Our system, in that respect, is so very different from (that of) the French. All *that* work is done by non-commissioned officers of the Guards'.

Of those non-commissioned officers he candidly admitted, 'It is true that they regularly get drunk by eight in the evening, and go to bed soon after, but they always take care to do first whatever they are bid', and—as he later made clear—in his opinion there was no-one in the armies of the world, 'so intelligent and so valuable as an English sergeant', provided, 'you get him sober, which *is* possible'.

It was fortunate that it always had been possible, because, from the 1660's to the 1890's, officers never did any of the regimental things that needed to be done, rarely went near their men in peace-time, occasionally omitted to do so even in war-time, and contributed nothing at any time except an occasional air of gallantry, swagger and dash.

Many of their casualties they suffered not on the field of battle, from foreign shot and shell, but in Hyde Park from English duelling swords and pistols. Though expected to know nothing of military drill and tactics, they were obliged to be wholly familiar with a vast catalogue of insults to their honour, and to respond to any of them instantly.

No one was excused, no matter what his rank, how oblique the insult, or how murderous the insulting party. Thus, in 1712 the Duke of Hamilton, then colonel of the Blues, unhesitatingly fought the notorious Lord Mohun, killed him and himself died of wounds as he was being carried to his carriage; and in 1789 Lieutenant

Colonel Lennox of the Coldstream was even obliged to challenge the Duke of York, His Royal Highness having accused him of suffering words to be spoken to him at Daubigny's Club 'to which no gentleman ought to have submitted'.

His reputation at stake, Lennox circularised the members of Daubigny's, asking what words they might remember being addressed to him; but Daubigny's membership proved amnesiac. Accordingly Lennox required His Royal Highness either to 'contradict the report as publicly as he had asserted it' or to offer him 'the satisfaction' he had promised when he uttered that report.

His Royal Highness having declined to recant, the two men, escorted by seconds, found themselves standing twelve paces apart on Wimbledon Common, awaiting the signal of an umpire.

When it came, Lennox fired, grazing the Duke's brown coat; but the Duke did not fire. Thereupon Lennox invited the Duke to fire; but the Duke replied that he had come to the Common only to give Lennox satisfaction and that he had never intended firing.

Now Lennox *insisted* that the Duke should fire; but still the Duke declined, suggesting instead that, if the colonel was not 'satisfied', *he* could fire again.

This suggestion rejected, the two men departed the Common, Lennox in such a state of perturbation that he assembled his officers and required them to adjudge 'whether he had behaved in the late dispute as became a gentleman and an officer'.

They, discreetly, decided that he had 'behaved with courage but, from the peculiar difficulty of his situation, not with judgment'. On the other hand, no-one suggested, or even considered, that the Duke of York had lacked judgment in passively exposing himself to the risk of death by pistol shot, still less that it was ludicrous that an alleged slight by a third party could lead a Lieutenant Colonel commanding a company of a Guards Regiment to a duel with the King's second son, least of all that it was positively unseemly that the Commander in Chief of the King's Army should have risked death simply to afford one of his father's subjects 'satisfaction' for an insult that need never have been uttered.

Though duelling was later made illegal, the system prevailed even into the reign of Victoria, because it was more disgraceful for an officer to refuse a challenge than to flout the law.

Almost as important for an officer as the pursuit of honour, in the mid-eighteenth century, was the need to avoid any contact with trade, which had become so socially repellent that letters of the period, found in the archives of the Household Cavalry, have had all references to it deleted by their late eighteenth century curator.

For the same reason, no doubt, surnames became first of all exotic and then double, or even treble barrelled, the better to proclaim a family untainted by any need to work. Thus the commanding officer of the First Battalion of the Coldstream Guards in 1758, was a Colonel Julius Caesar, while nineteenth century Coldstream records reveal the arrival of officers called Paulet St John Mildmay, Ely Duodecimus Wigram, Boyd Pollen Manningham and the Hon Frederick William Child Villiers.

Splendidly named though they were, and lavishly endowed with wealth (often inherited from unmentionable ancestors) few Guards or Household Cavalry officers deigned to marry while serving their Regiments—perhaps because the Season offered pickings too easy, and procureurs provided bed-mates too diverse for marriage to be attractive.

My Lord, wrote one such to Lord Alvanley, who had purchased a commission in the Coldstream Guards in 1804 and now, in 1808, was all of nineteen years old, *having just been informed you are going to Spain, I take the liberty to send you your account with me, owing since six months.*

I trust your generosity to take into consideration my situation in pecuniary account and to be so kind as to let me have the money before your departure or, if you are not in cash, to give me your note for as long a time as your Lordship thinks proper.

I wish you success and glory and a speedy return.

Your Lordship's very humble servant,
Derville.

Enclosed with this letter was the humble Derville's itemised account which, to some extent, explains why the Household officer of the past needed a large private income. As well as huge bills for drinking, gambling and hunting, there were also his bills for sexual pleasures: or, as Derville put it, for:–

	£.	s.
Lady	5	0
Ditto a country girl	2	2
The same	2	2
One night Mrs Dubois (grande blonde)	5	5
Few days after at daytime	2	2
11th June Modest girl	3	3
26th June Sunday morning	2	2
27th June By particular appointment	5	5
3rd July An American Lady	10	10
Lately one night with Eliza Farquhar	3	3
30th Nov	2	2
1st Dec	3	3
4th Dec	3	3
11th Dec All night Miss N from the		
* Boarding School Chelsea*	5	5

Lord Alvanley died unmarried aged sixty. As if wenching were some extraordinary proof of patrician virility, however, Guards officers allegedly continued to honour its practice for a century or more by regularly encouraging their adjutant to pay for a whore from the Mall, laying her on the Regimental Colours atop their dining table in St. James's Palace and requiring an ensign to have intercourse with her as they watched.

'I believe it *was* once the practice,' confessed a bored Lieutenant Colonel of the 1970's. 'Never saw it myself.'

'It's *still* the practice,' insists an over-emphatic and probably virginal subaltern. 'Why else do the Colours have to be replaced so often?'

Doubtless it did happen on occasions, because it is too silly a tradition to be entirely fictitious; but there is little evidence, either from documents of the past or from officers of the present, to suggest that its regular performances existed anywhere but in the fantasies of those who desired to proclaim themselves as lusty at least as the soldiers they commanded. Happily there is no evidence at all to suggest that today's subalterns would be prepared publicly to roger (the correct Guards terminology) a whore even if his fellow officers desired it and his adjutant could afford it.

Nevertheless, to this day, the junior officer of both Guards and Household Cavalry tends not to be married, and in the past would more than likely have resigned when he did marry because he had no intention of making the army his career. In those days, in fact, it was almost as vulgar to pursue a 'career' as to be in trade, and young men became Guards or Cavalry officers to enjoy themselves, hunt, preserve a family tradition and proclaim themselves members of an élite.

It was probably its horror of trade that led to the only anomaly in the officer's caste system of the early nineteenth century. The creation of barracks throughout Britain had transformed the army's housekeeping. Previously battalions had been billeted in small groups in alehouses and the like, each group in each billet supervised by a Quarter Master Sergeant, each paying for its own lodgings and victuals. Now food had to be bought for the whole battalion which resided under the one roof. Likewise its weapons, ammunition and uniforms had to be purchased and stored. And to perform this ungentlemanly but demanding duty non-commissioned officers were commissioned.

The custom still prevails. The Quarter Master of even the most fashionable regiment is still an officer promoted from the ranks who can rise to the rank of Lieutenant Colonel; but far from being made to feel uncomfortable in the rarified atmosphere of Household Division messes, he is invariably made to feel at home and is frequently accepted as the father figure who reminds high spirited junior officers of the standards with which they should conform.

Though the Duke of York, when he became Commander in Chief, did much to improve the army, it was probably Wellington who first campaigned for standards to which *officers* should conform. George I had understood nothing about the English, least of all their officers; George II had concerned himself with the drill of privates, which was no concern of officers; George III had merely perpetuated George

Parade of Scots Fusilier Guards at Buckingham
Palace prior to their departure for the Crimea,
March 2nd 1854 (Coloured lithograph by
G. H. Thomas and E. Walker)

The Saving of the Colours at the Alma: Scots
Guards (Painting by Lady Butler)

and of the Scots Guards: main entrance of Buckingham Palace

1st Battalion Welsh
Guards patrol the
Habilayn area in the
Radfan, Aden, 196[...]

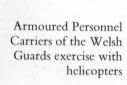

Armoured Personnel
Carriers of the Welsh
Guards exercise with
helicopters

II's snobberies as to officers; and George IV had contented himself with constantly altering their uniforms. It was Wellington who began the move that was to end the purchasing of commissions, just as it was Wellington who had first attempted to curb his officers' predilection for bad language.

Ironically, by so doing, he set in motion a process (hastened by the subsequent establishment of a Staff College and completed by the contemporary need even of 'gentlemen' to earn a living) that has led to today's officers being so much less gentlemanly than professional that they constantly speak to their men (and would be severely reprimanded if they did not) and frequently discuss the care they must take *not* to intrude *too much* upon what was once exclusively the N.C.O.'s domain.

But the process has been long and slow, and was probably as much affected by the mid-nineteenth century desire for social and political reform as by anyone's desire for military reform. At a time when Lord Shaftesbury was bringing Parliament's attention to social evils, it was inevitable that officers from the landed gentry should begin at last to feel some sense of responsibility for privates who were the sons of their tenant farmers.

At a time when the young officer, having dined sumptuously at one of London's great houses, was obliged to tip the butler a guinea, it began to be difficult for him to ignore the fact that, for his privates, a guinea was three weeks' pay.

Then, during the Crimean War, newspaper correspondents brought home to a middle-class readership not only the unforgiveable and unimagined hardships of the rank and file but also the frightening ineptitude of many of the officers who led them. Of that ineptitude, and of the fatal suffering of their ill-clad men, junior officers serving in the Crimea were well aware, and some of their letters home revealed a sense of shame at both.

Yet when they returned to England, they immediately resumed the ways of the past, because the two hundred year-old system was still perfectly designed for their social needs however unsuitable it had been for the needs of war.

'There are so many "good fellows" in the common acceptance of the word,' one officer complained of his non-Guards colleagues at the Crimea, 'who have "hair on the heels."'

'On looking back through your letters,' wrote a young officer whose mother had at last succeeded in getting him transferred to the Coldstream, 'I see that as far back as the middle of March you had a great wish to get me into the Guards.'

Not even other officers could understand the Crimea's Guards officer, who was inclined to use the term captain in its most archaic sense. 'Where is the Captain of this company?' a musketry inspector enquired.

'There isn't one,' he was blandly informed. 'The Colonel is away, the Senior Major is at breakfast and I am the *Junior* Major.'

Such gentlemen were unlikely to forget the more important things in life—

Practice in ceremonial for Officers just returned from foreign action

like 'hairless' heels, being in the Guards and maintaining the Guards' esoteric traditions—simply because their subordinates had suffered shamefully. Rather they reverted instantly to type. Once again they took their five months' leave each year to go fox hunting, the more enterprising among them even applying for an additional five months to go tiger hunting in India, and in 1857 at least one of them resigned because he was denied this extra leave.

The only qualifications needed to transform a gentleman into an officer were still, in the 1860's, the capital with which to purchase his commission and the income to sustain so expensive a way of life; and this right up to the time when the highly professional army of Bismarck's Prussia crushed France. Not surprisingly, however, the year after the Franco-Prussian war saw the abolition of the purchase of commissions. Thereafter officer-selection became slowly but steadily more discriminating and officer-training even more slowly but quite inevitably more sophisticated.

So far as the Guards and Household Cavalry were concerned, however, the reservoir for this new breed of officer would remain the same as it had always been. For another eighty years at least these regiments would draw their officer candidates from that class of rich young gentlemen who had just left a recognised Public School —preferably Eton or Harrow—but were insufficiently clever either to go into politics or to practise law.

Brilliant they may rarely have been, but they did frequently combine a tiny core of professionalism with a glossy veneer of almost studied eccentricity. It was an ex-Grenadier officer who, asked what his new (and unfashionable) regiment was, replied, 'I can never wemember, but they have gween facings and you get at 'em from Waterloo', an affectation of vagueness—particularly about geography—being an obligatory Guards characteristic.

'Early in 1964,' wrote a Brigadier, formerly of the Coldstream, 'I paid a short visit to Laos, having first sent out for a map of the world to find out where it was.'

Having just read an article about the Blues on service in Ezerum, an ex-lieutenant colonel of the Life Guards declared, 'We decline, frankly, to believe there *is* such a place.'

Listing the foreign parts it had visited in 1965, the Life Guards Band included 'the Channel Island and the Isle of Man;' and, ordered to attend a memorial service in Biarritz, a Coldstream officer packed cheerfully for an anticipated sojourn in the Lebanon.

It must not be imagined, however, that Guards eccentricity is confined to a vagueness about geography. Colonel Frederick Burnaby of the Blues, an enormous man whose hobby was ballooning, at which he was not very skilled, once took off in England, landed in France, and was rebuked for leaving the country without permission.

Colonel Cook of the Life Guards, in 1913, ordered all his officers to join Whites (one of London's most expensive clubs, and a hot bed of gambling) and when a subaltern complained that he belonged to several other clubs already, told him, 'Then resign'—though whether from those other clubs or from the Life Guards he did not stipulate. The Boer War, the internal combustion engine, new weapons and high explosives may radically have transformed the profession of soldiering, but some Guards traditions were inviolate, and autocratic commanding officers were one of them.

Thus the Rolls Royce, headlights blazing as it nosed its way towards the 'front line' during a manoeuvre, which was halted by a sentry who asked its chauffeur, 'Where the hell do you think you're going?'

'Taking up his Lordship's breakfast,' the chauffeur replied.

Thus a breed of officer during World War I conspicuous for its valour, and epitomised by the lieutenant colonel who, having seen two waves of his battalion scythed down as they advanced across no man's land at Ginchy, took personal command of the third, sounding a silver hunting horn and shouting 'Tally ho' as he led his men from their own trench to the German trench, which they captured, along with a number of enemy guns.

Thus, after 1918, a breed of officer conspicuous for its prompt resumption of such gentlemanly attributes as never carrying parcels, never travelling by public transport, never unfurling its umbrellas, and never going anywhere bareheaded.

Thus the Captain of a King's Guard at St. James's Palace who fell asleep with his face in his soup and slept right through to the savoury, because no one chose, or dared, to wake him up.

Thus the succeeding generations of young officers who sat silent in their mess, not daring to speak (still less to awaken a Captain of the King's Guard simply because he lay with his face in his soup), and never being spoken to except by their orderlies, who got them onto parade properly dressed, and their N.C.O.'s who preserved them from total humiliation in front of their men.

Thus an affectation of ignorance not only of all things geographic but, if it would achieve an effect, of all things mechanical as well—as with the Life Guards Officer who, during World War II, was told by one of his troops, 'Sir, the big end of my three tonner has gone.'

'Oh has it?' replied the officer. 'Then I shall give you a quarter of an hour to find it.'

Thus a splendid sense of rhetoric, as with the fiery Lieutenant Colonel of the Welsh Guards who, during that same war, was given to drawing his revolver, holding it at the temple of any defaulting Guardsman and bellowing, 'Men in convoys at sea are *dying* to bring you the food you eat. Can you give me *any* good reason why I shouldn't *shoot* you?'

Thus to this day a benevolent attitude toward antics in the mess which, in their subordinates, would be deemed hooliganism. 'High spirits' is the official description for it, and the fact that high spirits are less in evidence nowadays than of yore is positively regretted.

'One of the problems,' laments an officer of the 1970s, 'is that in the old days a chap could swing from the chandelier and break it and no one would bother about it. He'd always come up with the fruit. Nowadays there are damn few chaps around who can afford it.'

Which is why the subaltern who threw a bread roll at the Captain of the Guard at St. James's Palace, and hit Queen Victoria's portrait instead, is so fondly quoted. It cost him hundreds of pounds to restore Victoria but it was, after all, only high spirits. The trooper at Detmold who, in 1975, threw cutlery at the Kaiser's portrait, on the other hand, was severely punished for vandalism.

As soon as possible after the conclusion of World War II, the Guards officer in London resumed his leisurely ways. For the subaltern the battleground was once again the ballroom, his enemy the debutante. For company commanders, a weekly visit to the battalion, bowler hatted and wielding an impeccable umbrella, was once again sufficient. For the commanding officer, there was once again little to do but dispense summary and frightful justice upon the worst of the battalion's defaulters and lead its more prestigious parades.

Between times, of course, there were moments of such active service as were demanded by H.M. Government's desire to suppress terrorism in Palestine, Malaya, Cyprus or Kenya; but back in London the Household officer went to considerable pains to preserve his, by now, quite unwarranted reputation as a decorative, decadent and chinless wonder.

'You can always tell a Guards officer,' the witty used to jibe, 'but you can't tell him much.'

As late as 1957 a young officer newly arrived at Chelsea Barracks allegedly spent his first night sharing a small carpetless room with two others. On the floor above was a boiler, which vibrated violently, filling his room with heat, noise and flakes of plaster. He did not sleep well and the following morning felt that he must be dreaming when he saw an old Rolls Royce draw up, an orderly leap out to open its rear door and a bowler hatted gentleman, wearing an orchid in his button hole, emerge.

'Who's that?' he asked; and was told, 'The adjutant.'

That night, in the Mess, the adjutant spoke to him. 'I trust,' he murmured, 'you find your accommodation satisfactory?' and, not waiting for an answer, left him. Which was the last time anyone addressed him in the Mess for a full six months.

'"Who the bloody hell do you think you are?" seemed still to be the attitude, even in those days,' he was to reminisce as the battalion's commanding officer. 'Rather like being a fag at school. Today, of course, we're all more equal. Even in the Sergeant's Mess, awe no longer exists.'

In fact, the Welfare State has so influenced military attitudes that recently it became possible for the Welsh Guards to debate the correct way to pay compliments when on skis, one of their Warrant Officers having just been content simply to wave a vague alpenstock in the general direction of his Commanding Officer before crashing to the snow.

Likewise the Household officer has changed. Possibly he cannot ride at all; probably, if he can, he has to hire his horse. Probably he has no country estate: possibly, if he does, he prefers to live in the city. Possibly he may not be able both to buy a home *and* send his son to Eton: probably he will rent the sort of house his father would have scorned so that he *can* send his son to Eton.

He will probably not be an eccentric: he will certainly be a professional. He will be as élitist as ever; but he will not only look after his men, he will concern himself with the welfare of their families as well.

As one of his seniors put it, 'He must never be found wanting in either courage or old-fashioned honour; and even should he be rich enough to drive a flashy sports car with polo sticks in the back, he must bloody well *always* look after his men. See they get fed before he eats himself. Protect their privileges. If necessary even stand between them and an angry general.'

Thus the general who recently asked a guardsman how he found the battalion's food.

'It's all right, sir,' said the Guardsman.

'You're satisfied with it?'

'It's all right, sir,' said the Guardsman.

'But I bloody well want to know,' roared the general, 'is it good or is it bad?'

'It's *all right, sir*,' said the Guardsman—and his freedom to equivocate, though hardly welcomed, was respected.

Though several European princes, the son of Generalissimo Chiang Kai Shek, King Freddy of Buganda and the Maharajah of Jaipur (among other exotics) have been Guards officers, it will more likely be the son, relative or close friend of a Household Divisional officer who today successfully applies for selection by the Regimental Lieutenant Colonel; but if selected he will no longer accept all of his school contemporaries uncritically.

'Naturally all one's best friends are with one in the Army,' a Grenadier remarked. 'But one's Regimental friends tend not to be those who were one's contemporaries at Eton. Them, strangely, one tends to think of as absolute military shits.'

Some of those selected as potential officers for the Guards are first sent to Pirbright, where they are trained in a Brigade Squad to pass their Regular Commissions Board exam before Sandhurst. 'The main thing,' these unfortunates are warned, as the horrors of their course begin, 'is never to lose your sense of humour.'

Three Officers in a Guard of Honour Order. Their bearskins, taken from the soft hide of a female bear, will be
wrapped in damp towels when they come off duty.
Guardsmen's bearskins are made from the coarser fur of
the male bear, but are just as lovingly groomed

'Mother,' enquired a Brigadier's son over the telephone two days later, 'what is
a sense of humour?'

'Why?' she demanded.

'I've just spent three hours in the Guardroom for smiling,' he told her.

At both Pirbright and Sandhurst all will undergo the sort of systematic humiliation
to which only the product of an English Public School would willingly submit
himself. Indeed Pirbright, Sandhurst, the Regiment to which he proceeds on
passing out and the Army itself will all perpetuate the Public School pattern. At
school the potential Guards officer will have advanced from nonentity to exalted
Sixth Former. At Pirbright he will revert to being a nonentity, but go from it to
Sandhurst with a sixth former's sense of predestined glory. Only to be treated like
dirt at Sandhurst until, a sixth former once again, he passes out and enters his
Regiment—as a mere nothing—in the hope that some fifteen years later he might

become its Head Boy. As which, at the bottom of the hierarchy of Field officers
he will be almost a nonentity again.

From all of this long cycle, however, those who have completed it most vividly
remember the tyranny of Sandhurst, where first 'the gentlemen were sorted out
from the boys' and then were 'decivilianised' and metamorphosed into a type that
has no equivalent in civilian society; where the jargon, techniques and tactics of
conventional, nuclear, jungle and urban guerilla warfare became instinctive; where
the officer's role not only in the Army but in society as well was formally debated;
and where instruction in the social graces was as obligatory as it was for their
sisters in their finishing schools in Switzerland.

From first day to last, though, there had always been non-commissioned instructors and a terrifying R.S.M. to ensure that no one got above himself—not
even Royals.

'Will you hold your rifle straight, you silly little wog, Sir,' one R.S.M. once
bellowed at King Hussein of Jordan.

'*You*, Sir,' shrieked another at the Crown Prince of Tonga, 'are the most idle
prince I ever commanded. You yawned, Sir. You insulted Her Majesty'—pointing
his outraged stick at a statue of Queen Victoria. 'Insulted her by yawning. So
you will double down to Her Majesty, Sir, and *apologise* forthwith.'

Obediently the Crown Prince—an enormous, amiable man whose ancestors
would have eaten several R.S.M.s at a sitting—doubled off, paused before Queen
Victoria's statue and then doubled back.

'Did you apologise to Her Majesty, Sir?'

'Yes, Sergeant Major.'

'And what did Her Majesty say?'

'That I must have been a very tired Crown Prince to yawn on parade, and that
I should have the rest of the day off, Sergeant Major.'

'And so you shall, if that's what Her Majesty said,' declared the R.S.M. 'Get
fell out, Sir, and take off the rest of the day.'

Because of this capacity to absorb foreign blood, the Guards still manage to
surprise those who accuse them of being isolationist. The Birthday Parade in 1967,
for example, had as its Commanding Officer a colonel of Dutch extraction, as
its Brigade Major a Rumanian Prince and as its Colour Ensign a man of French
extraction. 'It could only,' sighed two foreign spectators, 'happen in England.'

Whatever his nationality, upon leaving Sandhurst and joining his battalion, the
new Guards officer will go to the store of the Regimental Quarter Master Sergeant
to be fitted with a ceremonial uniform, bearskin and sword which, had he to pay
for them, would cost him as much as a small car. The new Household Cavalry
Officer, if he goes to Knightsbridge to do mounted duties, will be issued with thigh-
length boots, a double cuirass, a helmet, a sword and a tunic heavily adorned

with braid, its velvet cuffs and collar exquisitely embroidered in gold, which will cost considerably more than a small car.

Having joined a Mess, the officer of today no longer waits six months before anyone speaks to him. On the other hand, should he be too outspoken, or persistently fall short of any of the standards required of him, he will be 'shaped', his shaping taking the form of anything from a mild dunking in camouflage paint to a bare-fisted hiding; and should he refuse to be shaped, he will be induced to resign and his career will be at an end.

'One doesn't like to be called a career officer,' a Welsh Guards officer explains, 'although, of course, one is. In the past one was supposed to sustain the myth that we all had so much money and such vast estates that careers were beneath us; but not any longer. Actually, I personally have no money at all, and no estates, and will try jolly hard to do well in my Staff College exams so that a career is precisely what I shall have.'

'In the past,' a Blues officer confirms, 'our officers tended either to be rather rich, or the heirs to enormous estates; but more recently death duties have struck, and the city does tend to lure our chaps away from polo and county marriages into stockbroking and insurance.'

'Mind you,' another Blues officer interrupts, 'not all of us like polo. Some of us don't even like horses—have as little to do with them as possible.'

Which can be disagreeable for those of them who are Regulars, because all Regulars in the Life Guards or the Blues and Royals do a stint of ceremonial mounted duties; and learning to ride to the standards required by the Household Cavalry is a kind of purgatory equalled only by the past purgatory of Sandhurst, involving as it does a skill that has no more to do with the playing of polo or the hunting of foxes than it has with the commanding of tanks or conducting a reconnaissance in an armoured car.

'It's probably balls,' admits a Grenadier major, 'that those of us who hunt have an instinctive feeling for the lie of the land; but I must admit that the Household Cavalry, who are pretty effete in most other respects, reveal a remarkable capacity for concealing their armoured cars in the most unpromising terrain.'

'A *Grenadier* told you we were effete?' a Life Guard challenges. 'But all *they* can say is "SIR". Weren't even allowed to vote in the referendum, you know. No box for them to tick marked SIR. And I suppose you've heard about their Picquet officer who was asked to Windsor Castle to make up the numbers at one of the Queen's dinners, have you? Wore Mess kit and a soft shirt, which was correct, but when one of the guests, a woman, asked him didn't Grenadier officers ever wear *boiled* shirts to dinner, he said, "Only on important occasions, Madam."'

'One has to be frightfully careful about dress in London,' complains an officer of the Scots Guards. 'I'll never forget being at Victoria Station, skis across my shoulder, wearing jeans and an open-necked shirt, when I heard this voice behind me saying, "I'll see you in my office when you get back", and turned to see the adjutant. I mean, one can hardly go on a skiing holiday wearing one's pin-striped suit and bowler hat, can one? No use telling *him*, though. I was improperly dressed in London and that was that. He roasted me and gave me masses of picquets.'

'And then,' chimes in a colleague, 'there are the rules relating to the Brigade tie, which really are frightfully confusing. It may only be worn at certain times, with certain collars, in certain places; and very few of us can ever remember when, which and where.'

'The rule as to caps, by comparison, is clarity itself: they must not be worn at all after six p.m. So there I was,' relates a smooth cheeked subaltern, 'having a pee with my forage cap on—looking, as I thought, absolutely splendid—when up came this seedy old stick of a captain who glanced at his watch and bellowed, "Take it off at ONCE". Most upsetting. I wasn't even sure to what exactly he was referring!'

For Life Guards officers in Germany the recent ruling about cigarettes was equally clear: they were only to be carried in cases of silver or gold. None of the Life Guards took the ruling amiss, and no one thought that they would, they being so fastidious a breed that anyone they suspect of being less than fastidious is described as 'the sort of chap who sleeps in his underpants.'

Indeed it is their casual conversation that reveals most about the officers of today's Household Division.

Talking about East Germany's agriculture, one said, 'It's pathetic. It's thirty years out of date.'

'Really?' responded another. 'I rather *approve* of that.'

'I've just been shooting a war dog,' one announced.

'Why?' he was challenged.

'I'm told it ate its handler.'

'It says here,' muttered an officer about to do service on the rock strewn slopes of the parched Radfan, 'to take absolutely basic kit. What do they mean by absolutely basic?'

'Dinner jacket and toothbrush,' he was told.

Asked why Life Guards officers click their heels to acknowledge the entry into the Mess of their Commanding Officer, Second-in-Command or Squadron Leader, one of those who had just clicked replied, 'I've no idea. Except, of course, one always has.'

'Prince Albert perhaps?' suggested a second.

'Shouldn't think so,' a third contradicted. 'He never took the faintest interest in *us*, did he?'

'Wasn't it that Brandenburg chap?' volunteered a fourth (conversations swiftly

Officers off duty

become general among the Life Guards).

'What Brandenburg chap?'

'Mountbatten's father?'

'He wasn't a Brandenburg.'

'What was he then?'

'No idea.'

A fifth officer entered, wearing his cap, which indicated that he did not wish to be talked to while he ate his breakfast.

'Who's billed me for a bottle of champagne?' he demanded, making it difficult for at least one subaltern (whose breakfast consisted of buttered toast and a bottle of champagne) to respect his cap.

'I did,' that subaltern replied.

'Why?'

'Because *your* dog ate *my* whip.' After which no one talked.

'They're the Mafia of the British Army,' an Irish Guards officer slandered the Life Guards. 'One great big family with connections everywhere. If they want anything, their lieutenant colonel rings their colonel, who rings his niece, who makes an offer no one can refuse.'

The layman may not instantly take the Irishman's point—which is that the Colonel of The Life Guards is Admiral of the Fleet the Earl Mountbatten whose niece is Her Majesty Queen Elizabeth II—but the Irishman was less than consistent in slandering only the Life Guards. Should the Scots Guards want something, *their* Colonel could ring his cousin; should the Welsh Guards want something, *their* Colonel could ring his mother; should the Grenadiers want something, *their* Colonel could ring his wife . . . and each would still be ringing Her Majesty Queen Elizabeth II, who is Colonel in Chief of them all.

But the Life Guards take no exception to the Irish canard. 'Delightful people,' they say of the Irish Guards. 'Peculiar, of course, but delightful. There's a swagger to them—a slight flick of the wrist when they march—that singles them out from the rest of the Guards.'

A Coldstream Colour Sergeant agrees. 'They're mad as arse-holes,' he confirms.

'One can tell at a glance if an officer comes from the Household Division and, if so, to which Regiment he belongs,' declared a recent Major General of the Division. 'Each in his manner bears his distinguishing mark.'

Perhaps so, but it is a mark that eludes the outsider, who notices only that Grenadier Officers seem less relaxed than Coldstream Officers, Scots Guards officers less gregarious than Irish and Welsh Guards officers, and all Foot Guard officers less sociable than officers of the Household Cavalry.

Grenadier, Coldstream and Scots Guard Messes, in fact, tend not to notice visitors, though their commanding officer does shake the guest warmly by the hand as he leaves and assure him, 'So good of you to have come. I do hope we shall see you again.'

Scots Guards officers at breakfast are a cross between a community of taciturn Trappist monks and a lodge of testy Trade Unionists upon whom has intruded an heretical blackleg. Under no circumstances, short of announcing a declaration of war, may anyone talk to anyone else.

Though less studiously mute, other Foot Guards messes maintain the kind of breakfast silence that betokens not so much family forebearance as the imminence of a ferociously contested petition for divorce during which the children will seek to avoid the custody of both parents.

Household Cavalry breakfasts, on the other hand, are remarkable only for being devoid of all affectation—and cheerful. And at dinner they will even go so far as to mention the name of a girl *before* the port has been circulated; but they always were frightfully precocious.

Their dining room in the Officers House at Detmold, in Germany, is perplexing because it features—as well as the expected portraits—the previously mentioned larger than life painting of Kaiser Wilhelm II. This, combined with the Teutonic practice of heel-clicking (a general practice throughout the Army in the nineteenth century), is apt to convince German visitors that they are the victims of a tasteless hoax; but the truth of the matter is that Kaiser Wilhelm (whose portrait also hangs in the barracks at Knightsbridge) was once Colonel of the Royal Dragoons, now amalgamated with the Blues, and nothing that he subsequently became has ever convinced the Household Cavalry that he should cease to preside over their meals.

In short, the officer of the Household Division remains incorrigibly élitist, however professional he may have become. The Foot Guards officer may jeer 'Hack on, Algy,' at the Horse Guards officer, and pray that 'one day he'll come an almighty cropper,' but Algy, slapping his shapely calf with his treasured whip, waiting for his inevitable appointment as A.D.C. to a Governor General or as equerry to someone Royal, will merely retort that it is his function, 'to give tone to an otherwise sordid business.'

Though he still plays croquet and backgammon, and reads *Horse and Hound* and *Field*, today's Household officer is a busy man whose every hour is filled with duties like training his guardsmen (who play dominos and darts and read comics), acting as welfare officer to his guardsmen and protecting London Airport with his guardsmen—duties that his predecessors would never even have contemplated.

Yet, as he rides to Horse Guards Parade, or dines at St. James's Palace, nothing seems to have changed. Marlborough's sword may have been removed from the Officer's Guard Room to the Museum in Birdcage Walk (because high spirited subalterns too often did damage with it) and a television set may stand glumly in one corner, but the atmosphere is as it always was. Scarlet tunics, gleaming wood, crystal and silver, Marengo's hoof, a silver box for cigars, a mahogany box for backgammon and historic portraits on the wall (Queen Victoria showing no signs of the extensive repairs necessitated by the subaltern's bread roll). A screen (half of which was originally the door of the First Battalion Scots Guards lavatory in the trenches during World War I) stands at the end of the table, but its presence is in no way anachronistic, because a screen is a screen, and because this one is kept closed and locked, thereby concealing its harmless contemporary pin-ups from eyes eager to confirm the carefully fostered myth of their extreme salacity.

The food and wines are excellent, the conversation better than London usually provides and the atmosphere urbane, because almost certainly the worst that the night will bring is a telephoned complaint that one of the sentries has failed to afford a Buckingham Palace official the courtesy to which he was entitled, or that two of the sentries are standing sixteen paces apart instead of fifteen, or that someone's car is improperly parked.

Complaints or not, the captain and his subaltern will prepare for their rounds at about 11.15, after which the subaltern will sleep at Buckingham Palace, the captain and the rest of his officers at St. James's, and nothing will happen. Even when Princess Anne and her husband were attacked a hundred yards away in the Mall, nothing happened at St. James's, because nowadays Scotland Yard holds itself responsible for the safety of Royals travelling about London by car—to which extent the prerogatives of the Household Division have been eroded.

Nevertheless the degree of co-operation between the Household Division and Scotland Yard is high, and the hypothesis that, in the event of an attempted coup, the defence of the Sovereign, the Government and the capital itself would mainly devolve upon them causes the Household Division no dismay at all. On the contrary, that, to the more thoughtful of them, is what defending the Sovereign has come to mean.

And fighting the Sovereign's wars? What has that come to mean? 'Something more complex,' replied a battalion commander with knowledge of fighting in Malaya, Aden, Cyprus, Kenya and Ulster, of service in Berlin, Manitoba, Hong Kong, Belize and Libya. 'It means soldiering with the utmost sophistication, not in order to kill the Government's enemies but to deter them from breaking what the Government chooses to describe as "the peace".'

*The first State Colour
presented to the Coldstream Guards by
King William IV*

THE GUARDS AT WAR, 1854–1901

17 *The Guards at War in Russia*

THE WORLD changed after 1815. What France had been to Europe for two hundred years Britain now became; and what Britain herself had been for even longer was soon to vanish in the smoke of industrialisation.

'The 2nd Battalion of the Coldstream Guards [is] to proceed by canal boats from Paddington to Manchester,' ran an order of 1 May, 1826. Thence it was to march to Liverpool and embark for Dublin. Not so long before it would have marched to Manchester as well; and not so much later it would travel to both Manchester and Liverpool by train.

In spite of her apparently unassailable military and technological superiority, Britain took no chances with the French. In Europe they had been rendered harmless, but in Canada they were still a danger, so a Guards presence was maintained at Quebec throughout the 1830s, doing endless fatigues, unloading endless ships and endlessly attending upon the Governor General. Its officers did little but sit upon courts martial, particularly of soldiers found wandering in Champlain Street, which was strictly out of bounds: and the whole detachment (like the whole English army) fossilised in the golden amber of Waterloo.

Unfortunately no one in Britain realised how inept the army had become, and when the Tsar of Russia demanded Turkey's recognition of himself as 'Protector of the Christians in the Turkish Domain of Europe,' the British public—who thought they liked the Turks—declared that Russia should be taught a lesson. When the unrepentant Russians went further, and destroyed a Turkish naval squadron, the British public confidently demanded war.

As the Russians crossed the Danube and advanced on Constantinople, the British and French sent armies to the Black Sea port of Varna, where they camped by the marshes and began at once to succumb to various virulent fevers. But before the Russians could attack Contantinople, or the British and French could attack the Russians, Austria threatened to intervene if the Tsar did not desist. Sensibly, the Tsar withdrew his armies into the homeland; only to find that the belligerent British public would not be denied its war. Russia's Black Sea Fleet and its bases in the Crimea must be destroyed, it demanded; and so began a most disastrous campaign.

It was disastrous not simply because Lord Raglan, who commanded the British army, was no Wellington; nor because he frequently referred to the Russians as the French; and not even because, as one officer complained, 'if he has any plans, he manages to keep them very dark'. Rather it was because most of his officers, and everyone in Whitehall, reverted to their worst practices of the past. Disturbed by a sentry's cries of 'All's well' throughout the night, a subaltern rushed out of his tent and rebuked him, 'My good man, I know all is well and I beg you will not make that horrid noise. If anything is the matter, pray go and report it, but I cannot have my slumbers disturbed.'

If the occasional Guards subaltern was somewhat peevish, more than a few Guards colonels were downright odd. One used to assert that, with the enemy before him and his own men behind him, his death was certain; another 'was not genial, though his men respected him'; and a third believed it beneath his dignity to speak to any of his subalterns 'unless perhaps he had known them intimately in private life'.

Though the Bulgarian summer of 1854 was hot beyond anything the Guards had ever known, they still wore their bearskins, tunics and waistcoats at all times, cursing the fact that there was so little water for them to drink, and disastrously unaware of the fact that much of that was cholera-infested.

No one spoke Bulgarian or Turkish, and few Bulgars or Turks spoke English—apart from the incorrigible hawkers who peddled their goods crying, 'Rotten eggies! Rotten eggies! Fine rotten eggies,' which nevertheless, to men whose rations consisted almost entirely of salt beef too tough to chew, proved irresistible.

The officers ate better than their men, but were disconcerted by the rats that swarmed through their mess huts. All sorts of remedies were suggested—including the strewing of broken glass under the floor boards to cut the rats' feet and persuade them to emigrate either to the French officers' mess or to that of the Russians. Undeterred, the rats stayed where they were.

When winter came, the officers naturally expected to go hunting. Foxes did not, however, abound on the coast of the Black Sea, so dog hunts were organised instead. Whooping and tally ho-ing, Guards officers pursued the hound of their choice on their expensively imported horses, though needless to say, the huntsmen being British, 'When the doggie was tired, we who whooped left him for another day.'

One officer wrote home that, 'None of us knew anything of the grim realities of war'; but their winter-time ablutions, according to another, were grim enough, being performed to the accompaniment of 'the cheerful jingle of ice as the bath was filled.'

Lamentably, the army that had roasted throughout the summer in its too thick uniforms froze throughout the winter for lack of overcoats, blankets, boots and proper shelter. In spite of which, it was ordered to attack the Russians, and did so bravely, ignoring the accurate fire of Russia's artillerymen.

According to a Guards officer on his staff, the whistle of shot and shell stimulated Lord Raglan 'like a glass of champagne', and whenever he heard it, he 'used to clutch himself under the stump of his right arm and chuckle'.

In September 1854 the Allies sailed to a point on the Crimean peninsula thirty miles north of the Russian Naval base, disembarked and began to march south across the vineyards toward Sebastopol.

Their initial obstacle was the Alma River whose far bank was high, steep and strongly held by the Russians. The British first line climbed the bank and occupied the main enemy redoubt. The Russians counter-attacked and evicted them. The Guards advanced through their retreating compatriots, retook the redoubt under heavy artillery fire and repelled another counter-attack by two enemy battalions.

'The fire was so hot,' a Scots Guards officer wrote to his mother, 'that you could hardly conceive it possible for anything the size of a rabbit not to be killed.' But, shouting, 'Forward Guards,' he had led his men on until a bullet pierced his cheek, knocked out all his teeth and silenced him. Thereupon two unflinching ensigns had held the Colours high while a viscount, two sergeants and a private rallied their comrades round them. The redoubt having been held, the whole British line advanced and the Russians fell back to Sebastopol, to warn of the siege that was coming.

To the surprise of the Allies, Sebastopol did not succumb to their immediate on-slaught. Though the Navy shelled it with their Lancaster guns, and though the British and French soldiers hurled themselves from their trenches to storm its defences, it did not surrender. 'The nut is rather harder to crack than some sanguine people expected,' a Coldstream officer admitted. Listing those in the mess who had been killed, he added with brutal frankness that 'Promotion, in a great measure, heals the sores that the loss of friends creates.' The charge of the Light Brigade, however, caused a disproportionate loss of friends.

To those on the spot, this charge lacked the fatal glamour with which Lord

Tennyson subsequently invested it. 'It went into action 680 strong and came out 390,' a letter home prosaically reported. 'The distance they had to charge was too far and consequently, when they had actually taken (they say) twenty-five guns, and destroyed all the gunners, they had not enough steam left to finish what they had begun so well, and were mowed down by the Russian artillery in sections.'

Though 390 survivors out of 680 was nothing remarkable in the annals of the Foot Guards, it came as a shock to the Light Cavalry. Back in England, the Life Guards and the Blues must have been glad that Queen Victoria had refused to allow them to go to the Crimea—if only because no one can really have regretted missing a war led by a one-armed Lord to whom the whistle of shot and shell was so stimulating that he clutched himself under his stump and chuckled.

In November came the battle on the heights that overlooked the Inkerman valley. The key point was held by the Guards Brigade, and against the allies in general and the Guards in particular the Russians despatched a vastly superior force. If they could capture the heights, they could relieve Sebastopol.

For six hours, in heavy mist, the Guards refused to be dislodged, wreaking fearful havoc with their new 'rifles'; throwing stones when their ammunition ran out; stabbing and clubbing their way out of defeat. Easily identifiable in their bearskins, they were attacked again and again. 'Our men never flinched but fought as cool as cool and were cut to pieces,' one of their officers recorded. 'We killed immense numbers of Russians, but our loss is frightful . . . Out of 17 officers, 4 came back not killed or wounded . . . Is it not too terrible? All our friends dead.'

'In hand to hand encounter,' another officer reported, 'the Guards proved themselves a match for any quantity of antagonists who could not stand the bayonet.'

About his fellow officers, he remarked, 'Such men as are lost are not replaced; but all one says out here is, "Poor fellow! Who gets his step?"'—and crossing his name off the Army List, his friends consoled themselves that *his* promotion might now become theirs.

The winter grew colder. 'The sickness is perfectly frightful,' wrote Surgeon Major Bostock. 'I believe the daily loss of the army has for some time been at the rate of two to three hundred men. All this is owing to the gross mismanagement and want of forethought of the Commissariat authorities generally.'

The Scots Guards received a draft of 101 replacements after the Battle of Inkerman. Dubbed the Dead Draft, it lost most of its number in the next eight weeks while waiting for a consignment of sheep skin coats and long boots.

'Of the many thousands of pairs of boots sent out from England,' an ensign complained, 'a few hundred are all that can be got to fit the men's swelled feet.' As if that were not fault enough, 'the boots are so badly made that the uppers and soles part company after only a day or two's wear.'

'The way the wounded are looked after is truly disgraceful. No surgeons, no

The Guards at Alma, 20th September 1854

The Charge of the Guards at Inkerman

nurses, no order, everything in confusion, no system, very bad indeed.'

The writer added a postscript to his parents. 'I ask as a most particular favour that my letters are not hawked about and shown to this person or that. I know that people are eager for news, but please tear them up when you have read them. God bless you all.'

Of Florence Nightingale, the men in the firing line apparently heard and knew nothing: she plays no part in their letters home. Medical innovations, however, did not go undiscussed.

'The question of chloroform was debated with acrimony,' a letter reveals. 'P.M.O Hall placed his objections to it on record, saying that he preferred "that a man should bawl lustily under the knife than sink silently into a grave" . . . I think that in General Napier's letters from the Peninsular there is mention of a Tommy Atkins having his arm off and walking away to see how his officer was going on. If he were allowed so to do nowadays (after chloroform), could he?'

'Lord Raglan,' complained a Guards ensign, 'knows nothing and cares less,' but 'he gets made a Field Marshal and we do not get the praise which is our due. After the supernatural courage displayed by our Brigade . . . we expected it would have been mentioned in the despatches—which of course were written by a Staff who always mention themselves no matter how they behave, whether skulking in the rear or sitting behind a stone or bush.'

Though the winter of 1855 was frightful, Sydney Herbert had hastened to reassure the House of Commons that all in the Crimea was well. Contradicting him bluntly, a Coldstream officer advised his mother. 'All I can say is that there is at present a foot of snow on the ground, and a hard frost, and our men have not even two blankets to cover them . . .When one goes to bed of a night one is frightened of breaking one's red coat of a morning, so stiff is it!"

Those conducting the war were daily lambasted in both the English press and London's clubland for their lack of aggression. 'Eventually,' promised a Grenadier, 'we shall satisfy the bloodthirsty *Times* and the rest of the warriors at home.'

In June another Guards officer reported, 'The Russians sold us terribly yesterday, the anniversary of Waterloo, and gave us a most severe drilling . . . (They) behaved in the coolest and most plucky way in the world . . . . (and) mauled the French to an immense extent.'

The French having constantly bragged of 'the incontestable superiority' of their brave soldiers', this mauling caused their allies little grief; but the attitude of the English soldier himself had begun to worry some of his officers.

'The men are getting like the French—very sensible,' one complained. 'They see their danger, and the effect which grape and canister can have upon them, and there is no longer that idea which there used to be that they could never be licked, and did not know when they were licked.'

Perhaps it was Lord Raglan who by his crass mis-handling of the June 18th attack had disillusioned them. He may even have disillusioned himself, because he uttered not a single word for eleven days thereafter—and then died.

'I think,' commented an ensign about his men, 'from what I have overheard . . . that they are glad he is out of the way.' They were. They were also tired of the war.

Of those who leaped out of the trenches to make the final Allied attack on Sebastopol 'nine tenths . . . were officers who had failed, by example or encourage-ment, to get the men on. Truly it disabuses one unpleasantly. But I hope that we shall not fall into the opposite extreme and underrate the British soldier as much as we have hitherto overrated him. It makes me almost think that true courage is *not* found in every hedge and ditch in England, or in every alley from which we recruit our army.'

In his shock at the refusal of his soldiers to follow him in this last charge, the writer forgot their previous steadfastness at Alma and Inkerman, and ignored the fact that the Crimea had glaringly demonstrated both the negligence of the commis-sariat and the frivolity of many of his brother officers who, by their own admission, had known nothing of the realities of war, had prepared for those realities by hunting 'doggies' and strewing glass under the tender feet of rats, and were much

more concerned with their chances of promotion than with the suffering of thei
men. Of the original 101 men of the Dead Draft, for example, only seventeen now
survived.

'We are so strong in officers and so weak in men,' a more sensitive subaltern
lamented. 'The men are in a sad condition. They have heaps and heaps of clothing
now, but too late, the mischief is done: they are shadows of what they were.'

Not for him the noble dream of true courage behind every hedge and ditch.
Describing his sharpshooters, he said, 'None are married and they are the most out
and out blackguards of the Regiment—rob a church and use language fit to frighten
a fellow into a fit.'

Despite all these British defects, the Russians—who had allegedly lost 500,000
men during the siege—finally withdrew. 'So Sebastopol is truly taken,' wrote
bemused Coldstream officer. 'Who would believe it? Abandoned would be
better word, for (they) seem to have retreated with the greatest dignity, dressing the
wounds of our men that were left in the Redan and putting water beside them . .

And so ended the first war to come under the daily scrutiny of Britain's news
paper readers—an experience Whitehall enjoyed no more than the White Hous
was to enjoy the cold eye of the television camera a century later in Vietnam.

Because of what it had read, the British public completely revised its attitud
towards the ordinary soldier. From that day to this, as a result, a steady improvemen
has been seen in his lot and a growing concern for him has been displayed by hi
officers. From that day to this, he has become steadily more urban and has grown
steadily younger.

Of the 2,060 men who served with the Coldstream in the Crimea between 185
and 1856, for example, 1,523 were either husbandmen, labourers or servants; of the
eleven N.C.O.'s invalided home, nine were agriculturalists; and of the 184 private
invalided home, 148 were agriculturalists.

The average age of those 11 N.C.O.'s was twenty-eight: of the 184 Private
twenty-seven. Today's N.C.O.'s and Privates are four or five years younger
most of them come from cities; and all of them fight a kind of war that wa
inconceivable in 1856.

18 The Guards at War in South Africa

'THAT ELECTRIC telegraph!' complained a staff officer during the Crimean War. 'What good has it done us? What harm? ... I don't believe that he (Lord Raglan) could now send 500 men anywhere without first being obliged to telegraph home to know if he might do so.'

For better or worse, the telegraph had changed the conduct of war. The Government had not only become instantly privy to every decision made, but was instantly able to countermand those decisions; and the events of every future war would be instantly communicated, via the Press, to the public at home. In other words, not only would all future Sovereign's wars be wars declared by the Government, but when the Guards fought them it would be with the Government breathing down their necks and the public sitting in daily judgment upon them.

The better to co-ordinate their training for such future wars, a General commanding the Brigade of Guards was appointed; and the better to improve the performance of the Army as a whole, Aldershot was expanded as a centre of training and education.

Indeed, in 1871, agitated by Prussia's swift annihilation of all French resistance in 1870, Britain even instituted the foreign and ungentlemanly practice of annual manoeuvres; but abandoned them in 1873 because they were expensive. Apart, in fact, from sending a Brigade of Guards to reinforce the Canadian border in 1862—during America's Civil War—Britain's militarism was almost entirely academic from the time the Crimean War ended until 1881.

Then, however, a mob rioted in Alexandria, slaughtered a hundred Europeans and (worst of all) insulted the British consul. At once a British army was despatched to Egypt, led by Sir Garnet Wolsey, whom the Queen most heartily disliked.

Adamant throughout her reign that neither the Life Guards nor the Blues should leave the country, Victoria would probably have ignored the urging of their Colonel in Chief, the Prince of Wales, that now they be sent to the Middle East had not Sir Garnet (who favoured *short* service soldiers) also advised that he did not want them. At which she gave her immediate approval, and off they went to the southernmost province of the sprawling Ottoman Empire, through which ran the thirteen year-old Suez Canal.

'Egypt,' Victoria unequivocally declared, 'can be in no other hands than ours if she is to be taken from Turkey—or rather,' since the proprieties of Royalty had to be observed, 'from the Khedive.'

In a moonlit charge, 'right gallantly led and executed', the Household Cavalry and the 7th Dragoon Guards duly chopped the unfortunate insurgents to pieces and escorted the Khedive back to his palace at Alexandria; but the Army did not then go home. Without actually *taking* Egypt from Turkey (or rather from the Khedive)

2nd Battalion Coldstream Guards embarking for active
service at Kingstown on Pacific Steam *Iberia*, 1882

the Army, by staying there till 1956, ensured that it remained in no other hands tha
England's for three-quarters of a century.

The Egyptian 'war' of 1882 had been as short as it was brutal, but Sir Garne
Wolsey was full of unexpected praise for the Life Guards and the Blues. 'Thes
Household Cavalrymen are teaching me a lesson. I wish I had more of them,' h
confessed.

'They are the best troops in the world,' he wrote to his wife. 'At least, none coul
be better.'

Such unstinted praise softened Victoria's heart toward him almost as much as th
fact that Gladstone—whom she detested—had attempted to interfere in his condu
of the campaign.

'Meddling from home,' she tartly advised her Prime Minister, 'might be injurious
while, forgetting no past slights, she wrote to Wolsey, 'The Queen is glad to he
that Sir Garnet Wolsey entertains such a high opinion of her Household Cavalr
She would remind him that they are the only *long* service corps in the Army.'

Needless to say the Household Cavalry had neither fought nor won the campaig alone: the Navy had bombarded Alexandria, and the infantry, which had marched from Ismailia to Cairo (sweltering in pith helmets and scarlet tunics while Indian troops were comfortable in sensible khaki) had contributed handsomely to the thirty-five minute battle.

As a result, the Duke of Connaught wrote to the Queen suggesting that in future the British Army, too, should fight in khaki.

'Café au lait,' snorted Victoria, and refused.

Though peace and the Khedive had been restored in Egypt, the Sudan remained restive. In particular, the Mahdi had bailed up General Gordon. To put an end to that impertinence, a brace of relief forces was despatched to relieve Khartoum.

Of these, one was to proceed as far up the Nile as possible by steamer, and paddle the rest of the way to Khartoum in canoes; the second was to proceed by camels, which were to be ridden by, among others, forty men from each of the Household Cavalry Regiments.

Both were intercepted—the so-called Heavy Camel Regiment a hundred lurching miles into the desert. Having killed about a thousand Dervishes, for the loss of seventy-four Household Cavalrymen, the Camel Regiment staggered on to the Nile—where it learned that Gordon had been murdered. Its camels exhausted, the force limped back to Egypt on foot.

An outraged Britain—concerned only with the murder of one of her generals and the need to punish the fuzzy-wuzzies responsible—paid no heed to any other aspect of the Household Cavalry's experiment than its failure; but the creation of a Heavy Camel Regiment was significant. For 222 years the Household Cavalry had changed nothing but its uniforms; now it had signalled its willingness to adapt and experiment.

Kitchener settled the Mahdi's hash two years later, leading an army clad at last in khaki and initiating, from 1885 to 1899, a period of comparative peace during which the Foot and Horse Guards were almost entirely occupied with ceremonial duties. But politicians in Whitehall and South Africa had done little to avert a clash since 1880, and it could not be delayed much longer.

The Boers wanted war because, having trekked so far north from the Cape Colony to find independence in 1836, they had only surrendered it to the British to buy protection from the Zulus. The Zulu danger dispelled, their urge to be independent had revived and they had both declared themselves a republic once again and successfully attacked the British forces in Natal. Worse, led by Kruger, they had had no difficulty in capturing an entire British raiding-party, had sentenced its members to death, commuted the sentence to a magnanimous but enormous fine, and bought arms with the proceeds. Though the Kaiser had congratulated them, Britain had continued to deny them recognition as an independent nation.

The British wanted war because the crisis had brought their trade in and with

South Africa to a stand-still and because the Kaiser had congratulated the Boers on their handling of the Jameson Raid. 'The state of affairs in South Africa cannot long be tolerated,' Chamberlain finally told the House of Commons. 'We have put our hands to the plough and shall not draw back.'

More interested in the fascinating events of the Dreyfus affair, the British public took little interest in Mr. Chamberlain's ploughing, even though his Government now proceeded to despatch 10,000 men from India to Natal and call up Britain's reserves.

Not so indifferent were the Boers, who delivered an ultimatum and, when Westminster ignored it, declared war in October 1899.

'All bright parts, except the blades of swords and bayonets, and all scabbards, are to be painted brown,' the Household Cavalry and the Guards Brigade were ordered when eventually they arrived on the Veld. All were dressed in khaki; infantry officers and N.C.O.'s had to wear the same equipment as their men; all their Sam Brown belts, swords and revolvers had to be handed in; and the day of the Conspicuous Redcoat was over.

So, it seemed, was the day of the crushing frontal attack, because the Boer would simply have shot it to ribbons and then mounted their ponies and galloped away rather than be over-run. To this evasive kind of warfare Britain's generals especially Buller, seemed unable to find any reply.

The Boers, for their part, found swift remedies for their every defect. Realising that their rifle fire from dominating heights tended to 'plunge', and cause few casualties, they sought such natural positions on the plains as creek beds from which to make the best use of the Mauser's flat trajectory.

Advancing against them, then, Methuen's force (mainly Guards) would see only the empty veld and an apparently harmless line of bushes. From behind which abruptly, would pour a storm of rifle bullets and one pound shells that ripped apart the British line, for whom there was no cover anywhere.

The Boer employed this tactic time after time, making the scrub his ally, the vastness of the land his strongest weapon.

'We must face the facts,' warned a journalist on the spot, called Winston Churchill, 'the individual Boer, mounted in suitable country, is worth from three to five regular soldiers . . . The only way of treating the problem is either to get men equal in character and intelligence as riflemen, or, failing the individual, huge masses of troops.'

Naturally his advice was rejected. The British continued to suffer constant ambushes, disproportionate losses and successive reverses. Finally Lord Roberts was sent out from England to take over the conduct of the war.

High summer brought fires, dysentery, reinforcements and further failures. 30,000 Britons could neither put down nor escape the taunting Boers. Their horses died by the hundred; Lord Roberts, at first, made mistakes; and even though the Guards

Coldstream Guards resting in redoubt, Boer War

distinguished themselves by the speed, discipline and endurance of the phenomenal marches they undertook, they won not a single significant victory because their Boer opponents invariably disappeared in the dust kicked up by their fleet-footed ponies.

Fortunately, Lord Roberts had not entirely forgotten the lessons of the American War of 1776, nor the tactics he had employed against the Pathans in India. He established blockhouses all along the railway and sent out mobile columns to protect the line and round up the Boers.

In February 1900, General French ordered his Cavalry, 'You must relieve Kimberley if it costs half your forces.' The attack lasted four days and victory came when 3,650 mounted men charged three miles through one Boer position after another. At last the cavalry—especially the Household Cavalry—had found themselves an effective role as an integral part of an army engaged in a general tactic. At Ladysmith, Kimberley and later at Mafeking the cavalry's tactical deficiencies of Minden, Fontenoy, Waterloo and the Crimea were all made good.

Meanwhile the process began of harrying the Boers from pillar to post. Even though De Wet took the war into the Cape Colony itself, creating havoc with a few thousand men, each of whom had at least five spare mounts, he could do no more than delay the inevitable. Roberts went home to become Commander-in-Chief. Queen Victoria died and the Household Cavalry went home to escort the new King. Kitchener took over the conduct of the war and the Boers continued their guerilla and commando tactics, denying victory to no less than a quarter of a million British soldiers for yet another frustrating year.

Eventually an honourable peace was negotiated and the Guards returned to England to escort King Edward VII to his Coronation. Over a period of three years they had re-learnt the arts of war and become an important part of the first of Europe's twentieth century armies. But their strenuous efforts must be seen in the light of the facts of the war they fought rather than the fervour that war aroused.

From 16 November 1899 to 12 September 1901 the 1st Battalion of the Coldstream Guards—whose case is typical of all the Guards Regiments—had no less than 132 Battalion Headquarters as it chased Boers all over South Africa. Yet, in all its battles, it lost only 21 killed in action and 7 who died of wounds. Enteric fever, on the other hand, killed 60; a train killed 2; 2 died by drowning; 8 succumbed to illness other than enteric fever; and one expired of alcoholism. The battalion lost only 2 of its officers, both from illness.

In other words, the Guards learnt only the motions of twentieth century warfare in South Africa between 1899 and 1902, just as they had learnt to take cover from artillery fire at Waterloo and how to fight from trenches in the Crimea. That modern warfare could mean not only taking cover from shell fire and fighting from trenches but carnage as well they did not learn. Of that they and the world were to be left in ignorance until 1914.

The Regimental Colour, 1st Battalion Scots Guards

THE GUARDS, THEIR SOVEREIGN AND LONDON, AFTER 1901

19   *Edward VII–Elizabeth II*

EDWARD VII was the last of Britain's kings to be able to influence Government, and the first of them to have travelled extensively and visited some of the Empire. He was the intimate and close relative of almost every Royal Household in Europe; through his ageing veins coursed a volatile mixture of disreputable Hanoverian and dutiful Saxe-Coburg blood; and his familiar world of Kings, Emperors and Tsars was about to be blown to extinction.

Nevertheless Britain under his rule retained its sense of divinely ordained greatness, and London—provided one was rich—maintained its air of dazzling gaiety. As in George II's time, the best people still did not work and their younger sons still joined the Guards or the Household Cavalry.

Of course it was a little more difficult, now that commissions could no longer be bought; but not so much more difficult that the same families were unable to get their sons into the same regiments. And once commissioned, of course, the emphasis lay as much on hunting, shooting, gambling and the Season's Balls as ever.

Following the King's example, double standards were more than ever the order of the day. Divorce was unacceptable, adulteries as notorious as they were rife. Duty was inescapable, self-indulgence a way of life. The greatest virtue was to be well-born, the cardinal sin to cheat at cards. The most savage deterrent was to be rejected by one's peers, the highest accolade to be accepted by the King.

Who was himself accepted by the world as Edward the Peacemaker, as he travelled from Royal Court to Royal Court, persuading a cousin here, a son-in-law there, a nephew somewhere else that *his* way—which he had usually agreed in advance with the Foreign Office—was best. Only the impossible Kaiser Wilhelm II resisted him, so that Edward, unable to win him over, was obliged to win over his friends instead.

On the domestic front his popularity was as much due to the serene beauty of his Danish wife, Alexandra, as it was to his own stout affability; and on the Imperial front he shrewdly sent his oldest surviving son, George, with his wife, Princess Mary, to visit Australia, New Zealand, South Africa and Canada.

A decade of such intense Royal activity precipitated numerous return visits by foreign Royals and an endless cycle of ceremonial for the Household troops—whose drill, discipline and turn-out had become stunningly impressive.

Yet one of their most colourful duties—the provision of a Sovereign's Escort of plumed and glittering horsemen—had become almost a formality, because of the advent of the motor car. Doubtless the Life Guards and Blues *could* have escorted

The tallest men in the 3rd Battalion Scots Guards, 1906,
with one of the youngest and smallest

the Royal motors at a gallop: sensibly they chose not to, surrendering that responsibility to the police, who have attended to it ever since.

Edward died in 1910 having, by a combination of professionalism and personality, made his own a decade which English history will probably, a hundred years hence, ascribe solely to the London activities of anarchists and suffragettes and the suburban scribblings of two insignificant refugees called Lenin and Marx.

The death of the King Emperor was marked by an impressive lying-in-state and a funeral of such pomp and circumstance as only the presence of nine kings, a cohort of archdukes and princes and the spectacle of the Guards and the Household Cavalry could provide.

This was no mere ritual. It was the last purple flowering of Europe's doomed but royal vine. Because they were all his relatives, kings and princes were very properly the closest mourners of the King Emperor. Because only God ranked higher than Edward, plumes, swords, helmets, cuirasses, glossy black horses, gleaming black boots and sleek black bearskins were fitting accoutrements for the cortège of England's King Emperor. Because cavalry charges and the thin red line were popularly deemed to be as effective still as they had been at Waterloo, the plumed Household Cavalry and bear-skinned Foot Guards were considered to be as up to date as the man they had served, the late and beloved King Emperor.

Which is not to say that Edward's successor, George v, was less regal or imperial than his father, but simply that time was running out for kings and emperors. World War I may have been a Royal War for George's first cousins, Kaiser Wilhelm and Tsar Nicholas, but for him and his subjects it was a Government war, during which, as an example to his subjects, he wore uniform to open Parliament and forswore alcohol.

At the conclusion of the war his cousins had lost their thrones, his subjects had been slaughtered by the hundred thousand and his Brigade of Guards and Household Cavalry had been wiped out ten times over. So long as there is a Royal Household, however, there will always be Household troops, and Britain's constitutional monarchy survived the blizzard of post-war revolution as the autocratic monarchies of Germany, Russia and Austria did not.

Having survived it, George v used pageantry as a panacea, encouraging his sons to marry at Westminster Abbey, himself opening Northern Ireland's new Parliament, attending great public functions, using the new medium of radio to reach all his subjects at Christmas-time and participating regally, with his even more regal Queen, in the celebration of his Silver Jubilee.

While thus deliberately preserving and exploiting the theatrical attributes of his Household troops, George v and his Queen assiduously obliterated the double standards of the past. Unlike Edward vii, George v lived a simple, respectable, private life and expected the same of others. He was a severe father, and so uncompromising an English king that during the war he had disclaimed all his German titles, adopted the family name of Windsor and ordered all those princes in his family who were British also to change their names.

The war over, he participated in none of the giddy frivolities of the Twenties and, declining to court popularity by making himself either accessible or approachable, became the most majestic king, married to the most formidable Queen, that England had ever known.

As such King George and Queen Mary were the perfect symbol of an imperial Britain noted for its honour and greatness. Embodying a myth, they were almost as intangible as the myth itself—and they were not at all their oldest son's idea of the monarchy that Britain needed in the Thirties.

Unfortunately for him, nor was he, as Edward VIII, the Government's idea of a suitable monarch. Obliged either to abandon his marriage plans or abdicate, he was succeeded by his brother, George—and a second world war.

At the end of which there were left in the world fewer monarchies than ever and, in victorious Britain, a weariness so intense, an economy so shattered and a colonial guilt so incurable that it became physically and morally impossible to retain the Empire. George VI was therefore obliged to preside over the beginning of that Imperial liquidation which Churchill, at Yalta, had rejected: Elizabeth II has seen the process completed.

Yet London remains. The London of the Royals, of the Guards, of Elizabeth I's 200,000 subjects and Elizabeth II's 7,000,000; the London of Horse Guards Parade and St. James's Park, round which, in one palace or another, the sovereign has lived since the time of Henry VIII.

And the park remains, with Nash's lake in the hollow where once there was a canal, the by-products of a sort of hockey pitch on one side and an aviary on the other, all of it the work of kings and queens from the time of Henry VIII to George IV.

And the monarchy remains, its residence being Buckingham Palace (which must still be guarded) whose formal entrance is Horse Guards Arch (which must still be guarded) through which will pass the sovereign's coach (which must still be guarded) on its way to the State Opening of Parliament (whose wars must still be fought).

After the death of Edward VII, 1910, Queen Alexandra
takes the salute in the gardens of Buckingham Palace

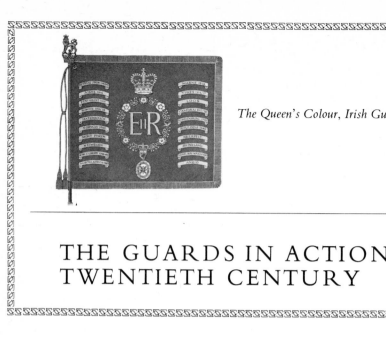

The Queen's Colour, Irish Guards

THE GUARDS IN ACTION IN THE TWENTIETH CENTURY

20 The Guards in Two World Wars

THROUGHOUT THE South African war the Boer had shown a decisive superiority over his enemy in marksmanship, fire tactics and rapid magazine fire. Colonel Maxse of the Coldstream therefore suggested that every man in his regiment should forego two days' pay to finance the construction of a miniature rifle range on which any man could practise whenever he was off duty.

His suggestion was enthusiastically endorsed and within a year the 2nd Battalion of the Coldstream—never before highly regarded for their musketry—were accepted as the best shooting battalion in the army. Miniature rifle ranges then became a standard army facility.

The Boer War had also revealed a tendency to fight according to the book rather than with initiative or flexibility, and in manoeuvres from 1903 onwards exercises to rectify this defect were studied—as were the results of and tactics employed in Russia's calamitous war against Japan.

Almost outweighing these military virtues were the inevitable post-war defence cuts, which, among other things as bad or worse, cost the Coldstream and the Scots Guards their third battalion. More cunning than the Scots, the Coldstream promptly contrived to have *their* 3rd Battalion posted to Egypt. There it became 'lost' until 1911, when, rearmament having become fashionable again, it was conveniently rediscovered.

The great European war that had been inevitable since 1870 finally broke out in 1914. It should—like the Boer War that preceded it, or the Second World War that followed it—have been a conflict of spectacular movement: instead, sustained by Europe's railway system and millions of doomed young men, it became, almost at once, a static killing match of hideous length and intensity.

'Dear me,' Lord Kitchener complained, as he entered his room in Whitehall for the first time, 'what a War Office! No army—no staff—and not even a pen that will write.'

But that was less a criticism of Britain's small Regular Army—whose standards were extremely high—than an admission that World War I demanded not thousands of men (as had previous wars) but millions, entailed battles that lasted not hours or days but weeks and months; and killed in an hour more men than other wars had killed from beginning to end.

It goes without saying that both the Brigade of Guards and the Household Cavalry fought with that degree of discipline and steadiness peculiar to themselves; but neither of these admirable qualities made their sacrifice one whit the less bloody or futile than that of any other regiment. Today's world, however, is more familiar with the monstrous details of death on the Western Front than with any other war in history, and not even as a memorial to the Guards is there any point in recapitulating anything but the barest outline of their four year involvement.

The 1914 Allied retreat from Mons was the last but one Household Cavalry operation to be executed on horseback. Having reached the Marne, the Allies dug in, trench warfare began (with millions of soldiers separated from each other by only a narrow, blasted, pock-marked strip of no man's land, hundreds of miles long) and horses became a liability.

Consequently cavalrymen soon grew accustomed to fighting on foot. Admittedly, at home, entire Cavalry divisions were still being formed; but with no intention of their ever fighting any other way than dismounted. Admittedly the Life Guards provided a *bicycle* battalion and some lorry-borne machine gunners; but mainly they served as trench-diggers and infantrymen, and the only indication that either they or the Blues had ever been colourful or glamorous came from the mounted guard of unfit men which, throughout all the years of muddy slaughter in Flanders, appeared daily in Whitehall in all its pristine splendour.

The last mounted charge of the Household Cavalry came in 1917, when Field Marshal the Earl Haig inexplicably decided that the Life Guards and Blues should carry out a diversionary attack on the Hindenburg Line at Arras. He could as justifiably have ordered them to attack Everest.

Across appallingly broken, snow-covered ground that had immobilised even the new fangled tank, the two regiments, swords drawn, charged undaunted through withering machine-gun fire and were sliced to ribbons on German

barbed wire. It was Easter Monday and the slaughter of horses and men was
horrific.

'It's all in the day's work,' a dying officer murmured; and grievously he spoke
nothing but his generation's epitaph. From 1914 to 1918 a man's work was to kill
for as long as possible and then to die; and the best he could hope for was that
at the end of the day, he might die quickly.

Even more horrific than the slaughter of the Household Cavalry at Arras in 1917
was the fate of the Foot Guards throughout the war. In the past their great battles
had lasted at most a week. Waterloo lasted less than a day. But the first battle of
Ypres, in 1914, lasted from 19 October to 22 November, and during those 34 days
the 2nd Battalion Scots Guards, whose fate was typical, was reduced from 31
officers and 970 men to 6 officers and 233 men.

Coldstream Guards leaving for the Front, August 1914

Determined to make use of the Guards' special qualities, Lord Kitchener announced the formation of a Guards Division in August 1915. Its lunatic role was 'to pierce the German wall' and it was first employed in this fatal capacity at Loos, in September 1915.

There, according to one observer, its 'advance brought tears to the eyes. Men dropped like flies, but they kept on as if marching up the Mall.' The battle lasted three weeks, cost the British 60,000 casualties, and failed. Poelcapelle and Passchendaele followed in 1917, killing a quarter of a million British soldiers; then came the Somme, Cambrai, St. Quentin and Arras in 1918, all of them cataclysmic examples of the madness of ordering frontal attacks against an entrenched enemy armed with magazine rifles and machine-guns.

By 1916 most of the world had become too obsessed with its own casualty lists

The Household Cavalry leaving for the Front, 1914

ever to identify with the losses of others, but the Americans were still not involved and their sympathies had at last begun to polarise. As a gesture of their growing good-will, they sent the Coldstream an old regimental buckle—a recently excavated relic of England's eighteenth-century occupation of Manhattan Island; but what the Allies needed in 1916 was not a sympathetic gesture but a massive transfusion of American blood.

Eventually it came, and by its mere arrival transformed a war of murderous equipoise into an unequal conflict that the Germans had to lose. Only the most stubborn Allied courage, however, had held the Central Powers to three years of equipoise; and the Guards had been conspicuous for their courage throughout those years, having won between them no less than twenty-three Victoria Crosses.

Six were won by officers, seventeen by N.C.O.s and men, and almost all were awarded for a persistent refusal to be deterred by odds that should have been paralysing. The Guards who had once marched majestically up the slope of Fontenoy, not even stepping aside to avoid the careering cannon ball, might not easily have recognised as their descendants the Guards Division's mud-stained ranks of tall men with short hair; the Guards who had stood on the ridge at Mont St. Jean calmly delaying the moment when they would destroy the reputation of Napoleon's legendary Grenadiers might not easily have identified with those to whom Kitchener had assigned the task of 'piercing the German walls'; the Guards who had fought the French hand-to-hand in Hougoumont's soggy orchard and hurled stones at the Russians on the misty heights of Inkerman might not have approved of a war where millions of men were blown apart by remotely propelled high explosives or mown down like flies by invisible machine-gunners; but none of them, reading the citations for those twenty-three Victoria Crosses, would have been surprised to learn that all the recipients were men of the Foot Guards. In each case the award had been made for courage based on discipline, steadiness and contempt for the enemy; and these had always been the very special qualities of the Brigade of Guards.

Victory in World War I was not marked by magnanimity toward the vanquished. Exhausted, impoverished and vindictive, most of the Allies demanded that Germany should pay ruinous reparations. Thus Versailles set the stage for World War II.

Whose opening Hitler timed perfectly. In 1914 Britain had faced an Irish Home Rule crisis so severe that Mr. Asquith had finally confessed that his conference to resolve it had been unable to agree 'either in principle or in detail'.

'To hell with Serbia,' *John Bull* had therefore proclaimed when Austria's Archduke was assassinated; and had the Kaiser not persisted in the long-planned invasion of neutral Belgium he might well have found his most stubborn enemy too embroiled in an Irish conflict to care about any war in Europe. But the moment

Corporal Major M. G. Tench,
later Captain and Adjutant of the
Blues, 1915

Belgium's neutrality was violated, Britain had sprung indignantly to her defence.

In 1938 and 1939, Hitler made no such mistake, virtually paralysing Britain's will to resist as he marched from strength to strength. When war did come, he had achieved such a diplomatic and military dominance in Europe as Frederick the Great, Bismarck and Kaiser Wilhelm II combined had never attained.

To say that Britain was unprepared for a war with Hitler in 1939 is rather like saying that America was not particularly happy to have Nixon as its President in 1974. Since 1919 Britain's defence capacity had been hacked to pieces by what had been dubbed the Geddes Axe, and her belated attempts to re-arm had amounted to little more than gestures like allowing the Life Guards to return to their Knightsbridge Barracks.

When war broke out, the Household Cavalry found itself mounted on horses (which it knew from its experiences in World War I, and the recent fate of Poland's cavalry, to be useless) and armed with a few Bren guns (which were promptly taken from it and given to the infantry).

Grenadiers supported by Bren Gun carriers on
reconnaissance at the Kasserine Pass, Tunisia, March 1943

In February 1940, Life Guards and Blues were shipped to Palestine as a composite
regiment, leaving the Whitehall Guard to be mounted (on weekdays only) by
reservists who had at their disposal a furniture van, an old motorbike, four buses
and sixty elderly horses.

For a year the Household Cavalry and the Cavalry Division of which it was
part did nothing in the Middle East—to Churchill's fury. Then Iraq's premier
ordered an attack on the R.A.F. base at Habbaniya and the Vichy French in Syria
began to harbour 'technicians' who were in fact Nazis: so a British force was
despatched to save Iraq from itself and its oil for the Allies.

Spearheaded by the 1st Essex Regiment and a detachment of the Household
Cavalry (who had shot their horses and mounted trucks instead), and led by a
cavalry officer in a yellow taxi, this force relieved Habbaniya, occupied Baghdad,

helped occupy Syria, and entered Teheran, thereby encouraging the Shah of Persia to adopt a less ambiguous posture.

The Household Cavalry reservists in England, meantime—making full use of their four buses, sixty horses, furniture van and motorbike—had manned what was euphemistically known as the Acton Line, from which they were under orders to repel any Wehrmacht advance on London.

Both in the Middle East and on the Acton Line, an élitist regiment had thus been seen at its eccentric best; but in February of 1942 the Household Cavalry Regiment became an Armoured Car Regiment and the days of eccentricity were over. Superbly trained to combine technical skill with cavalry dash, they probed, reconnoitred, spied and raided first of all as far north as Turkey, then from Alamein to Tripoli and Italy, and finally from Normandy to Belgium and into the very heart of Germany.

Between 1939 and 1945 the Household Brigade expanded to two composite regiments of Household Cavalry and twenty-five active battalions of Foot Guards. In 1941, a Guards Armoured Division was formed, to the dismay of many an armchair critic who pointed out the folly of putting, big, brainless Guardsmen into cramped, complex tanks and allowing them to crash around the world's battlefields in the wake of armoured cars commanded by idiot Household cavalry-men who had never driven anything but polo ponies.

Once ashore at Normandy the Guards Armoured Division swiftly silenced its armchair critics. Though its Sherman tanks burst into flames so easily that the Germans dubbed them 'Tommy Cookers', the Guards never once shirked driving them. Similarly the Household Cavalry silenced their critics by providing the Armoured Division with a large number of 'polo players' who performed ad-mirably in armoured cars and were affectionately known to their Guards' colleagues as 'The Stable Boys'.

On 3 September 1944, both Guards and Stable Boys particularly distinguished themselves. 'My intention,' General Adair had instructed his Armoured Division the day before, 'is to advance and liberate Brussels, and that is a grand intention!'

Indeed it was: Brussels lay ninety miles away and no one knew what opposition would be encountered en route. Nevertheless, at 7 a.m. on the fifth anniversary of the declaration of war, two groups of tank and lorry borne Guards, led by Household Cavalry armoured cars, set off.

Driving flat-out, they crossed the Belgian frontier at 10.30, demolished an enemy rearguard position at Lenze, dashed on all day, brushed aside another enemy obstacle at 6.15 p.m. and finally entered Brussels—the Welsh Guards in their tanks slightly in the lead.

'It's a long way to Tipperary,' sang the normally dour townspeople of Brussels, and 'God save the King'—stuffing the barrels of the tanks' guns with fruit, throwing

The Guards Armoured Division enters Brussels, 3rd September 1944

flowers and installing a girl in each turret to chant 'Vive les Anglais' over the radio.

For once the Welsh took no exception to being called English. Nor did the Company of Scots Guards attached to them. Nor did the Grenadiers, who had just entered the outskirts of Brussels, begrudge the youngest of the Guards Regiment the honour of liberating Belgium's capital. It was a happy occasion; and on its anniversary Brussels still dresses the Manneken Pis in the uniform of a Welsh Guardsman.

As to the rest of the war, the Guards Armoured Division strove valiantly to link up with the besieged and doomed paratroopers (many of them Guardsmen) of the 1st Airborne Division who had landed at Arnhem; helped repel von Runsted's final thrust in the Ardennes; and pushed constantly forward from the Rhine, supported by American infantry.

The first stage of this thrust into Hitler's Reich was a fifty-mile advance to Münster. Since it was the initial fifty miles, and Münster was the first German town of significance beyond the Rhine, resistance was stubborn. But Münster fell to tanks crewed by Scots Guardsmen and supported by American infantrymen only eight days after they had left the Rhine.

'The liaison with the Americans has been quite splendid,' acknowledged the Scots Guard's C.O.

'Come on, boys, let's go,' the American colonel had been constantly heard to exhort his troops.

'They are some of the finest fighters I have ever met and we got on like a house on fire,' said the Scots Guards colonel.

As the tanks crashed ever deeper into Germany, their constant inquiry was, 'Is Gerry up the road?' And usually the answer came, 'No idea. Why don't you ask the Household Cavalry to go and see?'

Constantly screening the way ahead, the Household Cavalry's armoured cars had already won high praise for such diverse successes as capturing three vital bridges called Faith, Hope and Charity, being the first to enter Holland, accepting the surrender of a German destroyer at Cuxhaven and having one of its officers arrested as Otto Skorzenny. By the end of the war it had become the acknowledged master of mobile operations in Europe. At Minden its regiments had failed to attack when they should have done; at Waterloo they had attacked with a minimum of tactical sense; during the Crimean war they had been kept at home; during the Boer war they had come into their own, only to be dismounted during the Great War; in World War II they found their true role.

As Hitler's Reich suffered its death-throes, the full force of His Majesty's House-hold Cavalry, in armoured cars and scout cars, was thus deployed on German soil, and the vast bulk of the Brigade of Guards, either in tanks or on foot, was close behind them.

★   ★   ★

The war of the Foot Guards who fought as infantrymen was very different from that of their brothers in tanks and their cousins in armoured cars. Just as Haigh had asked the impossible of them during the Great War, so were many of the worst and maddest tasks assigned to them between 1939 and 1945.

The 5th Battalion Scots Guards, for example, was formed as a Ski Battalion to support the Finns in their war against the Russians. Fortunately the Finns surrendered before the 5th Battalion could reach them; but unfortunately Norway was next on the list of Britain's doomed Allies, so the Scots Guards skiers were sent there—to fight, retreat and be evacuated.

Though the Guards Brigade embarked on many an unorthodox venture before hostilities ended, their wartime training at Pirbright remained as orthodox as ever. 'I often wondered,' a Guardsman wrote to R.S.M. Freddie Archer in 1943, 'what you meant by a hundred plus 10%. I found out at Medjez-el-Bas when I watched Left Flank go into action. You, sir, would have been as proud as I if you had been able to see what I saw. Most of the men that died I remembered from Pirbright. They died as you said they would, taking all before them. I remember one day when the [German] tanks broke through, a sergeant shouted, "Do what Freddie says—don't give an inch." Everybody stayed, though I must admit I didn't want to. I can't say even now what made me.'

Rommel declared of the Guards, 'They are almost a living embodiment of the virtues and faults of the British soldier. [They display] tremendous courage and tenacity combined with a rigid lack of mobility.'

Strangely he delivered himself of these words just after he had captured Tobruk: yet it was when Tobruk surrendered that the Guards were seen at their most unrigid and mobile best. Flagrantly disobeying their superior's order to capitulate, 15 officers and 183 men of the Coldstream Regiment seized some trucks, collected several hundred like-minded non-conformists, shot their way out of the German encirclement, careered through a minefield and reached the safety of the next defensive line.

Although the remainder of Tobruk's garrison was obliged to surrender, one of them, a Scots Guardsman, escaped by sea and another, an ex-Scots Guards officer, found his way to freedom on foot. In fact all through both the Desert and the Italian campaign an astonishing number of captured Guardsmen instantly liberated themselves, in spite of the fact that the moment of capture is so stupefying that apathy is the mood most likely to prevail for days. More than any other soldier during World War II, the Guardsman, though completely conditioned to obey, was the man who spontaneously overcame both stupefaction and apathy in an immediate bid for freedom. Probably he did so because his dignity was outraged.

An earlier refutation of any 'rigid lack of mobility' had come at the end of 1940 with the formation of a section of the Long Range Desert Group known as G Patrol. Composed of volunteers from the Scots and Coldstream Guards, G Patrol set out on its first foray, crossed the Western Desert, Libya and French Equatorial Africa, and then returned to Cairo—having travelled 4,300 miles in 45 days. Its last patrol in mid-1943 lasted thirty-seven days and covered 3,400 miles. And these and every other patrol involved raids on Rommel's supply-lines and airfields, and radioing back to Cairo details of all enemy movements.

The Guards in the Desert did not, however, rely on vehicles alone to achieve mobility. When one of G Patrol's ventures into French Equatorial Africa was ambushed, Guardsman Easton, who was wounded, had to be left behind. He then walked more than two hundred miles until he stumbled upon some French troops, in whose company he at last died of exposure.

No one would deny that Caterham created a strange breed of war-time soldier:

but he was not without his charm. At the height of the German shelling at Medinine in Tunisia in 1943, a platoon H.Q. that was dug-in beneath a tree was being showered with leaves. Commented a sergeant to his officer, 'Quite like autumn, sir.' By the time that whimsical autumn fall of leaves had ended, the Germans had lost 52 tanks (a third of Rommel's available strength) in what Montgomery later described as 'a model defensive engagement and a great triumph for the infantry and the anti-tank gun'.

Even in the face of almost intolerable provocation, the Guards maintained an appearance of impeccable courtesy. Admittedly those of the First Army considered those of the Eighth Army 'horribly above themselves', while those of the Eighth Army found those of the First Army 'a lot of rank amateurs', but each group was unfailingly civil to the other.

South of Medjez, in April 1943, two German divisions attacked positions held by the 5th Battalion Grenadiers and three companies of the Duke of Wellington's Regiment. A Company of Scots Guards was sent to reinforce them and, finding the Grenadiers in good heart, proceeded across open ground to help the Dukes.

6th Battalion Grenadier Guards evacuating casualties, Monte Cassino, May 1944

'It was magnificent to see them advancing steadily, and keeping their formation exactly, under heavy mortar and shell fire,' a Grenadier acknowledged.

'Thank you,' the Dukes greeted them, 'but we can manage very well by ourselves!'

And without a word of recrimination for either Dukes or Grenadiers, the Scots Guards returned to their wadi to report the loss of two men killed and four wounded.

After victory in arid North Africa came the winter invasion of Italy. 'It's nice,' a Guards officer then wrote home, 'to be in Europe again.' But he must soon have changed his mind.

Instead of heat, thirst and flies there were snow, mud and mountains. Wrapped in gas capes against night's icy chill, living in slit trenches and stone sangars, keeping awake on benzedrine and free of malaria on mepacrine, and fighting a slogging war, the Guardsmen in Europe found life no less uncivilised than it had been in Africa. But he lost neither his self-control nor his self-reliance. Asked how he had

Men of the H.L.I. advancing through Cleves, 11th February 1945, supported by tanks of 3rd Battalion Scots Guards

cured himself of diarrhoea, for example, a Guards colonel replied, 'By consuming an entire tin of treacle duff followed instantly by another tin of rice.'

After the triumph of the Western Desert and Libya, Italy proved a costly, frustrating theatre of war. Salerno was desperate and the landing at Anzio was worse—because an American general refused to allow anyone to budge from the beach-head for so long that, as Churchill complained, the invading force became less 'a wild cat' than 'a stranded whale'.

A battalion of Irish Guards was so nearly murdered at Anzio that it never recovered; but it retained its good humour and its swagger to the last. Its pride in General (later Field Marshal) Alexander—as one of its own whom it had worshipped ever since their 1923 sojourn in Constantinople, when he was their angry commanding officer—it never lost. But Anzio still means more and worse to the Irish Guards than to anyone else.

Those Guards Battalions who had been overseas for five years were shuttled home from Italy to take leave, train for the invasion of Normandy and see their chapel in Wellington Barracks destroyed by a flying bomb. The rest remained— to fight alongside Americans, Poles, New Zealanders, Canadians, Indians and South Africans. To this day (whatever politicians may say) Guardsmen speak highly of the support they received in Italy from the South African armour which enabled them, with their Allies, to inflict huge losses on Kesselring's Wehrmacht.

When the Italian war was won, the Guards celebrated by catching the Germans' abandoned horses and selling them to the locals. Who, being wary peasants, naturally demanded a deed of title from the vendors. Who, being arrogant Guardsmen, naturally provided documents that read, 'This wop paid me 2,000 lire for a horse. He's had it.' They signed these deeds of title 'Donald Duck' and 'Harry Lauder'.

And so to Normandy, from whose beach-heads Guardsmen fought their way inland in tanks and on foot. To the Welsh Guards—who had defended Arras so gallantly in 1940—fell the privilege of liberating Arras in 1944. So grateful were its townspeople, and so liberally were the Guards entertained, that reveille next day was sounded at an unprecedented 9 a.m.

From the Lowlands to the Rhine, and then from the Rhine to the Baltic, the Guards Brigade and the Guards Armoured Division fought their way to the final victory. Fought across battlefields familiar to Guardsmen since the days of William III and George II. And having defeated one enemy, settled down at once to the responsibilities of victory in Europe and the continuing war against Japan.

But even as a Guards Brigade was being formed for despatch to the Far East, Japan surrendered and six years of war ended. At a third of the cost in lives, the Guards had fought half as long again as they had in World War I—and had achieved a hundred times as much.

At Rotenburg Airfield, Field Marshal Montgomery said farewell to those who

General Alexander presents the ribbon of the Victoria
Cross to Major the Hon. William Philip Sydney of the
5th Battalion Grenadier Guards for his conspicuous
bravery at Anzio

had fought in tanks:

'We need you in the *infantry*,' he told them. 'We need your high standards,
your great efficiency in all matters, and your old traditions of duty and service.
All these are needed to help weld the infantry arm into a firm and solid basis on
which to build . . . The Guards have shown that whatever they are asked to do,
whatever they take on, they do well, maintaining always the highest standards,
and giving the lead to all others. You will long be remembered for your prowess
in armoured war.'

They would also, of course, be immediately required to resume their role of
defending the Sovereign and fighting the Sovereign's wars.

THE PEACE that came on 15 August 1945, and has allegedly endured since, has proved singularly unpeaceful for the Guards. At first they merely attended to such by-products of the war as occupying Berlin, preventing the outbreak of a new war in Trieste and supervising the enforced repatriation of Russian ex-prisoners of war; but all too soon they were in Palestine, endeavouring to keep Arabs and Jews from each others' throats—and from that day to this they have done little but career round the world interposing themselves between rival factions in one ex-British colony after another.

In the process, the seven Household Regiments of today have evolved into a Division that bears almost no resemblance to the Guards formations of 1945; and one of the first of these evolutionary developments came with the inevitable disbanding of war-time units that followed Germany's surrender.

Of these units perhaps the most colourful had been the 1st Airborne Division, formed in 1941, at Churchill's behest, by General Browning, an ex-Grenadier and commander of a Guards Independent Brigade Group.

In 1945 Browning's Airborne Division (which had naturally included many Guardsmen) was disbanded and its remnants transferred to Palestine to help keep the so-called peace. A year later these remnants—mostly Guardsmen—were re-designated a Parachute Battalion and as such spent two more years in Palestine, endlessly cordoning off one area or another and constantly searching, ambushing and raiding before returning to England.

There the marriage of Guards and Airborne techniques seemed as unlikely a union of spit and polish with the rough and ready as any of the innovations of the past (from the Camel Regiment to the Armoured Division); but, like all its predecessors, it worked.

Those Guardsmen who volunteered and were selected for training in the Parachute Battalion were first sent on a hardening course to Pirbright (where the instructors were notorious for their contemptuous rudeness) and then sent to Aldershot to learn the art of jumping out of aeroplanes (attached by a length of rope to all their kit) from as high as 800 and as low as 350 feet. At the latter height, they were told, there was no point their wearing a reserve parachute. Should their first parachute misbehave, they would be dead before any reserve could retard their fall.

Because his kit was attached to him by twenty feet of rope it hit the ground two seconds before the parachuting guardsman. Because he and his comrades jumped alternately out of each side of the night-flying aircraft, all left it within forty seconds and each (theoretically) landed fifty metres from the next. Once landed, their role was to march as far as twenty miles through the darkness to mark out a Dropping

Zone (and if necessary to hold it intact) for the main airborne group that would join them some hours, or even a day, later.

Thus trained—and seventy-five per cent of those on the course were weeded out—they became members of the 1st (Guards) Parachute Battalion and acquired an air of breezy super confidence that marked them out from their earth-bound Regimental brothers. Only they, for example, could have rid themselves of the obligatory Drill Sergeant by displaying so unanimous an aversion to square bashing that his appointment was discreetly cancelled.

A month after their inauguration parade they changed their designation (as the Guards are apt to do) to the 1st (Guards) Independent Company, the Parachute Regiment, and moved to Germany, where they practised their path-finding techniques and from time to time patrolled the East German border. They had become a fully fledged member of the Guards family of peace-keepers.

★   ★   ★

No sooner, it seemed, had the Army been allowed to quit Palestine in 1948 than the Russians were blockading Berlin. Inevitably, when the Allied Airlift broke that blockade, it was from the Household Division (in fact the Blues) that a detachment was chosen to lead the first convoy of supplies into the divided and isolated city.

And meantime, in 1948, in Malaya, highly organised groups of Chinese communists had been making so effective and murderous a bid to cripple the tin and rubber industries that three battalions of Guards had to be sent out to help contain them. That Guards presence was to be maintained for almost six years.

In 1951 the Guards Parachute Company went briefly to Cyprus and thence to the Egyptian Canal Zone, where it from time to time put on a show of force for the benefit of the Egyptian army, which was thought to be contemplating the annexation of the Canal.

Convinced that the Canal was for the moment safe, the Parachute Company took part in an exercise in Transjordan and then practised its path-finding role in the Sinai Desert.

By 1953 the Al Fatah movement had begun to launch minor but irritating attacks on British troops in the Canal Zone and the Parachute Company were assigned the proposed task of dropping onto Cairo Airfield and seizing the nearby Al Fatah camp in broad daylight. They prepared and practised for this operation for four months, and were within days of putting it into effect, when it was called off by the politicians.

The Emergency having ended in Malaya, trouble broke out in Cyprus, where a Greek Colonel called Grivas was organising and training a terrorist movement

In training, Aldershot 1872—forming a square, soon to be outmoded

dedicated to the principle of self (or Greek Cypriot)-government. As part of the Parachute Brigade, the Guards Parachute Company flew to Cyprus and spent four almost fruitless months scouring the Hilarion mountains for Grivas and his E.O.K.A. supporters; but then Nasser nationalised the Suez Canal and Grivas was forgotten as French and British troops poured into the island preparatory to an invasion of Egypt.

After much hesitation Britain and France committed themselves to war and the Guards Parachute Company jumped with the French 'paras' into Port Said. Their success was almost immediately absolute. But forty-eight hours later, bowing to international pressure, the Government ordered them back to Cyprus.

Cyprus (an island of 3,572 square miles) was inhabited by about 450,000 adherents of the Greek Orthodox Church and some 120,000 Turks. Greeks and Turks disliked each other intensely, their dislike having been in no way diminished by the E.O.K.A. preachings of Archbishop Makarios and the terrorist tactics of Colonel Grivas. The State of Emergency announced by Field Marshal Sir John Harding acknowledged the fact. The presence of a Commando of Royal Marines, a detachment of Life Guards and the whole of the Blues, did not change it. And the deportation to the Seychelles, in March 1956, of the Archbishop, seemed merely to

The beginnings of mechanisation: a Life Guards N.C.O. training with a Gatling gun early this century

exacerbate it, followed as it was by three years of murders, arrests, truces and more murders.

As a sop to Greek feelings, Makarios was allowed to leave the Seychelles and live in Athens. Alarmed, the Turkish minority began to riot. Massacres and the burning of villages were then inflicted by each ethnic group upon the other.

On one occasion, the Blues found themselves being viciously stoned by villagers determined to prevent them from arresting a terrorist. When one of the villagers attempted to brain the Troop leader with a rock, the officer concerned shot him dead. Unfortunately the bullet passed through his assailant and dislodged some stones from the wall of a house. These killed a local woman. Three days later the Cypriots took their revenge: a Blues Officer and a trooper were murdered.

The Blues mounted donkey patrols to hunt down mountain terrorists who previously had always fled at the sound of approaching armoured cars.

They also strapped two-inch mortars to the turrets of their Scout cars and fired parachute flares as they patrolled at night, thus abruptly terminating the E.O.K.A. habit of staging nocturnal ambushes.

And finally they arrested many wanted terrorists, among them Nicos Samson. Samson was tried and condemned to death, had his sentence commuted, was subsequently amnestied, and in July 1974 led the coup that briefly ousted Archbishop Makarios—who was, by that time, President of Cyprus. The Blues relate these facts without emotion. Though one of Samson's earliest victims was their unarmed Medical Officer, it is not their job to comment upon the futility of the tasks they are required to perform.

In July 1959, at the request of King Hussein, the Parachute Brigade was flown to Jordan to help suppress a revolution. In 1960 the Guards were shipped to Kenya to help stabilise a society still reeling from the effects of Mau Mau. In 1963 Makarios' Cypriot Government asked Britain to help prevent bloodshed between Greeks and Turks. Early in 1964 President Sukarno's Indonesian challenge to the newly independent states of Brunei and Sarawak had to be resisted. Late in 1964 the authority of the Sheik to whom Britain intended handing over Aden had to be upheld.

Fortunately for its peace of mind the Household Division does not ask itself why Britain's politicians require it to make such interventions. King Hussein subsequently evinced no particular gratitude for the help of the Parachute Brigade. A Mau Mau detainee called Jomo Kenyatta subsequently became his country's President. A troop of Life Guards, having been fired on by the Turks as it evacuated Greek children from their school in the hills above Kyrenia, was subsequently stoned by the same Greek children in Nicosia. Turkey subsequently invaded Cyprus. And so on, interminably, through the 1960s and into the Seventies—when two Scots Guards were killed by an I.R.A. bomb in a pub at Guildford, and five Welsh Guards were maimed by an I.R.A. bomb in a pub at Caterham, and Chinese communists blew up the memorial erected in Kuala Lumpur at the end of the Malayan Emergency, and the Guards Parachute Company was disbanded to save a million pounds or so for a government that had habitually overspent by billions.

Not once though, has the Household Division been heard to complain. Rather it has attended to all these tasks and, at the same time, fulfilled everyone of its Public Duties in London (including Winston Churchill's funeral), honoured Britain's obligation to N.A.T.O., provided two battalions a year for service in Ulster and despatched regular garrisons to Hong Kong and Belize.

'One of our worst problems in Germany,' confessed the Brigade Major of the Guards Armoured Brigade at Munster, 'has been that to provide two battalions a year for Ulster means removing them from their N.A.T.O. training here for at least seven months.

'Take the 1st Scots Guards. They were ordered to go to Ulster in April. That meant they all had to be given leave in *January*, then do their shooting practice and guerilla training till *March*, and then put their armoured vehicles into what we call "light preservation state" before they flew off to Belfast.

'Of course, their wives had to stay behind in Münster, which made them feel frightfully isolated, so a weekly T.V. video tape had to be made of the battalion in Ulster and sent back here.

'Their four months' tour of Ulster finished, the battalion went on leave till *September*, so that it was *October* before they resumed their duty here, and virtually nine months' training for a European war had been lost to put them in Ulster for four months of urban guerilla warfare.'

They train in Germany, of course, for service in the next European war. Their enemies, of course, will be the Warsaw Powers. And, although their equipment is stunningly sophisticated, and their ability to handle it unsurpassed, they are, of course, part of a force that is quite appallingly outnumbered and outgunned. Their annihilation, in the event of a war, would be so swift as to remind of eighteenth-century wars rather than the protracted campaigns of the twentieth century. But World War II was so long ago that even the most senior among them knew it only as boys. They, the most experienced fighting troops in the Western World, know nothing of mass slaughter and react to every mention of it with the flippancy of young men who cannot really believe in it—to which flippancy is added the political reticence of all professional British soldiers.

Should the next European war come to pass, however, there can be no doubt that they will resist spectacularly and die heroically. They were prepared for that by their training at Pirbright, where the likes of R.S.M. Freddie Archer have for generations convinced them that Guardsmen 'don't give an inch'.

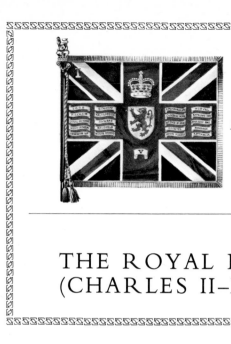

THE ROYAL RELATIONSHIP (CHARLES II–ELIZABETH II)

22   *The Royal Relationship with the Guards*

FOR ALMOST everything that the Guards have ever done, or been, there is a Royal explanation; and almost every Sovereign since 1660 has—by the nature of his or her relationship with the Guards—helped to make the Household Division what it is today.

Gold Stick and Silver Stick exist today because Charles II's life was allegedly threatened three hundred years ago; acorns are embroidered on Life Guards' tunics to this day because of the oak that once concealed a defeated king; finger bowls are absent from Scots Guards' messes to this day because Scottish officers who sympathised first with exiled James II and then with his son used to make symbolic use of them as they drank the Loyal Toast; and, oldest precedent of all perhaps, annual hunting leaves existed almost to this day because Henry VIII—detesting the paperwork of kingship—once went hunting for a whole five months instead.

The debt of today's Household Division to Charles II is as obvious as that of Charles II to General George Monck and his Regiment of Coldstreamers: yet Charles' brother, James II, failed to use these Foot and Horse Guards when William of Orange invaded England. Though as brave as he was stubborn, though he had led the Guards with incisive courage during the Great Fire of 1666, he proved so apathetic in 1688 that his son-in-law and his daughter easily deprived him of his throne. His apathy seems inexplicable until one recollects that, for three vital days, he suffered a continuous nose-bleed.

William III, on the other hand, suffered from asthma and an implacable hostility to Louis XIV. Because of the one, new palaces were built; because of the other, England's Household troops spent about twenty years fighting William's anti-Catholic wars.

Throughout those wars William found himself much better served by his English soldiers than by his English officers—whose practice of purchasing their commissions caused him concern because it encouraged the offer of a bribe in addition to the purchase price. This he sought to prevent by requiring each new officer to swear that in purchasing his commission, he had made, and would make, no 'present or gratuity'. A hundred years later the Duke of York was to find himself involved in a major scandal because this simple precaution of William's had been abandoned.

Largely to please Sarah Churchill, Queen Anne revived the office of Captain General, her choice for the post being that one-time Grenadier officer, and Sarah's husband, the Earl of Marlborough. Thus Marlborough gained the coveted command that William had always denied him, England gained some famous victories against the French, and Wellington inherited a master tactician's reconnaissance of the ridges of Mt. St. Jean which were to contribute to his victory at Waterloo.

As the last of the Stuarts, Anne had always had an affection for the Royal Regiment of Scots Guards raised by her grandfather, decimated in futile support of her uncle and reformed soon after the Restoration. She therefore ordered that, as the oldest of the Guards Regiments, it be listed as the First of her three Regiments of Foot Guards.

To which the existing First and Second Regiments took such violent exception that the Queen for once changed her mind and made the Scots her Third Regiment of Foot Guards instead.

Having dismissed Marlborough from all his offices, Anne established a new Royal precedent by creating her husband, Prince George, a Field Marshal so that he would outrank the ex-Captain General.

Her successor, George I, brought with him to England a German respect for order which found expression in his ruling that henceforth the rates for the purchase of commissions would be:

> Major £3,600
> Captain £2,400
> Lieutenant £900
> Ensign £450
> Adjutant £200
> Quarter Master . . . £150

The late Duke of Windsor, then Edward VIII, at the
Birthday Parade in 1936. He was still in mourning for his
father, George V

Orderliness became, in George II, a passion for the brilliance of the Prussian troops of King Frederic William—whose gigantic Guards were smartly uniformed, superbly drilled and often completely moronic. Unable to recruit giants (in whom Frederic William had cornered the market) George II nevertheless demanded tall men for his Foot Guards, put them all in colourful uniforms and added to their English drill—which he had standardised—the Hanoverian refinement of a slow march (for which they should be ever grateful because it could just as easily have been the goose step—which the Prussians were using as an early morning test of a soldier's sobriety).

Though George III left the conduct and leadership of the army to his son, the Duke of York, his reign bequeathed to posterity one of the world's most brilliant military ceremonies. Because all Guard mountings (for whichever of the palaces) had always taken place on Horse Guards Parade, and because the Sovereign's birthday had always been celebrated with a parade, the two were combined to mark one of the birthdays of George III. It was not a very big occasion, that first birthday Trooping of the Colour on Horse Guards Parade, but it did create a precedent—from which springs today's stunning performance by a complete Sovereign's Escort of Household Cavalry and divisions from the entire Brigade of Guards.

The appointment of the Duke of York as Commander in Chief affected the Army in general and the Guards in particular in such a variety of ways as only a Hanoverian could achieve.

The Life Guards, for example, owe their very existence to the fact that the Duke of York and the King between them decided to abolish the anomalous rank of Private Gentleman and to interpose between their new privates and the old Horse Guards officers a layer of non-commissioned officers whose unique distinction it was (and remains) to be called not Sergeant and Sergeant Major but Corporal of Horse and Corporal Major.

The Duke of York led England to no victories against the French and has been much derided because of it (in spite of the fact that only Marlborough ever had achieved and Wellington ever would achieve great victories for England over France), but His Royal Highness had done much to reform the Army with which Wellington was to alter the course of Europe's history, and he did display an interest in the conduct, fate and well-being of mere rankers that was unprecedented at the time and remained so for many years.

Nowadays the Household Division prides itself on its 'family' closeness and the manner in which its officers involve themselves in the welfare of their men. For them that involvement probably began in Flanders during World War I: the Duke of York displayed it in Flanders in 1793.

In which year Sergeant Major Darley of the Coldstream, though his arm had

The 1st Battalion Grenadier Guards during a rehearsal for
the Royal Funeral Guard of Honour, upon the death of
George VI in 1952

been shattered, continued to fight 'with the most animated and determined bravery'
for several hours, at the end of which, having just killed a French officer, his leg
was smashed by a cannon ball and he fell into enemy hands.

At once the Duke of York, as Commander in Chief of the Army and Colonel
of the Coldstream, sent a message to the French that no expense was to be spared
in treating Darley. Not satisfied with that, he also instructed his Adjutant General
to write to Darley's father-in-law, another Coldstream Sergeant Major, so that
the news of her husband's survival in captivity could be passed on to Mrs. Darley.

Naturally enough the Army's rank and file were fond of their compassionate
Commander in Chief. Its officers, on the other hand, were awed by his insistence
that they adhere absolutely to the prevailing code of honour. Yet that same honourable, compassionate soldier Prince had taken unto himself a young mistress, Mrs.
Mary Anne Clarke, and had permitted her to supplement his allowance to her by
trafficking in commissions and promotions.

Princess Elizabeth inspects the 1st Battalion Grenadier
Guards, Brighton 1944

Mrs. Clarke's system was simplicity itself. If a gentleman wanted a Major's commission, for which the going rate was £3,600, she would 'recommend' her Royal lover, the Commander in Chief, to give it to him—provided the would-be major gave her a 'pecuniary compliment' of, say, £2,000.

This arrangement suited his Royal Highness—whose payments of Mrs. Clarke's allowance were regally erratic—quite as well as it did his mistress, who thereby contrived to run a large London house in which she entertained most lavishly.

Mrs. Clarke regarded the Duke of York as a 'big baby', was never faithful to him and dealt in promotions to non-commissioned as well as commissioned ranks.

It was Colonel Wardle, a Radical M.P. (not to mention one of Mrs. Clarke's less patrician but more possessive lovers) who exploited the suspicions of some London journalists sufficiently to bring about a House of Commons enquiry into the Duke of York's management of the Army he commanded. To this enquiry, held in 1809, Mrs. Clarke was summoned as a star witness. She was questioned only about the exchange of two colonels' appointments procured by her in 1805.

Her contact with them had been her doctor, who was asked, 'Was it not under the consideration and conviction of her at that time being under the protection of the Commander in Chief that such application was made to her?'

'Of course,' the doctor replied. 'If Mrs. Clarke was not thought likely to expedite the thing, no application would have been made to her.'

Her bona fides, as it were, thus established, the Committee called for Mrs. Clarke; and must often, in the ensuing hours, have wished that it had not.

'What is your husband's name?' she was asked.

'Clarke.'

'What is his Christian name?'

'Joseph, I believe.'

'What *is* your husband?'

'He is nothing but a man.'

'What *business?*'

'No business.' Mrs. Clarke was an extremely composed witness.

'Did you ever live in Tavistock Place?' she was asked.

'Yes, I did.'

'When did you live there?'

Mrs. Clarke considered the matter briefly; then answered, 'I do not recollect.'

'How many years ago?'

'I do not recollect.'

'When did you go to Gloucester Place?'

'I do not recollect,' Mrs. Clarke declared; but added, apparently anxious to help, 'I was with the Duke in Park Lane before.'

'And when did you go to Park Lane?' asked her foolish interrogator.

'I do not recollect,' she told him.

Three further questions having provoked only three further failures to recollect, the Committee tried a different tack.

'Where did you live when first you knew the Duke?' Mrs. Clarke was asked.

'You will excuse me,' she responded primly, 'if I do not mention it.'

The Chairman told her she must mention it; but Mrs. Clarke had an answer to that.

'I do not,' she declared, 'recollect.'

'If you do not recollect,' she was challenged, 'why did you desire to be excused from answering the question?'

'*Because* I did not recollect,' explained Mrs. Clarke.

'*Do* you recollect,' she was then asked, 'that an application was made to you by Dr. Thynne to effect an exchange between Lt. Colonel Knight and Lt. Colonel Brooke?'

'Yes, I do.'

'Do you recollect that he urged great despatch?'

'Yes.'

'Did he hold out any expectation of a pecuniary compliment provided you

2nd Battalion Coldstream Guards during the final rehearsal
for Trooping the Colour, 1968

effected the exchange?'

'Certainly he did,' replied Mrs. Clarke.

A note for £200, it seemed, had been delivered to her, and £200 notes being rather more than petty cash in those days, she had despatched one of the Duke's servants to the bank to change it for her into notes of a smaller denomination. Mrs Clarke was asked the name of the messenger.

'I do not know I am sure,' she answered. 'It is a very unusual thing to ask servants their name!'

Rebuffed, the questioner again switched his line of attack. 'Did you afterwards speak to the Commander in Chief upon the subject?'

'Yes, I did,' replied Mrs Clarke, having clearly decided to abandon all discretion. 'Just after dinner. His Royal Highness asked me if I knew the parties and I said that I did not—but that they would make me a compliment.'

In fact, the exchange of appointments had been effected in a matter of days, she had been as promptly paid, and almost at once, prying into her papers, the Duke's rival, Colonel Wardle, had found out about it and taxed her with the suggestion that the Commander in Chief was allowing her to traffick in commissions and promotions.

'Had you any knowledge of Colonel Wardle before he attacked you upon (this matter)?' Mrs. Clarke was asked.

'Yes, I had.'

'What led to your knowledge of Colonel Wardle before that time?'

'Himself,' she primly replied.

'Are you speaking of a time before the attack he made upon you with respect to this transaction?'

'Yes, I knew him before ever he attacked me upon this subject.'

'How long?'

'I suppose six months.'

'Had you ever mentioned the transaction voluntarily to Colonel Wardle till he attacked you upon it?'

Shaking her head, Mrs. Clarke explained, 'He asked me if it was true and I told him yes. That was all I said. I did not think,' she explained, 'I should be brought here upon it, or I might have been very apt to deny it.'

Asked if she had given Colonel Wardle exactly the same account of the transaction as that which she had just given the committee, she replied, 'No, I did not.'

'Which is the true account?'

'Both.'

'In what way do the two accounts differ?'

'I do not see that they differ at all. I simply did not enter so much into detail then as I do now.'

'Was the difference between your two accounts that you were *shorter* in the account you gave Colonel Wardle than in the account you have given today?'

As always, Mrs. Clarke had the last word. 'Considerably,' she replied.

Though Mrs. Clarke's performance delighted London, there was no escaping the damage she had done the Duke of York, who resigned his various appointments and repudiated his mistress. Thus provoked, Mrs. Clarke threatened to publish his numerous letters to her—among which was many an indiscretion about the Royal Family. The Duke was therefore obliged to buy back his own letters and Mrs. Clarke was thereby enabled to retire to Paris, where she lived extravagantly ever after.

The following year the King went mad and the Prince of Wales became England's Regent and precipitated an era of sartorial splendour that inevitably affected the Guards. Lieutenant Colonel Kelly, of the First Regiment of Foot Guards, for example, had boots of unsurpassable brilliance of which he was so inordinately proud that when his house set on fire he died trying to rescue them.

Though never an innovator in civilian fashion, the Prince Regent made frequent alterations and additions to the uniform of his father's Household troops, some of which hitherto—for officers—had been little more than a rather severe modification of civilian dress. Most noticeable were the decorative helmets, jackboots and breeches he decreed; most elegant were the officers' leg-shaping trousers, strapped tight under the foot and tailored to fit the calf and knee; and most ludicrous were the officers' cocked hats, sometimes worn fore and aft, at other times sideways, but constantly increasing in size until they became sufficiently grotesque to satisfy even the most rapacious of today's publicity-hunting ladies at Royal Ascot.

In 1812, the Prince Regent replaced the Household Cavalry officer's sideways worn cocked hat, which constantly blew off, with a helmet: and in 1814, he decreed that the Second Regiment of Life Guards should wear a cuirass of black lacquered metal. But when he saw it, he decided that he did not like it; so the cuirass, for the moment, was abandoned.

In 1816, Waterloo won and the world at peace, the Blues returned to Windsor, to the delight of poor, mad George III whose conversation had become more eccentric than ever.

'Fine man, fine man,' he said when someone mentioned Major General Sir John Elley, a Blues officer who had joined the Regiment as a trooper in 1791 and, almost uniquely, achieved high rank. 'Fine soldier,' the King rambled on. 'No family, no family.'

Quite soon the same was virtually true of himself. His condition having deteriorated, even Queen Charlotte became frightened of him and tried to avoid him. Incarcerated on the Castle's North terrace, he degenerated into a blind and solitary old man with long white hair and a long white beard who tottered round in a dirty robe.

When he died, in 1820, the Prince Regent succeeded him and, as the so-called First Gentleman of Europe, held court not only in London but also at Windsor and Brighton, and was escorted everywhere either by the Life Guards or by the Blues.

To those attending him in Brighton, he issued the order 'During the period of His Majesty's residence, officers are required never to appear in Town otherwise than in Full Dress'; and those who were invited to join him in the Pavilion itself (where he was apt to sing to them in the Music Room) had to wear epaulettes as well.

The bearskins that he had made the official headwear first of the Grenadiers and then of all the Foot Guards grew bigger and bigger at his instigation; and metal cuirasses much more decorative than those last worn in the days of William III were, upon his instructions, slapped on to the chests and backs of his Household Cavalrymen, whose helmets had by now run the gamut of Roman to Grecian and back again to Roman, because the Grecian ones so often fell off.

The Irish Guards cheer the Princess Royal and Field
Marshal the Earl Alexander at their St. Patrick's Day
celebrations at Windsor in 1960

George IV, in fact, was at times not much saner than his late mad father, being given to relating, when drunk, how he had led the Household Cavalry at Waterloo, and constantly demanding that members of his family send back to him any details of Hanoverian and Prussian military dress that he might not already have pirated for use by the British Army.

At the same time he appointed himself Colonel in Chief of the three Regiments of Household Cavalry, demanded that all his Foot Guard rankers be between the heights of five foot ten inches and six foot one (so that their lines would look uniform) and insisted that wherever he moved—to open Parliament, attend a theatre, bathe at the seaside or visit another town—his Household Cavalry would escort him.

When his brother William succeeded him, Britain acquired her most inept

Hanoverian King who, trained as a sailor, once took advantage of his Admiral's rank to assume command of the Home Fleet off Weymouth and almost totally unnerved the Royal Navy. Fortunately for his Household troops, he was not much interested in things military and had none of his brother's mania for uniforms. Instead, he was content to become Colonel in Chief of the Household Cavalry; to present the Life Guards with the superb silver kettle drums they carry to this day; to acknowledge the ethnic origins of the Third Foot Guards by re-titling them the Scots Fusilier Guards; to present the Blues with an enormously heavy Guidon; and so to modify those various forms of headwear designed by his brother that they were always thereafter, because of their size, apt to blow off all trotting Cavalrymen and most stationary Guardsmen.

These harmless contributions to posterity effected, he died, leaving behind him no legitimate progeny, so that the throne passed to the late Duke of Kent's only legitimate child, Princess Victoria.

Alone of all the sovereigns since George IV, Victoria did not appoint herself Colonel in Chief of the Life Guards and Blues and never displayed much inclination to appear publicly before her Foot and Horse Guards.

Landseer sketched her inspecting the Life Guards in 1838, and when the occasion required it—such as the Birthday Parade at Horse Guards—she would ride side-saddle; but mainly she delegated such military tasks to male members of her family.

Which is not to say that she had no interest in her Brigade of Guards and Household Cavalry. On the contrary, she was pleased that the First Life Guards slow marched to a composition by her mother; she had, and expected, a Cavalry escort wherever she moved; and whenever she left Buckingham Palace there was only one route she would tolerate, which was the route out of the Park taken by every sovereign since the days of William and Mary—which was down the Mall, across Horse Guards Parade, under Horse Guards Arch and out into Whitehall. The newly created exits from St. James's Park into Trafalgar Square or up to Hyde Park Corner simply did not exist as far as Victoria was concerned.

When she travelled by rail from Paddington to Slough, the windows of the Royal train were always (whatever the weather) open, and her Blues were always waiting for her at Slough, ready to escort her carriage (after a short rest at the hotel opposite the station) to Windsor Castle. The train journey from Paddington to Slough took thirty minutes then and takes thirty minutes today. The Queen could have saved herself the carriage journey to the castle had she been prepared to allow the line to be extended from Slough to Windsor, through her park: but she was not, so the carriage journeys continued and her relationship with the Blues grew closer.

Close enough for her to visit Combermere Barracks in the early years of her widowhood, declare herself horrified by their airlessness and demand not only

Outside Buckingham Palace: after the Queen's Birthday Parade

that they be rebuilt—with higher ceilings and bigger windows—but that some married quarters, for the wives and children of privates and non-commisioned officers, be added as well.

Her relationship with her Guards was not so close, however, that after Albert's death she would ever again agree to appear at a Birthday Parade. This duty she delegated to her uncle, the Duke of Cambridge; most of her other public duties she simply allowed to lapse. Behind the scenes, though, she allowed almost no detail that concerned her Household troops to escape her.

Thus, in 1871, her Royal Warrant abolished the practice of buying commissions; in 1877 she granted to the Third Foot Guards, whom William IV had dubbed the Scots Fusilier Guards, the title they had always wanted—the Scots Guards; in 1887, having reluctantly celebrated her Jubilee in London, she retired the Blues' Guidon which (topped by a solid gilt finial of St. George and the Dragon) was so heavy that very few men of the Regiment could properly support it: in 1897 she approved the enlargement from two to three battalions of the Coldstream Regiment, noting that there were now nine Guards battalions, three of them stationed in Gibraltar and Malta: and in 1898 she agreed to present the new Third Battalion of the Coldstream and Scots Guards Regiment with their Colours.

Speaking from her carriage, the Old Queen proclaimed, 'It gives me great pleasure to present these colours to the young battalion of the Coldstream here (at Aldershot) where, forty-two years ago, I last addressed the Guards on their return from the Crimea. I feel certain that you will ever maintain the high reputation of the other battalions of the Guards who have always been so closely connected with the sovereign.'

Two addresses in forty-two years would not seem the surest way of winning the esteem of the Brigade of Guards: yet Victoria was esteemed to such a degree that she alone, of the sovereigns of the past, is real to the Guardsmen and Troopers of today.

Ask a Corporal of Horse today why he has that rank, rather than the rank of Sergeant, and he will probably repeat the myth that it was Victoria's doing—that Victoria (quite inaccurately) once declared, 'Sergeant means servant, and there will be no servants in my Household Cavalry.'

Ask a Guardsman today why there are apparently no Lance Corporals in any of the Regiments of Foot Guards and he will probably reply that it was Queen Victoria's doing—that Victoria once said, 'I dislike my sentries at Buckingham Palace being marched to their posts by anyone wearing only one stripe. In future, let them wear two.'

Ask most of the Household troops of today why detachments of Foot Guards had once to attend the Haymarket Theatre, there to prevent acts of indecency and rudeness, and almost certainly they will hazard a guess that it was upon the orders of Queen Victoria. They know it was she who commanded Guardsmen to perform at Covent Garden's Royal Opera House, because she disliked unmilitary-looking extras playing soldiers; and they know she was opposed to acts of indecency and rudeness; so they plump for her as the instigator of detachments in the Haymarket. Tell them it was George i's doing, not Victoria's, and they will at once lose interest.

Doubtless she maddened her advisers by so consistently refusing to make public appearances during her long widowhood, but she cannot be accused of making no impact upon her troops. Addressing the Blues Squadron that was about to serve in South Africa as a part of a composite Regiment, she said, 'I have asked you, who have always served near me, to come here that I may take leave of you before you start on your voyage to a distant part of my Empire.'

No wonder they remember her. 'I know that you will always do your duty to your sovereign and country, wherever that duty may lead you, and I pray God,' she concluded, 'to protect you and bring you safely home.'

Happily her prayer was heard and most of her Blues came safely back to Windsor; but by then the Queen was dead and it was to the service of a King that they returned.

At the very end of her reign, Victoria authorised the creation of a Regiment of Irish Guards, which makes her memory particularly significant to them; but she is no more real to them than to each of the other Regiments. Perhaps—like Garbo—she achieved immortality by becoming a recluse.

Certainly there was nothing of the recluse about her son, Edward vii. Yet—in spite of being militarily well-informed and influential—he is remembered not at all by the Household Division of today, even though it was he who declared that the rank of Private in the Household Cavalry should be changed to Trooper: even though it was his wife, Queen Alexandra, who, on the first St Patrick's Day after their creation, sent boxes of shamrock for distribution to every member of the Irish Guards; and even though it was he who, when defence cuts deprived the Scots Guard of their Third Battalion, first articulated the continuing relationship that exists between the Monarchy and the Guards.

Speaking of the Colours of that disbanded Battalion, he said, 'I shall always preserve them, religiously and carefully, at Buckingham Palace, and I hope it may be possible for me—or at any rate my successor—to see a Third Battalion of the Scots Guards carrying the same Colours again.'

In fact it became possible only too soon and too tragically: George v saw it when World War i broke out in 1914, and George vi saw it when World War ii seemed lost in 1940.

George v's time as Colonel in Chief of all the Regiments of Guards and Household Cavalry produced three changes. In 1913, watching manoeuvres, and observing that his Blues had no badge on their service caps, the king offered his own cypher.

His offer (as king's offers tend to be) was at once accepted and his cypher, encircled with the Blues' full Regimental title, became their first badge.

A year later the Blues marched from their camp to Victoria Station, to go to war. Queen Alexandra, the Queen Mother, said farewell to them from Regent's Park: Queen Mary took her leave of them in Hyde Park. For almost a quarter of a century the Blues had escorted both Queens constantly. Not many of those who marched that day survived to escort a queen again.

In 1915 the Brigade of Guards grew from four Regiments to five, the new Regiment being that of the Welsh Guards; and some three years later, on 11 November, 1918, George v declared, with his usual brevity, 'Soldiers of the Empire, with your Allied comrades, you have won the war,' and, in honour of their contribution to that victory, ordered that privates of all five Regiments of Foot Guards should thereafter be titled 'Guardsmen'.

Thus, by 1918, the evolution of all the components of today's Household Division —as London sees it—was virtually complete. It had begun with the creation of a Scots Regiment by Charles I and ended with the creation of a Welsh Regiment by George v. It had begun with Charles II's Private Gentlemen in the Horse Guards and Privates in the Foot Guards, and ended with Edward vII's Troopers and George v's Guardsmen. It had begun with a multiplicity of uniforms and ended with bearskins, red tunics, dark blue trousers and white belts for the Guardsmen; helmets, plumes, cuirasses, white breeches and black jackboots for the Trooper. It had begun at Henry vIII's Whitehall Palace, and ended at George IV's Buckingham Palace. It had begun in billets, and ended in barracks. It had begun with a variety of English drills devised to move men quickly into battle and ended with George II's standardised Anglo-Prussian drill specially choreographed for Royal and State occasions.

After the Great War the Life Guards' participation in these occasions was rendered somewhat the less convenient by virtue of the fact that their various Kings Guards and Sovereign's Escorts rode to Horse Guards and the Palace not from the barracks in Knightsbridge but from another barrack at Regent's Park. When motor traffic began to impede these constant tasks, the Household Cavalry asked King George v to move them back to Knightsbridge. It is typical of the relationship that exists between a Sovereign and his Household Troops that when the Life Guards did re-enter Knightsbridge Barracks in 1932 a telegram awaited them from their King and Colonel in Chief. 'I welcome my Life Guards back to their old home,' it said.

A Jubilee, a King's funeral and a Coronation stole the limelight from the Birthday Parades of the 1930's; but then came World War II, and for six years the Brigade of Guards and the Household Cavalry forsook their ceremonial skills.

Victory brought Britain not the spoils of war but so austere a peace that it was three years before a sufficient number of full-dress uniforms could be scraped together to enliven London with its first proper Birthday Parade in almost a decade.

Just as George V had taken advantage of his son's wedding to lighten the gloom that followed World War I, so did George VI relieve the austerity that followed World War II by ordering a spectacular wedding for his daughter, Princess Elizabeth. For the first time in England's history the Sovereign was known to be as good a husband and as beloved a father as he was a good and much loved king; and his quiet but special contribution to his people was that he bridged with such dignity the gap between pre-war and cold war Britain, between the Empire and the Commonwealth, the Monarchy and the Welfare State. If there has never been an effective Left Wing move to dismantle the élitist Household Division, much of the credit for it must go to George VI.

The rest must go to his daughter, Elizabeth II, whose professionalism in every aspect of the art of being the Head of a modern State will not quickly be surpassed.

Not the least important aspect of her role as Queen is her work as the Household Division's Colonel in Chief. In this she has received massive support from her mother, her husband, two of her uncles, one of her cousins and her oldest son. Queen Elizabeth the Queen Mother has created an extraordinary bond between herself and the Irish Guards, the Duke of Edinburgh was Colonel of the Welsh Guards for a record of twenty-two years and is now Colonel of the Grenadiers, the late Duke of Gloucester was Colonel of the Scots Guards, Earl Mountbatten is Colonel of the Life Guards, the Duke of Kent succeeded the late Duke of Gloucester as Colonel of the Scots Guards and the Prince of Wales took over from his father as Colonel of the Welsh Guards.

Indeed, since George VI's time, the relationship between Royals and Regiments has been more than merely nominal. In 1942, the twenty-second colonel of the Scots Guards died, having held the post for twenty-one years. He was H.R.H. the Duke of Connaught—or Queen Victoria's son, and the Duke of Wellington's godson, Arthur.

'The Duke of Wellington,' tiny Prince Arthur had prattled at the great man's funeral. 'Little Arta's godpapa.' Nine months after Little Arta died, Hitler was to receive the first intimations of *his* Waterloo at Alamein.

And eleven years after Alamein, Queen Mary, as was her wont, was browsing round Christies when she remarked a walking cane upon which were carvings of two Life Guards Colonels, the Lords Combermere and Anglesey. Purchasing the cane, she presented it to the Regiment.

And thirty years after Alamein the Princess who had been the Grenadier's Colonel was crowned Queen and became their Colonel in Chief.

And almost every year for many years, on St Patrick's Day, Queen Elizabeth, the Queen Mother, has personally presented the Irish Guards with the shamrock that first was presented to them, in 1901, by Queen Alexandra.

And whenever the Royal Family is in residence at Windsor Castle its male

members discard the conventional dinner jacket for a blue one with scarlet cuffs and
lapels, because that is the jacket of the Blues, as worn by George III, who was
devoted to them, which—even if he was deranged—is not to be forgotten.

And when it comes to Birthday Parades, no one in the Household Division is
more familiar with the intricacies of its traditions and mechanics than Elizabeth II.
Her eye for the details of a uniform is as sharp as George IV's, her knowledge of the
drills involved as demanding as George II's, her horsemanship vastly superior to
that of either Queen Anne or Queen Victoria, and her insistence upon proper
spacing, as she rides down the Mall with her Sovereign's Escort, notorious.

The Armoured Squadrons of the Household Cavalry drive
past the Queen, who has just presented the Household
Cavalry with new standards

'The Queen is known to be punctilious about spacing,' the Knightsbridge Barrack adjutant will warn her escort. 'She doesn't like to be hemmed in. And she knows every move to the second.'

Since she is equally punctilious when riding in her State Carriage, Escort commanders must be careful not to let their horses stray even slightly forward of the rear wheel—as one learned to his cost when, having offended for the third time, Her Majesty, nodding towards the cheering crowd, whose view of her he obstructed, remarked, 'Actually, Captain, I *think* they've come to see *me*.'

Such is the quality, for the Household Division, of the special relationship it has always had with its sovereign. It is evidenced by an awareness of Royal characteristics such as only generations of Sovereign's Guards and Escorts could have attained —from James II's nose-bleed to William III's asthma: from George III's dislike of Nottingham to Victoria's affection for Mountain Dew: from Anne's pleasure in food to Elizabeth II's passion for fresh air, which, her Guards will tell you, she inherits from her great-great-grandmother, Victoria. Elizabeth, they will tell you, ignoring icy blasts and all objections, flings open the window of her bedroom at Windsor Castle—and plays havoc with the air-conditioning.

Though the role of both the Sovereign and the Household Division has radically changed since Charles II's reign, it still takes more than the highest standards of professionalism alone to make of a soldier a fully qualified Guardsman—as one Military Secretary discovered when he decided to promote to Lieutenant Colonel a Guards officer who had distinguished himself in both Staff and Imperial College exams.

'But you can't *possibly*,' a furious Regimental Colonel told him.

'Why not?' demanded the Military Secretary.

'Because,' said the Regimental Colonel, 'he has never done a Palace Guard.'

The Regimental Badges of the
Life Guards (left) and the
Blues and Royals (right)

THE GUARDS TODAY

23   *Twentieth-Century Guardsmen*

IT WAS THE Boer War that transformed the Guards and Household Cavalry from soldiers whose uniform and drill were virtually the same for a battle as they were for a State occasion into khaki-clad exponents of modern war on the one hand and the colourfully-clad cast of London's longest running outdoor entertainment on the other.

These divergent roles—dichotomous and dichromatic—have in common only the discipline on which both are based; and few of those who peer round the bearskins of scarlet tunicked Guardsmen, to watch the Household Cavalry escorting the Sovereign down the Mall to her Birthday Parade, appreciate that, only a fortnight earlier, the Guardsmen of one battalion may have been on active service in Ulster, and that a week later the Guardsmen of another may be protecting the citizens of Belize from the dreaded covetousness of the Guatemalese.

At the beginning of the twentieth century the Guardsman's career—though committed to its present course—had not yet become so sophisticated. In 1905, for example, recruits were offered five shillings and two pence a week on enlistment and twelve shillings and fourpence a week after five years service; no Guards Regiments served East of Suez; and all were tyrannised by their N.C.O.s in the good name of discipline.

World War I, with its hideous casualties and its filthy conditions, saw the emergence of the contemporary Guardsman—erect, short haired, rigidly disciplined and no less than ever imbued with the philosophy of the thin red line.

Neither Foot nor Horse Guards won any great victories between 1914 and 1918 because there were no such victories to be won; but the Great War enhanced their reputation because they were mainly committed in major battles, suffered stoically and even more appallingly than most other regiments because of it, and never failed the officers who led them—even if it was impossible to satisfy the generals who commanded them.

1915 saw the birth of the Welsh Guards and 1918 saw all privates in the Guards honoured (by Royal command) with the new rank of Guardsmen. The hopelessness and drabness of unemployment in the 1920s lured young men into the colourful, well-fed ranks of the various Guards regiments where they attained unprecedented pinnacles of discipline, smartness and drill.

For that, it is alleged by some, they owed little to their officers, the odd one of whom may occasionally have rolled up in a hansom cab and ordered everyone onto parade in full kit so that he could practise his drill on them, but the majority of whom stayed away as much as possible—mindful, barrack room historians insist, of the fact that snap drills in full kit were so detested that a battalion of Grenadiers, of all regiments, once refused to oblige the officer concerned, with the result that their ring-leaders were imprisoned for two years while the rest of the battalion was packed off to Bermuda.

Left in the hands of N.C.O.s, however, the Brigade of Guards and the Household Cavalry of the twenties more than maintained their impeccable London standards. On duty, they were miracles of precision; off duty, wearing their special walking out caps, they strutted the 'Monkey Parade' that ran from Hyde Park Gate to Marble Arch and flaunted their vivid red tunics at anyone willing to supplement their meagre pay of four shillings a day.

'You were so much in the public eye,' a veteran recalls, 'and you were never out of uniform. You walked out from the barracks only when you'd passed inspection. And the moment you got out, the girls and the men were waiting for you.'

More commonly, when they left their barracks, it was to mount guard at Buckingham Palace, or St. James's Palace, or Kensington Palace, or the Tower. Of them all, the posts outside the front railings of Buckingham Palace were the most taxing.

'You had to keep your wits about you all the time. You were so close to Wellington Barracks there was bound to be an officer or an N.C.O. in civvies somewhere among the crowd. And if you were the least bit idle, they'd report you—and then you were on a charge. For turning your head, or talking, or shifting about, or not paying attention to your mate's signals to come to the slope or turn to the front and halt. You see, there were two of you on duty in front of the Palace and everything you did had to be perfectly synchronised. So we had all these signals. A tap

Scots Guards on captured
enemy motorcycles, Western
Desert 1941

of the rifle butt on the paving stone and you both sloped arms, turned about and
marched off. Two taps, you both gave a butt salute. Three, you presented arms.

'Then there were finger signals, for when you were on the march. One finger,
turn to the front and halt. Two fingers, turn to the front and salute. Three fingers,
turn to the front and present arms. People would watch us for hours and never
twig how we managed to synchronise all our moves without a word being spoken.
But an N.C.O. or an officer in civvies watching you, *he'd* find something wrong—
and report you. For me, a day in the Guards was perfect if I finished it without
being reported.'

For those who became Guardsmen and Troopers in the Thirties, life was no
different from that of the man who had joined in the Twenties—though war was
soon to change everything for all of them.

'Of those who joined with me,' one of them relates, 'about twenty per cent
were killed in the war; and of the rest, some became N.C.O.s within the Regiment,
some took commissions and moved to other regiments, some left the Regiment
to become policemen, and practically none was equipped to cope with London
in the Forties and Fifties.'

As late as the 1950s there remained extraordinary relics of the feudal past. All
Other Ranks had to sign the Bath Book, thereby assuring their uneasy superiors

that that week they had taken a bath. Though no one objected to them being picked up outside the barrack gates by prostitutes and homosexuals, junior Guardsmen were forbidden to smoke until they were sixteen. And let any man get into trouble and his N.C.O.s would find him guilty of one offence after the other so that he remained in trouble for weeks on end. In other words, the old tyranny prevailed.

But not for much longer. Just as the social reforms of the mid-nineteenth century eventually prompted better conditions for servicemen, so the social revolution of the mid-twentieth century was to create a new breed of guardsmen by the Seventies. Today's guardsman, like his officer and N.C.O.s, is a professional; but so was yesterday's. Today's guardsman differs from yesterday's because he no longer fears his superiors.

He is tall and fit, because his medical examination was stringent and his initial training severe. During that training he will have done eleven weeks drill, three weeks war training and a final spell of foot drill (if destined for a Guards Regiment) or tank drill (if destined for the Household Cavalry). He joins the Household Division for a variety of motives, of which patriotism is not, at the moment, one. He joins because he has been persuaded that he will be doing 'a man's job'; or because he has been promised that he will travel; or because he wants to experience danger; or because he can find no other employment; or even because he is offered marvellous facilities for adventure and sport.

Gone are the days when soldiers simply boxed, played football and cricket and indulged in occasional outbursts of incompetent athletics. Today, in addition, they can indulge in softball, squash, badminton, fishing, archery, swimming, rock-climbing, yachting, free-fall parachuting, trans-ocean yachting and more besides.

Today's Guardsman seldom marches anywhere, except in London, and even then he only marches furlongs where his precedessor covered miles. For the rest of the time, he trains and functions as the most mobile of infantrymen, being consistently transported to his zone of operations in lorries, armoured carriers, helicopters and aeroplanes.

Today's Guardsman or Trooper enlists either as a junior or, if he is over seventeen and a half, as an adult soldier. The Guardsman will be so intensively trained as a recruit that, within six months, he will be capable of appearing on ceremonial parades for which his predecessors trained for eighteen months. The Junior Trooper will train for sixteen months, and an adult for eight months.

Today's Guardsman no longer goes on sentry duty outside the railings of Buckingham Palace because tourists with cameras finally drove him off that traditional beat and into the Palace forecourt, a particularly persistent American lady even claiming that one of the sentries had kicked her. No one believed her, of course, because kicking Guardsmen are even rarer at Buckingham Palace than cigar

Ready to Jump: Parachute Company

smoking capitalists in the Kremlin, but the time had clearly come when Her Majesty's unmounted sentries needed protection from demanding, thoughtless, or importunate civilians of whatever nationality.

And finally today's Guardsman or Trooper is neither an intellectual nor a moron. Ask him what a man needs to be, to make good in a Household Regiment, and he will answer, 'Thick!' By which he means that it is no job for the sensitive, the imaginative or the fastidious.

His average age is twenty-one. He will probably serve for nine years—though it could be for twenty-two. His wife, far from being the cowed creature of the past, has opinions of her own and lives in adequate married quarters. Her husband is likely to be affected by *her* reaction to Army life and, if she is displeased, he will usually require one of his officers to mollify her.

If he is unmarried, he lives, on the whole, in well-appointed barracks which he keeps reasonably clean, unless he is a trooper at Knightsbridge, in which case the room he shares with two or three others will be decidedly and inexplicably scruffy.

On duty as a sentry at Buckingham Palace, he will occasionally see members of the Royal family walking in the garden. He will present arms: they will nod and murmur good afternoon. He will not have been aware of the Guardsman's relationship with them when he enlisted; but he will soon become so, and will take a perverse pride in retailing anecdotes which prove the Queen to be as eagle-eyed as any R.S.M. when it comes to noticing faults of dress or drill.

Of all the royal residences he guards he will prefer Windsor, even though old hands insist that the ghost of George III—white haired and bearded, and wearing a long robe—occasionally prowls the North Terrace. He himself will swear that—looking down from the East Terrace— you can see thirteen statues in the gardens. In fact, there are only twelve: the thirteenth, of course, is George III.

Indeed, for so phlegmatic a race, Guardsmen are very susceptible to ghosts. At the Tower of London they are frequently conscious of the presence of Anne Boleyn; at St. Margaret's Chapel in Edinburgh a Scots Guardsman was notoriously so perturbed by a supernatural presence that he was actually taken off duty; and at Münster—where some of the barracks are the original huts of a Displaced Persons' Camp—two eighteen year-old Guardsmen recently reported the presence of a ghost in Block 49.

Whether it be ghosts or domestic problems that worry them, their N.C.O.s will advice them, the N.C.O. of today being a blander, more subtle man than the disciplinarian of a mere twenty years ago.

In 1952, in Germany, a Household Cavalry N.C.O.'s Mess debated whether or not to buy a candelabra. 'It's all very well *buying* it' a Regimental Corporal Major finally declared, 'but who's going to *play* the bastard?'

The Queen's Birthday only a fortnight away, the daily
Drill Parades are characterised by bearskins worn with
battledress to accustom everyone to their tiring weight.
Officers' horses are seen in the background

That sort of N.C.O.—one of whose gimmicks it was consistently to murder
the Queen's English—is vanishing. Today's N.C.O. in the Household Division
must know as much about man-management as about Queen's Regulations, and
is more likely to get results by somewhat mawkishly extolling the virtues of solidarity
('One man's failure can threaten the safety/reputation/performance of *all* his
mates') than by any threat of disciplinary reprisals. What distinguishes him from
those he commands is not now an air of comic frightfulness but the demeanour of
a conscientious junior executive combined with the patient skill of a born teacher.
'Put the weapon on your knees,' instructs a typical Scots Sergeant. 'Don't fiddle
about with it, just put it on your knees. O.K.? Right! . . .' and a superbly confident, natural discourse begins.

Though Guardsmen and Troopers dress like civilians of their own age when
they walk out, they remain a separate breed. Not only are their haircuts shorter
and their backs straighter than those of their civilian contemporaries, they are
(like off-duty policemen) indefinably different in their bearing and almost alien
in their attitudes. They accept authority. They expect orders—even though
training and danger have taught them initiative. They seldom get into trouble,

but when they do, the trouble is bad. And when in trouble they invent infantile defences which they refuse to change by so much as a syllable.

They are members of an élite, of which they are more overtly conscious than most of their officers, and they are snobs. To have an Honourable as their Platoon Commander pleases them: to have a peer delights them; to have a peer of the rank of viscount or above positively enchants them. They may, of course, loathe him as a man; but they will still be delighted to have him as their officer.

During his years in the Regiment, the Guardsman's officers will use him and care for him as efficiently as *he* will use and care for his weapons. They will not cherish him, or like him, or even know him as an individual, because that is not how the system upon which the regiment is based works; but they will no longer abuse the respect he is obliged to afford them and he will seldom find himself under the command of an officer who is less than competent at their common profession of soldiering.

He himself will be self-reliant and literate enough to comprehend a variety of manuals relating to the weaponry of hot and cold wars. He will be phlegmatic

Coldstream Guards getting ready for the Birthday Parade

enough not to ask upon occasions, 'What the bloody hell am I doing standing here guarding the Queen when I know bloody well she's touring Australia?' He will be proud enough to groom his bearskin into a fringe and to pester the Regimental tailor until his tunic fits and flatters him to perfection. He will be fastidious enough, whenever he returns to barracks, to remove his tunic, dust it, ask the tailor for some cleaning fluid, remove any stains, and hang it up. He will be independent enough to know his rights but practical enough to obey orders rather than be fined.

When he leaves the regiment, and looks for a job in civilian life, he will be as adaptable as he is pliable, and will be unfashionably ready to do what he is told. He will make a good policeman and a bad trade unionist. And after about five years he will become a nostalgic ex-Guardsman, so that his son, when he reaches the age of sixteen, will probably follow him into the Household Division. Un-reasonably, it has been happening for generations: there seems to be no reason now to believe that it will ever stop.

The Regimental Badges of the Grenadier Guards (left), the Coldstream Guards (centre) and the Scots Guards (right)

THE GUARDS AND TUMULTS OVERSEAS

24 *Malaya*

IN 1948 CHINESE Communists began murdering Malaya's rubber planters and tin miners and slashing its rubber trees so that they bled to death. Britain, in the grip of post-war austerity and near bankruptcy, could afford the loss neither of such skilled men nor of the millions of dollars the rubber and tin industries earned her. Furthermore she was not—then—in the habit of tolerating colonial disturbances. Accordingly the Labour Government decided to send out the Guards to stop the rot.

Three Guards battalions arrived in the last quarter of 1948—the Scots, the Coldstream and the Grenadiers—and it was the 2nd Battalion Scots Guards (under-trained after two and a half years of London duties, its numbers made up with recent recruits and National Servicemen) that stayed the longest.

On arrival, half the junior commanders were sent to a jungle warfare training centre in Johore Bahru: the rest of the battalion—after a brief pause at Nee Soon Camp in Singapore—went up to the peninsular, some as far as the Slim River.

Neither destination was auspicious. Nee Soon was first used in 1941 by Australian troops destined for captivity, and it was at the Slim River that the Japanese chopped to ribbons the first British line of defence and began their rampage through Malaya, Singapore, the Dutch East Indies, Timor and New Guinea.

Now, too stunned by humidity to care about such seven year-old precedents, those who found themselves on the frontier of Thailand started searching the jungle for another, more elusive enemy—and found nothing of him except a hammer and sickle motif carved on a tree, which they ignored, and an abandoned camp, to which they set fire.

They shot an elephant and captured its calf, shot a wild pig and tried to bleed it, learnt that Malaya's roads are narrow and dangerous, and adapted slowly to the climate. Their Minister of Defence in far away Whitehall was meanwhile letting it be known that he considered Guardsmen too tall for the jungle, and local arm-chair tacticians were grumbling about the folly of big white men crashing round the ulu in pursuit of little yellow men and making absolute idiots of themselves in the process.

In fact, from the beginning, the Guards neither crashed nor made idiots of themselves. They did, at first, frequently mistake the sound of a pig rooting in the darkness for a bandit creeping up on them through the lalang; they did, at first, occasionally mistake distant glow-worms for Chinese miners' lamps or Tamil tappers' torches; and they did, for a long time, have to suffer many official lunacies.

Living for weeks at a time in the jungle, fighting a murderously determined enemy, they were still on what was called 'peace time accounting', which meant that if they used a field dressing on a wound they had to pay for it; that if they wanted a brew-up they had to buy their own tea; and that when, as swiftly happened, their clothes rotted, they had to purchase replacements.

Nor were they the most handsomely accommodated of troops. Disused factories, abandoned schools and parts of police stations were the best they could hope for: the worst was tents, which were intolerably hot and inclined first to rot and then to disintegrate.

Consistent to the last, a devoted Government made sure that they were properly sustained on their long slogs through some of the hottest jungle in the world by issuing them with cold climate rations, which were almost inedible.

In spite of which—and the swamps, leeches, snakes, poisonous leaves and hornets —they began to stop the murders, even if they did not often kill the murderers. Those of their junior leaders who had finished their jungle warfare training returned to them; and the remaining junior leaders went to Johore Bahru in their turn; and at the end of the year the battalion had been transformed into a number of packs of lean, tanned, patient bandit hunters, among whom the conscript Guardsman surprisingly proved himself no less efficient than the regular.

Most operations were carried out by a platoon of twenty-six men and their one officer, who lived and co-operated with a British policeman and such of his Malayan or Indian subordinates as might be available.

Officially the Army was in Malaya only to assist the Civil Power, so it was the white policeman—often little more than a boy—who had the final word in every sortie led by the platoon commander. Since it was also he, however, who had the local knowledge and spoke the language, and since he and the platoon commander —who was not much more than a boy himself—shared a room, their whisky, their cigarettes and occasionally even their shaving kit, the system worked very well.

But the comradely policeman and platoon commander represented only the bottom of the hierarchy: at the top was a chaos of competing Whitehall, Malayan and Military departments all of which may have had in mind the same objective, but none of which, unfortunately, was of the same mind.

Thus, the platoon commander might protest, 'You *know* those bashas shouldn't be there. The baddies *must* have been living in them. We really *should* burn them down.'

But his policeman would be obliged to demur. 'We can't. The Law doesn't allow it.'

And the Law being greater than both of them, that would be that. The conflicting requirements of Minister and Minister, of Ministers and Senior Policemen, and of Senior Policemen and Senior Army Officers (all of them a law unto themselves) confused everyone—especially the platoon commander and his policeman.

At last, though, the Minister of Defence announced that he would come out to Malaya from Whitehall to see for himself, his arrival being awaited by the Guards with a certain lack of rapture. They remembered that he had implied that they were big and clumsy and that, before being put in charge of Defence, he had been responsible for a quite catastrophic attempt to grow ground nuts in Africa. Also they had been inordinately amused by a Fleet Street cartoon depicting him on patrol with them in the jungle and their sergeant hissing at them, 'Quit telling Mr. Strachey to mind his *nut*. Mr. Strachey's very touchy about nuts.'

In fact, as those who accompanied him on that patrol were the first to confess, they had to admire his guts; and when he returned to England, he was obliged to admit that his doubts about them had been unjustified.

They knew what they were doing and were doing it as well as—albeit differently from—the renowned Ghurkas. Their Bren guns, of which there were four to a platoon, could cut swathes through the jungle; their rifles may have been longer than ideal but then so were they; their Sten guns, when properly looked after, were efficient; their three inch mortars, used from the jungle's edge and exploding noisily if fairly harmlessly in the treetops, were splendid for flushing out or diverting the bandit; and they rendered their inadequate radios adequate either by climbing trees and draping long aerials of copper wire from branch to branch or, if reception remained too bad for voice, by using good, old-fashioned morse.

Only their dogs proved lacking. Savage they certainly were, and well trained; but in the jungle, unlike the Guardsmen, they were so inclined to become discouraged that eventually they were replaced by stocky, tattooed, Iban trackers from Borneo, who were just as savage and marvellously tenacious as well.

Month succeeded month and the slog went on. Sometimes patrols would spend thirty-six hours in a swamp, blood-streaked from leeches; at others it would be hacking clear a Dropping Zone in the jungle so that it could be resupplied by air. Sometimes they would blast all the foliage off a dozen tree tops to drive any bandits below back into an ambush; at others they would play marbles with native children on the hard earth in front of their jungle huts.

They became expert at making themselves bashas for cover and comfort each night in the jungle; they swam; they ate coconuts, papaya and pineapple; they reconoitred the dangerous roads between towns and villages; they experimented with flame-throwers; they killed and were killed.

That their enemy was determined as well as tough they had learned way back in December 1948, when one of their subalterns, nicknamed the Iron Duke, and two scouts were leading a patrol along a jungle track. This track had last been trod by British boots when Spencer Chapman used it in World War II; and suddenly subaltern and scouts found themselves almost face to face with two Chinese who opened fire on them with pistols and fled.

As the patrol behind him dropped to its knees, and the scouts flung themselves to either side of the track, the Iron Duke set off in pursuit, blazing away with his Sten.

One bandit escaped, but the second was hit and fell into a ditch. As his pursuer drew level, he raised his arm and threw.

'Grenade!' shouted the Iron Duke—flinging himself into the ditch, on top of the bandit.

As the grenade exploded, the wounded bandit, a powerfully built young man, fought bitterly: so the subaltern shot him. His name was Pan Poh, he was a courier, and in his pocket was a package of letters from the woman who was his leader to various gangs in the north.

Translated, those letters reveal something of the temperament and training of the Chinese communist in Malaya.

> *Dear Comrade Kin,*
>
>   *Foh Kwai and Brother Ho have left for your place. Foh Kwai appears a quiet chap, reluctant to talk much. He thinks more of his family than his work. He cannot work well, though he is obedient. Unless he receives more instruction and training he will find it hard to fight independently.*
>
>   *Swee Peng.*

Not the most sentimental of ladies, Miss Swee Peng; but for a communist she had her priorities right. Work always came before family, even where 'work'

A leave party from a jungle location in Malaya depart by boat

was a euphemism for ambushing men in the jungle or convoys on the roads, murdering isolated European civilians and terrorising native villagers into feeding and financing bandit gangs.

Nor was she given to hyperbole or immodesty; though clearly an idealist, she was quite prepared to pay the price of her ideals. To another gang leader she wrote:

Dear Comrade Chew Tang,

During these few days I have been in a bad situation. The enemy has searched this area for four days and it is said they will not leave it for a week. This hinders my work.

Comrade, it would be better if someone could assist me here. I am a female comrade and tackle the job alone. I can only read books to pass my leisure hours. When I feel sad I sing songs. Copy some new songs for me, please . . .

Swee Peng.

To another leader she revealed the successes the Army had scored in seducing away from her cause the disgruntled and the homesick; but at the same time—a year before Mao Tse Tung actually came to power in China— she never wavered in her belief that the lonely battle she fought would be won.

Dear Brother Kim

> *. . . my not writing to you is due to problems of transport.* [A problem the Iron Duke had not improved by shooting dead Pan Poh.] *When I heard of the enemy's round-up, and of the activities of the traitors, I was anxious about our comrades' safety.*
>
> *I am grateful to you for the help you rendered me during the fighting and I am sorry I showed you my temper so often.*
>
> *I am surprised to learn that comrades of ours have become traitors. I am sure such wicked people will not die peacefully. Their surrender to the enemy pollutes our revolutionary work and brings us shame . . .*
>
> *I assert that the proletarian party can never be suppressed. Rather, it will expand. The work of the communists in China is our example, don't you agree? We do our best. Victory will be ours.*
>
> *I read in the papers that victory in China will soon come to pass. Madam Chiang has gone to America; Foo Chok has suggested that Chiang Kai Shek should leave China so that peace talks with the Red Army can begin. All these things imply a surrender. We must prepare to celebrate the inevitable victory.*
>
> *Swee Peng.*

Until victory came, however, there were the day-to-day details of local movements and tactics to relate.

Dear Comrade Lin Hou,

> *. . . Recently the enemy attacked Ah Sow's area for four days . . . Poon San's house was burnt down. Now Ah Sow, Poon San and Yap Lin are somewhere in my area. Ah Sow wrote me that he has moved to another place and all his comrades are safe . . . although Yap Choy's wife was arrested.*
>
> *The enemy used new tactics in this attack . . . making it stealthily, searching Ngu Cheng Poh then suddenly charging from the rear without first warning the masses. In future we must be specially careful of this.*
>
> *It seems that work is difficult at the moment. Ah Sow is prepared to co-operate with Poon San to build a new camp. A man called Hew has agreed to contribute three hundred dollars and make a monthly contribution of sixty dollars. As this is all he can afford, I decided to accept it . . .*
>
> *As regards the regulations relating to discipline, reward and punishment, I will study these with Mr. Ngan . . .*

Herewith one box of hand grenades and eight pairs of socks. Please acknowledge.
                                    Swee Peng.

'The masses', as Swee Peng called them, were there to be exploited. Anything they learned from the police or the army they were expected to repeat to her agents. Any profits they made from their small businesses they were expected to contribute to the cause. Even so, the cause was hardly prospering.

Dear Comrade Peng Sang,
                           It is now many days since I left you. I understand you were wounded in the hand. How is it now?

Comrade, it is sheer luck that we have escaped and are still safe. Enemy attacks, and traitors informing on us, have brought us untold hardships.

Be sure we will suffer worse hardship in the future; but, if we persist, victory will be ours . . . The liberation of China is imminent and that situation affects the revolution in Malaya.

We must make every effort to hasten the imminent victory.

If your hand does not improve, see the doctor and take a rest. If it is better, pay attention to your studies during your leisure.
                                    Swee Peng.

It was in her last letter, though, that Swee Peng revealed the disruptive effect the British Army was having on the revolutionary war effort.

Dear Comrade Ah Choo,
                         I am sorry but there is no chance of our meeting you as you asked in your note of the 20th. For four days now the enemy has been searching my area and I understand their search will continue for a week.

Conditions here are bad. Two of my comrades were spotted by the enemy, who fired on them and now pay particular attention to this area.

Many of the masses have been moved into the towns.

Please excuse my inability to meet you, but the time allowed us is insufficient.

Regarding the education of comrades, Mr. Ngan's is very inadequate. When the situation improves, our work will be resumed.
                                    Swee Peng.

P.S.   Please inform Long Peng that there are no firearms in my camp. It is extremely dangerous for the few of us staying together here to proceed into villages unarmed. Ask them to send us weapons.

Hard-pressed though the bandits frequently were, no train was safe from derailment by them; no jungle road was safe from their ambushes; no jungle community could be regarded as anything but their involuntary ally; no telephone

Scots Guards on Patrol in the Malaysian Borneo Jungle

wire remained long uncut by them; and 1949 saw them no closer to extinction or surrender than they had been in 1948.

For the Scots Guards, as for everyone else, life became an endless series of one day patrols, the vast majority of which were fruitless. Returning from such patrols they were lucky to be able to report anything as significant as an old soap container lying in the bottom of a jungle pool, let alone a kill.

Many of them had still to glimpse a bandit—or, as they put it, 'to get a shot in' —and, of those who had, few had any idea whether or not they had hit their man. Their main weapon was not the Bren, the Sten, or even the new short rifle with which they had just been issued, but their feet. It was their eternal patrolling that most inhibited the bandits; but nothing, it seemed, would eradicate them.

As one of their officers put it, 'There was no relationship between effort and results—between tips acted upon and arrests—between intelligence gathered and results. Operation Lemon, for example, had the entire battalion in the jungle for three months, and got us three terrorists for the loss of three guardsmen.

'Yet on another occasion a company headquarters heard rumours of terrorists in the area, collected together six cooks, clerks and bottlewashers, made their way into the jungle, found a little camp, killed five bandits and were back at headquarters within the hour.'

But if they were not allowed to go out and win the war in 1949, at least the Guards made themselves as much at home—and vastly more comfortably at home —than the bandits they harried. When not in the jungle, they held company sports meetings (which included a blindfold sack race that could well have been intended as symbolic of the way they were required to fight) shot turtles, captured pythons, made pets of monkeys and occasionally went south to Singapore and Selarang Barracks.

There, on its impressive parade ground, they refurbished those ceremonial skills which, it was feared, months in the jungle might have rusted. Dismissed from parade, they took care not to tread on the grass verge that surrounded the barrack square because it was hallowed ground, sacred to the memory of the many British and Australian prisoners of war who were allegedly buried there.

In fact, British and Australian P.O.W.s were not buried there; but—as with many Army traditions—today's British soldier finds myth more acceptable than truth, so the grass verge remains sacred.

Refurbished, rested and refitted, many of them were glad to leave Selarang's comfortable barracks and return to the jungle. 'Too much spit and polish down there,' they complained. 'Up here, in the ulu, you know where you stand.'

Which, in 1950, was very much where they had stood in 1948 and 1949—on their two big feet, endlessly slogging against an enemy who continued to elude both death and capture.

On a June Sunday of that year, for example, the Iron Duke (promoted now to Captain) and two brother officers were being driven in a jeep from Kuala Lumpur to their village camp. Thirteen miles out of the capital, just as night fell, and in pouring rain, they ran into heavy fire. Bullets ripped through the canopy; the youngest officer was hit in the throat and blood from his severed artery spurted over his companions.

Then the second officer toppled forward. As the driver accelerated, the Iron Duke grabbed the first victim by his shirt, to stop him falling out, and fired four shots into the darkness. A bullet struck his hand and he lost his revolver. The driver, hurtling round a bend, found his way blocked by a parked lorry and careered down the twenty foot embankment. The Iron Duke was flung one way, the driver and the two wounded officers another.

The driver saw one of the wounded officers stagger to his feet and lurch towards the nearest of about sixteen bandits, who promptly shot him dead. Aware that his own chances of survival were nil, the driver feigned death.

It was the Iron Duke, though, who next came under the bandits' scrutiny. Unable to see either his comrades or the jeep, he had stood up, and had been immediately fired upon. Unarmed, bleeding from his hand wound and covered in his youthful colleague's arterial blood, he had run, then stumbled and finally fallen into a pool. There he lay motionless and spreadeagled; and seconds later felt his body being cursorily frisked by one of the bandits—who obviously decided, since he wore no watch and had no revolver, that he was not only dead but worthless as well. Shouting to his men, the bandit moved back up to the road.

At which moment another of the gang approached the motionless driver and kicked him in the face. The big Scotsman endured the first kick and waited for those that would follow. Instead he heard a whistle. It came from the leader of the gang, all of whom at once obediently withdrew.

Waiting a moment, the captain headed on hands and knees toward the embankment. The driver saw him and waved at him urgently.

'What happened to the other two?' the captain asked the driver.

'They're both dead,' the driver told him. Another of the Emergency's hundreds of incidents was over.

General Sir John Harding, now in command of all the troops in Malaya, at once wrote a graceful letter of sympathy to the commanding officer of the 2nd Battalion Scots Guards: the War Office rather belatedly wrote a typical civil service effusion to the Iron Duke's father.

Sir, this letter advised, *I am directed to inform you, with regret, that a report has been received from Far East Land Forces that your son ... was injured on 5th September 1950.*

The report does not indicate that the injuries are serious. The report states that the injuries were sustained as the result of wounds received whilst on operations in aid of the Civil Power.

I am to say that unless information is received from overseas that the condition of your son has become serious (and in such case you would be notified by telegram immediately) no further communication on this matter will be sent to you from the War Office.

> *I am, sir,*
> *Your Obedient Servant.*

The War Office should have taken lessons in the art of letter writing from Swee Peng. Little wonder, with syntax so woolly, that by the end of 1950 Whitehall's campaign—involving 10,000 troops and 45,000 policemen in pursuit of only 5,000 terrorists—was costing £36,000 a day and had inflicted upon the enemy no more casualties than the numerically inferior enemy had inflicted upon civilians, police and army.

Not surprisingly the Press complained of 'official obtuseness and niggardliness', of 'a war at half cock' and even of 'a horse being pulled by some jockey in Whitehall'.

It also complained of the shortage in Malaya of Army surgeons and armoured vehicles, of the need for American carbines to replace 'the erratic Sten', of the fact that soldiers were still having to buy their own tea 'for jungle brew-ups', and of army brusqueness to natives generally and all Chinese in particular.

As to the latter charge, it might in fairness have been added that, fast as the army arrested suspects, the Law released them. Let the army halt a delightful old Chinese lady on her bicycle, search in her basket and find, under the pineapples and papaya, half a dozen hand grenades: still, by morning, swearing that she had no idea who could have put hand grenades under her pineapples and papaya, she would be released.

A few top terrorists were so well known, their crimes so well documented, informers against them so readily available, that their arrest 'stuck'; but those who supported, condoned, informed and abetted them simply could not be held. They invariably pleaded innocence, and equally invariably there were no witnesses available to contradict them.

If, therefore, the Army had become brusque to most Tamils and Malays, and to all Chinese, there is little room for surprise. It suspected all three races and—incapable of mastering their languages—could only communicate with those Tamils and Chinese who spoke English. Moreover, the brusqueness of British soldiers towards the Chinese was more than matched by the contempt of the Chinese for British soldiers.

These factors combined had to result in tragedy. It came when—acting upon information—a twenty-two year-old Scots Guard sergeant, an Indian policeman, a Chinese detective and a fourteen man patrol were guided one Saturday to a small village in an acknowledged bandit area three miles from Ulu Yam Bahru.

Arriving there undetected, they observed three large kongsis, a smoke house, a rubber store and a few sheds. The men were working and the women cooking. According to the patrol's information, all the men were either bandits or bandit sympathisers.

Having surrounded the village, the sergeant and the police went in, segregated the men from the women, and detained twenty-five of the males in a large hut.

Searching the other huts, they found thirteen rounds of Sten gun ammunition and were told by the women that bandits had been extorting food and money from the village—for months. A lorry was due the very next morning to collect yet another consignment of food, they said.

The Guardsmen set up an ambush for this lorry. The twenty-five suspects in the hut were to be taken back to town for questioning after the lorry and its crew had been captured.

During the night one of the detainees attempted to escape and was shot dead.

Early in the morning, the lorry arrived, was halted and searched, and its driver and passengers were interrogated. The lorry was already heavily laden and neither the driver nor any of his passengers aroused any suspicions. Orders were accordingly given that the women and children, with as many of their belongings as possible, should leave the village at once on the lorry.

When they had gone, the patrol began to burn down the village huts. From the large shed they brought out their suspects. One of whom suddenly shouted something in Chinese, at which all twenty-four of them bolted in different directions for the jungle.

Those Guardsmen who surrounded the village had been ordered to shoot only when and if someone passed them—to avoid firing into the village.

They therefore allowed the twenty-four bolting Chinese to break out of their cordon before they opened fire and despatched all of them. Returning to Kuala Kubu, the patrol reported to their company commander who released the figures of this splendid weekend bag without a qualm. At once the Malayan Press was in an uproar.

'The public,' it proclaimed, 'wish to be satisfied that when men are killed they are killed for good reason and not for the sake of killing ... The affair at Kuala Kubu ... has the macabre air of an execution.

'Surely,' admonished another editorial, 'the patrol, outnumbered two to one, must have anticipated that an attempt to escape would be made? Could they not have bound the prisoners?'

In fairness, the Press might equally have asked why, unless they were guilty, all twenty-four men had attempted simultaneously to escape? And how, unless their escape was premeditated, did it happen that they all ran in different directions?

Suffice to say that the Ministry of Defence subsequently investigated the affair and decided that no one had behaved improperly. In spite of the efforts of a section of Fleet Street, many years later, 'The Affair at Kuala Kubu' did not become Britain's My Lai, nor was anyone prosecuted because of it.

At the time of the affair the 2nd Battalion was delighted with the patrol's success. The fact that bandit activity in that area thereafter decreased dramatically and permanently did nothing to change its mind. Today, dealing with the affair as a matter of history, the Regiment neither gloats nor recants. 'Question whom you like,' it declares. 'We have nothing to conceal.'

Thus 1950 ended, as it had begun, in stalemate. Some armour had been added to the driver's cab of military lorries; patrols now lasted weeks rather than days, and took men fifty miles or more from their company headquarters; and trains carried military escorts; but, as the *Daily Mail* commented, there was 'no hope of ending this vicious little war in 1951.'

That hopelessness took its toll not among the Guards' rank and file, but among their officers. Provided it was well led, the rank and file would put up with vicious little wars for an eternity; but to lead well in the jungle was no easy task.

Ambushed, it was the officer who, when everyone else was lying flat in the lalang, had to raise his head above the waist-high grass to see where the enemy was and in what strength. More officers had in fact been killed than N.C.O.s.

Setting off on a long patrol, it was the officer who had to give it point and keep it credible, though almost invariably it turned out to be pointless and futile.

Back in the infrequent comfort of his mess, it was officer who discussed with officer what the rank and file never bothered even to learn—that 30,000 British, Ghurka and Malayan troops, as well as the police, were now deployed against the surviving 3,000 bandits—that those bandits continued to live on extortion and the produce of their jungle gardens—that between seven and ten thousand rubber trees a week were still being slashed to bleed to death—and that damage caused by bandits was now running at £1,000,000 a month.

Suffering casualties on patrol, it was the officer who had to ensure that the dead—sometimes for days—were carried back to the company base. And if it was for days, it was the officer who had to open the corpse with a bayonet to allow the bloating gases to escape.

So not a few of the officers got sick of one another, of their men and of the responsibilities they bore. Of his platoon, one wrote to another at the time: '*The usual number of boring faces, the yawns, the belches, the farts; all the things that made a guardsman what he is, and his officer's life a living hell, doubled.*' Perhaps it takes a Scot to confess so frankly that in the Guards the relationship between officer and man is compounded not only of noblesse oblige, loyalty and respect, but also of contempt.

The 2nd Battalion stayed in Malaya for three years. It stayed there longer than anyone else; suffered thirteen killed, which was more than anyone else; and earned more decorations than anyone else.

Guards battalions stayed in Malaya till the emergency ended three and a half years later. To their honour, and to the honour of all the Commonwealth soldiers who fought and finally defeated their enemy in the jungle, a statue was erected in Kuala Lumpur.

Twenty years later, in August of 1975, a new generation of Chinese Communist insurgents blew it up.

25   *Aden*

GUARDS REGIMENTS are accustomed to being mucked about: in the Fifties and Sixties, they endured it all the time. One moment they would be on guard at the Palace, the next they would be flying off to some so-called emergent nation to keep the so-called peace.

In 1958 the First Battalion of the Irish Guards was Reserve Strategic Battalion and had nothing more exciting on its books than the running of the rifle championships at Bisley; but it ended up chasing terrorists in Cyprus for five hectic months, and during that time was twice warned that it was about to be shipped to the Middle East—once to help King Hussein in Jordan, later to help the Americans in the Lebanon.

In fact, it was November 1966 before the Micks were sent to the Middle East, and then it was neither to Jordan nor to the Lebanon they went, but to Aden, whose once thriving port had been moribund, whose arid hinterland had become a breeding-ground for dissidents, ever since Nasser closed the Suez Canal. As a Protectorate, it had been of no value at all to Britain for a decade: as a posting it came only slightly higher in the estimation of British soldiers than the glasshouse at Colchester: and as the setting for a very minor though rather nasty civil war it was about as newsworthy in 1966 as the suggestion that the United States might lose the war in Vietnam.

Until she could disengage from her now odious responsibilities, however, Britain was obliged to protect the Protectorate. Until she could hand Aden over, in tolerable running order, she must continue to garrison it with a thousand troops or so while the local dissidents (egged on by the southern Yemenis, trained by the Egyptians and armed by the Russians) sought to thwart her and kill them.

Early in 1966 the First Battalion Irish Guards had received their new colours from the Queen; in June they had trooped those colours at her Birthday Parade; in the autumn they had done some training in the wet clean mountains of Wales (allegedly to prepare them for service in the parched heights and filthy streets of Aden); and finally they had flown from England to Aden, there to relieve the Welsh Guards, and, in collaboration with the Marines, to suppress the Protectorate's nocturnal dissidents.

Arrived there, however, they learned that, instead of patrolling the town's dusty streets and stinking alleys, or picqueting its outlying hills, they were at once to board H.M.S. *Fearless* and go on a landing exercise.

The next forty-eight hours were as puzzling as they were exhausting for the battalion's rank and file. Not even the Army was in the habit of springing surprises like an immediate amphibious exercise on men who had just flown all the way to Aden from England; yet the Commanding Officer and the Adjutant both insisted that an exercise was all it was. Though food and ammunition in vast quantities were being loaded into *Fearless* under their very eyes, though she was stacked with landing craft and helicopters, all of it, they were told, was simply for an exercise.

Actually, all of it was to assist the battalion in an amphibious landing at a coastal village somewhere near the northern border, there to round up a group of Dhofari rebels who were said to be on the point of crossing back into Muscat.

The plan was that *Fearless* would sail up the coast and, just before her second dawn at sea, disgorge the Irish Guards, who would swarm ashore in landing craft, and into the hinterland by helicopter, thus cordoning off the rebellious Dhofaris. The area within the cordon would then be searched, the prisoners within the area would be screened (by accompanying informers) and those denounced by the informers would be flown from *Fearless* to the merciless hands of the authorities in Muscat.

Security, of course, had to be tight: the Irish are fearful talkers and all news travels fast in the Middle East. Accordingly, when the acting adjutant of the battalion boarded *Fearless*, and saw a minesweeper which he recognised as his brother's, he naturally visited it, but he admitted nothing.

'Hello,' he greeted his brother, who was supposed to be in the Persian Gulf. 'What are you doing here?'

'Oh,' said his brother, who had no intention of revealing the Navy's role in an imminent secret operation against some people called Dhofaris, 'just waiting. What are *you* doing?'

'Just visiting.'

'Didn't I see you a few minutes ago on *Fearless*?'

'Yes. But I was just visiting.'

Once well out to sea, though, the truth was revealed. The advance party would leave *Fearless* at first light; four landing craft transporting a platoon of Guardsmen each, and six Wessex helicopters, each depositing an outlying picquet, would follow; a number of rubber boats, with outboard motors, would patrol the sea to cut off any Dhofari who might decide to swim to Egypt; and all would co-operate to cordon off and search the suspect village.

And so, as their second night on board *Fearless* drew to a close, some of the Micks prepared to fly off in the Wessex helicopters at first light—only to find their pilots unprepared, because 'first light' for the R.A.F. comes an hour later than it does for the Army.

This contretemps resolved, and the advance party ashore, the adjutant was gazing down from *Fearless*'s deck, wondering what the Dhofaris had made of all those helicopters, and thinking how shallow the sea was, when, abruptly, the ship was plunged into darkness. No lights, no power, no generators; and, worst of all, no radio contact with the advance party ashore.

For the next twenty minutes, while Naval gentlemen scrabbled in *Fearless's* bowels, one of Her Majesty's most valued warships was not only immobilised but deprived of radio communication with the outside world as well. Then on came the lights, the power, the generators and the radio, and up came the explanation. Jellyfish. Sucked in. Gummed everything up. Never happened before.

The Micks went in—landing craft, helicopters, mortars and rubber boats every-where—one guardsman standing sound asleep in his landing craft all the way to the beach, and a company commander landing in his helicopter no less than two thousand yards from where he was supposed to land. But *that* had happened on the best of amphibious operations, not excluding Normandy, and anyway, there was the village, neatly bisected by a wadi, and all of it tightly cordoned off by picquets on the hill tops at the rear, and mortars and helicopters on the beach in front, and buzzing rubber boats in the sea beyond. Needless to say there was not a Dhofari to be found. Not a shot fired, either. The birds had flown, in spite of all the security. So making the best of it, the battalion rounded up some fifty locals whose only previous contact with the outside world had been by dhow. They had never seen men like the Micks before, nor anything like the massive Michegan tractors which had just forklifted rolls of barbed wire on to the beach to form the cage into which they were now being herded, and they were terrified.

Of the fifty thus detained, the imported informers screened out twenty, who were packed into helicopters and flown to whatever fate awaited them in Muscat. Something less than elated, the battalion sailed back at dusk to Aden.

There, for the rest of their tour, they did six weeks up country and six weeks in Aden town, alternating with the Marines. Up country they lived in tents on barren slopes, picqueting the four corners of their camp from sangars, built with

Even in Zanzibar pipers must keep in practice

rocks, on outlying hill tops.

The terrain was all hills and wadis, bare except for cacti and some primitive cultivation; and the battalion's role was to show the flag, to ambush rebels against the authority of the Sheik, and to prevent arms and ammunition being smuggled down to Aden.

The difficulty was that the enemy was the same illiterate farmer who worked so hard all day to scratch a living from the stony fields. Each night he became a skilled and well trained guerilla, armed with the latest weapons from Russia, Czechoslovakia and Britain.

There was a R.A.F. station at Khormaksar, with an airstrip, beside which were some wells drilled by the Army's engineers. Food and water were convoyed from it to the outlying picquets by trucks driving along the Dhala Road, which also was being built by the Army.

From time to time, always at night, the guerillas attacked the airstrip, the outlying camps and the patrols sent out to attack them. They invariably removed their dead and once, cornered by the Micks, had even had the temerity to withdraw down the R.A.F.'s airstrip, confident that their pursuers would not dare to fire for fear of hitting any of the seven helicopters parked on it.

In short, the Micks were fighting a typical Frontier war for which no one thanked them and about which almost nothing was printed in the British Press except reports of the more lurid kind that emanated from Egypt.

Thus, on 9 January 1967, an Egyptian news agency claimed that at Dhala thirty-six British officers and men had been killed, and fourteen seriously injured by commandos of the Front for the Liberation of South Yemen. Given this opportunity not only to deny the Egyptian claim but also to release some facts about the conflict in Aden, London's Ministry of Defence said expansively, 'It did not happen.'

Nor did it; but constant attacks *were* made by dissidents on targets in Little Aden, Big Aden and the hinterland; eight men of the First Battalion Irish Guards *were* killed during their tour; and some sort of coverage by Fleet Street's Press would have been reassuring.

Whenever they were relieved by the Marines from their up-country duties, the battalion assumed responsibility for patrolling the town. Here the dissident's chief weapon was the hand-grenade; and here the dissident was a town-dweller, with little of the skill and daring of the hinterland peasant.

'Dem wogs,' an Irish guardsman complained, 'dey don't tink before dey trow dose grenades.'

But even thoughtlessly thrown, a grenade is terrifying. Several hundred of Aden's servicemen were pouring out of the Astra Cinema at Steamer Point one night when a bomb landed in their midst. 'It was one of dem *hypnotic* grenades,' a Mick sergeant reported. 'You know the kind, the worst there are. You can't take yer eyes off 'em but neither can you tear yerself away.'

To the last the Micks in Aden remained cheerful and incorrigibly Irish. Told there were too many flies in his kitchen, one of their cooks demanded, 'Well how many *should* there be?'

Asked by a company commander, 'Was the trouble drink?' one of their number, who was on half a dozen charges, replied, 'No, sir, I wasn't drunk.'

'I didn't ask were you drunk. I asked was the trouble drink?'

'No, sir,' said the Mick. 'I'd only had eighteen pints and one Bacardi.'

Advised that Intelligence gathering was just as important in Aden as it had been in Malaya, Kenya and Cyprus, a Mick sergeant objected, 'The trouble is, every Tom, Dick and Harry round here is called Achmed.'

Their tour over, the battalion departed. Eight Irish lives had been lost in the alien cause of Middle Eastern peace and Britain's overseas reputation. All too soon the one would be shattered, the other a matter for anguished reappraisal. Like so many of the minor but nasty campaigns waged in and on behalf of emerging and emergent nations at that time, the Mick's tour of Aden had delayed much that was unacceptable, but ultimately prevented none of it. From their own experience in a dozen other countries the rest of the Household Division knew exactly how they felt.

In the event, then, the endless tiny 'wars' of the Fifties and Sixties achieved nothing;

but that did not concern the Household Division. Each episode was a Government, and therefore, a Sovereign's war: each had therefore to be fought. If none could be won, because the rules did not allow it, at least the Guards ensured that none was lost. And if all were microcosmic in the macrocosm of global war, at least the Guards were better prepared for global war than most. They still are.

Specifically they train for it in Germany, and when the Irish Guards are there they are housed at Münster, in what was once a Displaced Persons Camp.

The Irish Guardsman's attitude to N.A.T.O. service is as uncomplicated as it is unsophisticated. 'We're here to keep out the Communists, aren't we?' he says. 'If we weren't, they'd be across the Channel by now, wouldn't they?'

His officer does not jeer at such an over-simplification. For one thing, he is a less complex person than his peers in the other Guards regiments (not altogether objectively, he describes himself as less languid than they, and less foppish); for another, he is closer to his men.

'They're difficult to handle, for those who don't know them,' one of their majors admits. 'There's a magic method to which they respond. Try to ride or pressure them and they'll become not insubordinate but dull, uninspired and resentful. Let them feel that their officer isn't looking after them, and there's big trouble. Let them see that an officer's patronising them, or treating them with contempt, and he'll never be forgiven. And let an officer alienate his N.C.O.'s and you've got the formula for disaster.'

A Grenadier, Coldstream or Scots Guards officer would more likely resign his commission, or shoot his men, than handle them with such delicacy. Not even a Welsh Guards officer, with his strong sense of the battalion 'family', would be so careful to maintain a rapport with those he led. But Irishmen, whether from Ulster or Eire or Glasgow, have never been easy to handle; and if the Irish Guards of the 1970's can be so skilfully led as to lose only one deserter to the cause of the I.R.A., it is a rash Briton who criticises their system of leadership.

Actually, the Micks have always served Britain loyally, provided they were properly handled. Only the threat of unemployment, in fact, has ever persuaded them to accept discipline that was harsh and untouched by the magic of understanding. It did so between the two World Wars.

'Oh Jesus,' recalls an Irish Guardsman of the Twenties, 'it was terrible. At Windsor it was bad; but at Wellington Barracks in London it was terrible.

'Every frigging day you had a parade. And every frigging day you had stew. Stew, stew, stew. If you didn't like it, leave it; but there was never anything else.

'You knew nothing of what the outside world was doing. You were too busy for that—and anyway you were just a guardsman. Even going out, you had your red tunic on. At least it fitted you, because you had your regimental tailor, and he was good. He had to be.'

An Irish Guards Patrol in the main shopping area, Aden, 1967

'You were happy enough, just so long as you weren't in clink, or confined to barracks. And as for your pleasure—you picked up your dame, or you went up the Monkey Parade looking for someone to take you to the Victoria Palace, or the local pub.

'You'd no intention of getting married. All you were interested in was avoiding jankers, not losing your name, keeping off adjutant's orders if possible, and commander's orders by any means at all, because that meant C.B. or worse, for sure.

'And the N.C.O.'s were hard men like you never see any more. "What sort of a man is he, Sergeant Major?" the C.O. would ask; and the R.S.M. would say, "One of the worst, Sir—a Liverpool Irishman."' And him, like all of us, an Irishman.

'Mind, you were lucky if there was one soldier in a section—well, in a platoon— or a company, come to that—who had a brain in his head. Our lads enlisted from the streets, or from Borstal, not to see the world or anything funny like that, but from pure necessity. The country was in a hell of a state, you see. There was no work— nothing like that—the Army was your only chance.

'So you enlisted. And had the shit knocked out of you at Caterham. But still you were glad to be there, getting three meals a day. Of course many of them that joined were on the small side, and were sent to Number Two or Number Three Company—Number One and Four are for the tallest—but still they were glad to have got in at all—because you're not getting in till you've seen the Regimental Colonel, you know. Oh no. It's the Colonel who decides. Which is why, maybe, there was a Gorman in the Regiment who got an M.C. in World War I, a Gorman, his son, who got an M.C. in World War II, and a Gorman, his grandson, who got decorated in Hong Kong, not so very long ago.

'Anyway, once we'd got in, and survived Caterham, and been sent to a battalion, we soon learned to keep out of trouble—not to 'lose our names'—never 'to show arrogance'—and never to be 'done dirty on parade'. Oh, and you could be done dirty for so many things. For your buttons, your boots, your rifle, your sling— even for some sleep in the corner of your eye.

'Of course, you never saw your officers. Oh no, you could *apply* to see your company commander; but usually you only saw whichever subaltern was acting for him. The Company Commander himself, he only strolled in about once a week.

'Otherwise you never saw officers except on parade, or at guard mountings, or during inspections. They all lived out, you see. We never gave them a thought.'

And yet even then some of the magic method must have been applied, because this chronicler of the ruthless past continues: 'All the same, we took a great delight in the Regiment. We were proud of it—of ourselves and our officers and our Regiment. We knew we were better than the Bill Browns and the Coolies; the Jocks were just foreigners; the Welsh could sing a bit and play Rugby but otherwise were no frigging good for anything; and about the Household Cavalry we knew nothing and cared even less. They were bloody good ornaments and nothing else.

'And we were prepared to fight for our reputation at any time, with any of these characters. Oh yes. And many a bloody night we did, turning some convenient argument into a full-scale Donnybrook in a matter of seconds. But I suppose, really, we were only trying to convince ourselves, because the fact of the matter was it was a terrible life.

'Though funnily enough you came to like being a guardsman. When you had that tailored tunic on, you felt great. When you had on a bearskin, you felt terrific. When you marched to Buckingham Palace, you felt you were someone. I suppose that was it, really. Really we were nobodies; but no man who mounted guard at the Palace, unless he was a bloody clown, could help feeling "now I'm someone."

'And don't forget, those were bad times in Ireland. 1922 that was, and us stationed at Windsor while at home in Ireland there were the Troubles.

'But only *one* man failed the Regiment. Tried to take two stolen machine-guns to Ireland, he did, so he hired a cab to Euston Station; but when the cabbie wanted extra money for carrying two such heavy parcels, he refused. Well, one thing led to another, the police were called, the parcels were opened and the Irish Guards were packed off to Constantinople, where they so generally misbehaved that their C.O. paraded them and, flinging off his cap and Sam Brown, said, "I will not command such a battalion of blackguards."

'That was Alexander, who later became a Field Marshal! But back in those days he was our lieutenant colonel. Anyway, Kemal didn't want foreign troops in Turkey, so we were shipped off again, to Gibraltar this time, for a few years, four I think, before we came back to England.'

So Alexander, too, knew the magic method to which the Micks respond. At the Irish Guards Regimental Headquarters there is a glass case containing his muddied boots and bullet torn tunic from World War 1: also a letter addressed to Jumbo to which he appended a small but very bad painting. All of them, to the Micks, are priceless relics. Today's Irish Guards admit that as a colonel Alexander delivered a diatribe to his battalion in Constantinople. They even add that he offered to fight anyone who disagreed with him ('and he was only a little chap too'). But they deny quite blankly that any Irish Guardsman was ever caught at Euston Station trying to smuggle two machine-guns across the water to Dublin.

Likewise, and miraculously, claim the officers, in spite of the situation in Ulster, there exist today no tensions between Irish Guardsmen who are Catholic and Irish Guardsmen who are Protestant.

'Well actually,' some N.C.O.'s will admit, 'if something horrific occurs in Ulster, or there's a bombing here in the U.K., we do get a little of what we call the Irish twitches. But throughout the Ulster trouble, we've had the lowest absentee rate of the whole Household Division.'

To the non-Irishman, the Micks' officers and N.C.O.'s seem unduly reticent. To him it seems almost incredible that in the Troubles of the Twenties and the guerilla warfare of the Sixties and Seventies there should only have been one alleged and one actual defector from the Regiment.

But the Irish approach to such confessions always was oblique, and is no less so today. Recently a Guardsman approached his adjutant, seeking compassionate leave. His father, he said, was dying, and there was no-one at home to care for him.

'Isn't your mother there?' the adjutant enquired.

'Oh, she's getting on.'

'No brothers or sisters?'

'Ah well.'

'Come on.'

'Well, I do have a sister. But she's only ten.'

'No-one else?'

'Well, yes—a brother.'

'And how old is he?'

'Eleven.'

'No one else?'

'Well yes, sir—I have got another sister.'

'And how old is she?'

'Twelve, sir.'

'That all?'

'Not exactly, sir. I've a brother of fourteen, but he's away all day, working the fields.'

'I think,' said the adjutant, 'you'd better tell me exactly how many there are in your family.'

'Nineteen, sir,' said the Guardsman, totally unabashed. 'But they're all too young or too busy to look after my father, and *he's* dying.'

'Leave it with me,' said the adjutant.

Who then telephoned a friend in Ireland, who lived near the village where the guardsman's family lived. Enquiries were instituted—and the Guardsman recalled to the adjutant's office.

'I'm glad to be able to report to you,' the adjutant declared, 'that your father's not only fully recovered, he is *digging in his garden.*'

'Ah,' said the Guardsman with a wide smile, 'I tort you'd fluffed me, Sir.'

While, however, it is acceptable for an officer to 'fluff' a Guardsman, it is fatal for a Guardsman to 'fluff' an officer. When, therefore, the Micks complain that winter conditions in their appalling Münster barracks—for which pay is deducted —are 'shitty', the officer must not uphold the powers-that-be, he must agree. For him to deny that the D.P. huts were decades ago condemned, that the drains flood back, that the armoured vehicles are freezing to maintain and ankle deep in slush, and that the soccer pitch is a quagmire would be something the Mick would never forgive. But even less forgivable would be the confession by any Mick to any outsider that another Mick had been fluffed doing anything.

Yet handled the Irish way, this strange Regiment (few of whose members are English, many of whom would instantly confess a basic loyalty to Eire) loyally fulfils its twin duties of protecting the Sovereign and fighting the Sovereign's wars.

Its devotion to Elizabeth the Queen Mother is absolute. Its attitude to the possibility of having to fight in World War III is wholly professional. Should that war come, the Micks will clatter off to meet the enemy in personnel vehicles whose armour will keep out nothing bigger than small arms fire. Deposited at the point where they must fight, they will rely mainly on their own skills and courage as infantrymen—though they will be pleased to accept support from those other Micks whose personnel carriers contain either the two wheeled Wombat anti-tank gun or the solid fuel-propelled missile which can be electronically guided to its target by impulses transmitted to it along a silver wire it unreels spiderlike from its guts.

Thrusting ahead of them may be the brutish strength of the Chieftain tanks, and probing ahead of these will be the swift armoured cars; but still and always, as it has ever been, their main concern will be to ensure that the Regiment doesn't lose its name.

26   *Ulster*

EXCEPT FOR the Irish Guards, who have not been called upon, each of the Regiments of the Household Division has done more tours in Ulster than it cares to remember during the long, hate-filled years of Ireland's most recent crisis. Each has faced the same problems and dangers, and each has done it in its own way. The 1st Battalion Welsh Guards did it, where possible, gently.

They were in Germany in 1970 when first they were stood up for Ulster; but then they were stood down. Then, however, they were stood up again; but soon were definitely stood down.

'You're not going for twelve months,' their somewhat fretful commanding officer was finally assured: so he ordered his men back to training on their armoured personnel carriers while arranging that as many as possible of them should take their U.K. leave in time to support the battalion's Rugby team in its Army final at Aldershot.

It was at that match, during extra time, that he was called away and advised, 'You leave for Ulster on Monday'—and returned to see coachloads of triumphant Welsh Guardsmen, whose team had meanwhile won, streaming away to catch the train that would take them home to Wales. Somehow they had not only to be prevented from going home, they had also, and promptly, to be flown back to Germany.

Announcements over the public address system at all the relevant railway stations intercepted the leave-takers; that sense of discipline which had brought them back to England from the shambles of Dunkirk with buttons gleaming and in apparent perfect order now turned them round in their tracks; and planes took them back to Germany whence, by the Monday, the entire battalion had been flown to Belfast.

There, billeted in a disused factory, sleeping in double-tiered bunks, it spent the next four months in reserve. 'Our role,' the battalion subsequently explained without bitterness, 'was that of Rentacompany to anyone who needed us.'

Mainly it was an exhausting rather than a dangerous time, those being the comparatively halcyon Belfast days of the juvenile stone-thrower and the occasional I.R.A. or Provisional sniper rather than the indiscriminate bomber; but the battalion was delighted, after four months of it, to get back to armoured carriers and the dour but comprehensible Germans of Münster. Nine months later they were told they were to go to Ulster again—to do border patrols.

So they trained for a rural campaign, and in June of 1972 were despatched to the very centre of urban Belfast.

There, their four companies billeted in both Protestant and Catholic areas, they were no more incensed by the virulence of the Catholics than they were by the virtuousness of the Protestants who—tarring the entire battalion with the brush of Welsh nationalism—promptly rioted against the presence in their loyalist midst of what they chose to call 'Republicans'.

There was no time, however, to take umbrage. The better to avert the kind of car bombing that was currently paralysing Londonderry, the Welsh Guards were ordered to 'pedestrianise' Belfast. Keep out the cars, the theory was, and you'll keep down the explosions.

The battalion moved swiftly, blocking off with coils of barbed wire every road, lane and alley that led to the city centre, halting each oncoming vehicle and advising each motorist that, if he wished to proceed any further, he must walk. Few motorists were less than disgruntled and those who travelled by Rolls Royce were mostly outraged; but five hundred Welsh Guardsmen were not to be deterred and soon the city centre was not only virtually carless, it was virtually segmented as well.

Within these segments, individual companies, subject only to the overall policy laid down at each morning's battalion conference, conducted their own affairs. Each had its own Operations Room (an army euphemism for anything from a large cupboard to a partitioned corner of a disused warehouse); its own radio communications, its own Intelligence Room, and its own vehicles. Each sent out its own patrol, which was in radio contact with its company headquarters and, through that, with battalion headquarters and the police. Each got to know everyone who lived in its sector. Each did its work with one and a half hands tied behind its back by Westminster's political insistence that the slender possibility of a rapprochement between the warring Ulster factions should not be wrecked by any military affront to either side. And each knew that Belfast's volcanic antagonisms were in fact about to erupt.

Every day seemed to bring either a massive demonstration by the Protestants or provocative I.R.A. claims that yet another district was in their hands and inaccessable either to the Royal Ulster Constabulary or to the British army. Every day Mr. Whitelaw's futile negotiations demanded that the Army keep out of many a 'No Go' area it could easily have entered, and behave as little like soldiers as possible in those areas it did enter. And every day the proprietors of Belfast's various large stores pestered the battalion commander for better protection against the bombs they knew were coming.

The battalion did what it could, sending out random patrols, staging random searches, familiarising itself with every street, house and inhabitant in the various areas for which it was responsible.

Every day, for example, the Prince of Wales Company—billeted in a mill due for demolition—sent an eight man patrol into the Markets area for four hours. The Markets area was not so much a market as a slum which extended from the city centre to the river. Its population was wholly Catholic, hostile and frightened; yet, patrolling its sullen streets, the men of the Prince of Wales Company were required to adopt a demeanour of apparently insane casualness, their rifles slung over their shoulders lest, by carrying them at the ready, they offended the locals and caused a breakdown in Mr. Whitelaw's negotiations.

As anxious as Mr Whitelaw himself that peace should come to Ulster, they sought neither to provoke nor to respond to provocation. They greeted the sullen with cheery shouts of 'good-morning', gave the bleak-eyed, foul-mouthed children sweets and helped their slatternly mothers fill in their pools coupons. They ignored the taunts of passing paratroopers and marines that, because they carried their rifles slung, they didn't know their job. And whenever one of the numerous Market viragos screamed obscenities at them, they told her how pleased they were to see her again, and how well, or pretty, or tired, or hot, or cool she looked, so that, before long, most of the viragos were baffled. Indeed there was one, whose constant chant to them had been, 'Fuck off, you Welsh bastards,' who had been driven permanently indoors by the sergeant whose affectionate response to her had invariably been, 'Hello there, Mam'.

'When they abuse you, those awful I.R.A. women,' the Major commanding the Prince of Wales Company had ordered his men, 'you will not, repeat not, retaliate by shouting "fuck off home, you silly old cow".' But even he could not have hoped for quite such good natured self-control as appeared to come effortlessly to his subordinates.

Strangely, the Markets task suited the Welshmen. They came from cramped houses and mean streets themselves; but *their* houses were clean, their families intact, their streets properly lit and drained. In the Markets, the houses were rotting, most families were broken, the streets had been left uncleaned, with their drains blocked, for months, and it was impossible not to feel compassion for a sector of society so desperate that it had taught its infants to say 'fuck the British bastards' almost before they could walk.

Searching the houses of the Markets families increased that sense of compassion. Though their inhabitants had littered every street with derelict cars, bits of wood, broken bottles and rotting rubbish; though every filthy window pane might conceal a sniper; though half the filth outside was due to their own rent and rates strike (which in turn was a puny protest at their lack of any political power); though every fireplace flaunted its I.R.A. collecting box; though every staircase was likely to conceal either weapons or explosives, what every Welsh Guardsman resented most was the frightful stench of inescapable poverty.

It was the stench of sweat, excrement and urine—a stench worse than that of the neighbouring gas works and the nearby river combined—a stench that sent guardsmen who had become impervious to the squalor and stinks of Aden bolting for the street, there to be sick.

Strangely, though, they condemned not the people who produced the stench but rather the society that had produced the people. 'Fair do's,' the Welshman is wont to exclaim; and in Belfast he swiftly decided that fair do's were what the Catholics conspicuously had not got.

The Protestants meantime—as if deliberately to alienate what little sympathy the Welsh Guards still felt for them—were behaving with appalling immoderation. Union Jacks flew from every house in the Loyalist enclaves. A brief cease-fire having been negotiated by Whitelaw, Orangemen were busy ensuring its failure by celebrating William III's long ago defeat of James II with bonfires around which they sang and danced, with massive marches to the accompaniment of arrogantly taunting drums, and with volleys of nauseating abuse for any Catholics unfortunate enough to live in side-streets along the marchers' route.

'Sir,' commented an N.C.O. to his company commander, 'this must be just like the jackboots of Munich in 1938.'

Welsh sympathy did not, however, extend either to the I.R.A. or to the Provisionals, neither of whom, it considered, was doing any more to help the Catholic community than was its Catholic Church.

'We'll have no trouble with you,' I.R.A. agitators used to assure the Welsh Guardsman when first they entered the Markets. '*You*'re fighting for your language and *we*'re fighting for our religion.' But at the same time they were busy daubing every available wall with the slogan 'GO HOME THE TAFFS'. The Taffs rather enjoyed the inconsistency of it.

In fact they rather enjoyed many of the characteristics of the Catholic community—their mad humour, their mad logic, even the mad cadences of their madly unconvincing lies; and the Catholic community, as well as being hostile, saw nothing inconsistent in being, at times, friendly.

So they gave the musically inclined Welshmen long-playing records of some of the Republican songs for which they had expressed a liking. And they accepted from the Prince of Wales company summonses they refused to accept from the police. And when they were subsequently fined, they would hand a grubby envelope full of money to one of the Welsh Guardsmen for delivery to the court. And when their electricity failed, or their drains flooded, it was the Welsh Guards upon whom they relied to telephone for hated officialdom's maintenance men.

'GET OUT THE TAFFS' the slogans demanded—and from most of their billets round Belfast the Taffs were in fact *planning* to get out; but only to move into the Grand Central Hotel, which had been empty for nine months—in spite of the poster at the airport that continued to urge new arrivals to visit it and enjoy a happy holiday. Most of the First Battalion were due to move into it at the end of the week, on Friday, 23 July. But for that date the I.R.A. and Provisionals were planning something very different from a happy holiday.

Meanwhile, unable to break up the enormous Protestant marches, as in the past it had broken up the much smaller Catholic marches, the Army simply had to stand aside and watch. As a result, Protestant contempt for the Army's authority increased, Catholic confidence in its impartiality diminished, and patrolling in the Markets had to be intensified.

'I'm sorry, ma'am,' a sergeant apologised to a woman who was known both to run a business and to hold money for the I.R.A. 'I'll have to look in your safe.'

'It's under the stairs,' said the woman indifferently.

Also under the stairs he found roll upon roll of camouflage material.

'What's this then?' he demanded.

'Ah that,' she said. 'Yes. Yes, that's for wrapping the kiddies' Christmas presents.'

'In July?'

'I like to be ready.'

'And this?'—pointing to the thousands of pound notes stacked in the safe.

'For buying the presents with. What else?'

Over then to an even more derelict house than usual: one from which the original tenants had fled, in which tinkers were now squatting. Most of the floor boards had been torn up and used as fire wood.

'Why do you do it?' a Guardsman asked them.

'Because we're skint,' they replied. But before the search was over, hundreds of pounds were unearthed—I.R.A. money. And all the sergeant and his patrol could do was report every detail back to the Company Intelligence Room.

There was now very little about the Markets that the Intelligence Section didn't know. It knew which of the youths were the Provisionals, which of the women were rabble rousers, and which of their husbands were hard men who so terrorised the rest of the locals that they would offer sanctuary to snipers and succour to bombers, whatever the consequences from the Army. Most disquieting of all, though, was the knowledge that the enemy's tactics were becoming more sophisticated.

'There's something *different* about that house,' muttered the sergeant who had just searched it one day; but it was twenty minutes before he realised what it had been. New wallpaper. On *those* walls? He returned and ordered his men to rip it off.

The Welsh Guards are made welcome in Northern Ireland

To reveal a cupboard.

Which was empty.

'What was all that about, Sergeant?' asked one of his Guardsmen.

'That,' explained the sergeant, 'was a diversion. They knew we'd notice the new wallpaper. Relied on us to notice it, as a matter of fact. And when we noticed it, we did exactly what they wanted us to do—tore the place to bloody pieces—while *they* were shifting explosives or something into or out of one of the houses down the road.'

And so came 23 July, the day most of the First Battalion were to move into the Grand Central Hotel, the day the journalists were to dub Bloody Friday.

While each officer and every four men was allocated a room and bath, and while Reception was being transformed into a Headquarters, the Battalion commander was driving, in plain clothes and a private car, to a club where he was to lunch with an anxious store owner.

While the Colonel lunched, his Company commander in the Markets was discussing the problem of hoax bomb calls. To ignore any one of them might be to allow dozens of people to die; to treat all of them as genuine would be, time after time, unnecessarily to halt the city's life and to exhaust the army's bomb disposal experts.

As he talked, the radio in his operations room, and both the telephones, began to deliver message after message about bombs—where they were, and how soon they would explode.

'Something's up,' he commented; and decided that every call should be investigated.

A few miles away, the colonel, his lunch over, his host—he hoped—mollified, made his way back to his car.

'Anything doing?' he asked his driver.

'Lots of bomb *warnings*, sir,' said his driver, whose small radio was tuned into B.H.Q., 'but nothing else.'

They set off for the Grand Central Hotel, where the adjutant was taking a breather on the roof. It was a beautiful afternoon, he realised, and life in the Grand Central—even though, for the moment, it lacked carpets, curtains, beds and furniture—was going to be beautiful too.

Then he heard two explosions. His colonel, in his private car, also heard them. As did every other motorist in Belfast; so that the streets seized up in an instant traffic-jam, and it took the colonel half an hour to get back to the Grand Central. By which time there had been sixteen explosions in the city and the blue sky above it was streaked with black.

In the Markets, where the explosions had been just as clearly heard, orders were issued to cordon off and search areas where telephone calls had warned that further bombs were planted. The Company Commander had called in reserves from another battalion and even roused sleeping men from bed and sent them off, four at a time, in every available vehicle.

Then came a warning of a car-bomb by the Oxford Street bus depot, and he had no one to deal with it but his Intelligence Section. Reluctantly he ordered its sergeant, driver and three guardsmen to go and investigate.

They left in a squat armoured vehicle which weighs a ton and is unaffectionately known to soldiers as a Pig, although it more closely resembles a porcupine. Their progress was slow, despite the fact that they drove the wrong way down one-way streets and mounted the pavements without compunction. Eventually, though, they reached the bus depot and pulled up behind a parked car.

Having ordered the three Guardsmen to clear everyone out of the depot, the sergeant made enquiries about the parked car. An official said if it was an 1100, it was his. The hundreds of people milling round the depot, waiting for their buses, refused to believe that they were in danger. The I.R.A., they pointed out, were not in the habit of blowing up public property. Shops and pubs, yes, but not bus depots. Only after the sergeant and his men had insisted that they leave did the would-be bus passengers begin to disperse. Then the sergeant returned to his Pig, and he and his driver walked towards the innocent 1100.

At that moment, in the Albert Mill, trying to decide which of the many bomb calls being handled by his men he should personally supervise, the Company Commander heard an unusually loud explosion.

'Contact Sergeant Price,' he ordered his radio operator; but no answer came back from the Bus Depot. Not unduly surprised, he decided, nevertheless, to drive to Oxford Street and check for himself.

Approaching it in his Land Rover, he saw an ambulance; arrived at the Bus Depot, he beheld a scene of grotesque carnage. The 1100 had exploded, injuring more than a hundred and killing eleven—two of whom were the sergeant and his driver, their bodies relatively intact, despite their proximity to the explosion, because of their flack jackets. The nine other bodies were being collected piecemeal, like bloodied litter, in polythene bags.

By six o'clock Belfast was quiet again; but in the derelict Albert Mill and the unfurnished Grand Central the atmosphere was charged with vengefulness. The Battalion had suffered its first violent deaths since World War II and its rage was as tribal as it was intense.

'Let's go and sort them out,' the men begged their officers—who had to explain that sorting out the Provisional I.R.A. was not the role of the Welsh Guards. To their credit the Welsh Guards did not retort, 'Well, what *is* our role?', and to some extent events later that night eased their anguish. Brigade Headquarters notified Battalion Headquarters that two policemen needed rescuing from the Markets. At the same time the Prince of Wales Company radioed Battalion Headquarters that one of its Observation Posts having been fired upon from a car, a small three man patrol had given furious pursuit and radio contact with it had been lost. An hour later there was still no word from it. Worried both for the three Guardsmen and the two policemen, the Battalion commander sent two companies to invade the Markets. Thereafter a sporadic gun battle raged during which at least one Provisional gunman was seen to be killed, the lost patrol emerged triumphantly to claim three more and the Battalion's dead were felt to have been avenged.

The next day was spent planning a massive clean-out of the entire Markets area. This, with the help of two companies from a reserve battalion, was put into affect at dawn on Sunday.

It terrified the Market's community. Hitherto the Taffs had been so few and so amiably self-effacing: now they were there in their hundreds, bristling with arms and grimly business-like. The Catholics were not to know that it all seemed a bit Gestapo-like to the Guardsmen too, this business of bursting into sleeping households at dawn.

From one such house a naked man leapt out of a back window on to an outhouse roof, only to find himself confronted by a patrol in the neighbouring back yard.

The Welsh sergeant leading the patrol at once challenged him, and by way of an answer received a very rude sign indeed.

'Shoot him, shoot him,' shouted one of the men from the Reserve Battalion. But somehow the sergeant could not bring himself to shoot a naked man, so he fired to miss, and the naked man flung himself off the outhouse roof, into the back yard, over a wall, through a window and into another house where he was only cornered when he smashed a window and offered to fight. Then, without compunction, the sergeant shot him in the leg and he surrendered. The room in which he was captured contained a number of rifles. Elsewhere a bomb factory had been discovered, a mass of explosives and ammunition unearthed and a number of arrests made.

The following day the Battalion acquired a new commanding officer, but its prime duty remained the same, to prevent the bombing of Belfast's centre, which it sought to do by endlessly patrolling, segmenting and searching. In spite of all its efforts, however, there was usually an explosion each Wednesday (when the Provisionals issued their bombs) a crop of them on Thursday (when they collected their dole money and got recklessly drunk) isolated bombs on Friday, Saturday and Sunday (as their drinking money dwindled) and only rare explosions on Monday and Tuesday (when they were broke). But upon every mission the Provisionals sought to blow up newsworthy targets, and just as assiduously the Welsh Guards sought to deny them any targets at all.

As part of that process they sought also to intercept anyone carrying explosives to the targets of their choice. This involved searching shopping bags and parcels and, in the case of male pedestrians, making body searches. And body searches are useless if not thorough—which is no less embarrassing for the searcher than for the searchee.

On the whole, though, the public understood. One who did not was an American tourist. '*Sir,*' he wrote his consul, '*as a citizen of the U.S., I objected most strenuously to the handling of my person in the form of a search by an individual dressed in a military type uniform. No permission was granted or request issued. Just a blatant handling of my private parts by this individual.*'

The American Consul forwarded the letter without comment: the Welsh Guards marked the letter *No Further Action*: the letter itself is today a much read document in the regimental archives.

Apart from the impromptu and unsolicited handling of Americans' private parts, the Battalion was also required to clear the Markets of its hard men; and to that end the Prince of Wales Company moved out of its derelict mill, where it had always been vulnerable, and set itself up in a disused Protestant chapel, which

Welsh Guards on duty in Belfast, 1972

it transformed into a virtual block house in the very heart of the area.

From there, now that the cease-fire had been irrevocably breached, it moved out on boldly effective patrols. Assisted by a company of Marines and a troop of Hussars, the Prince of Wales Company would cordon off an area and then sieve it house by house. As soon as they moved in, hundreds of children would appear, led by dozens of frighteningly violent mothers and older sisters. They would fend off the children's missiles, close their ears to the women's obscenities and make their arrests; and in the process they not only came to appreciate that the women's foul language sprang more from fear (of everyone) than from depravity, but also they became preternaturally clean-mouthed themselves.

There were, of course, other duties to be performed—like policeing I.R.A. funerals, at which the large Welshmen were astonished as much by the comparative smallness of the Catholic mourners as by their restraint and decency. Indeed, they found it difficult to reconcile these qualities with what they now knew to be equally inherent traits of idleness and lack of civic pride. Amusing the Catholics might have been, but even rehoused, they lacked civic pride. The Protestants, on the other hand, were fanatically houseproud and totally humourless. To the Welshmen the two breeds of Ulstermen seemed eternally irreconcilable and, as the gunmen of both factions shot one another and anyone in between to ribbons, not a few of them began to wonder, 'How can democracy be defended against this sort of thing without resorting to methods that are equally undemocratic?'

Upon that question their second tour of Ulster drew to a close. At the Grand Central they were now infinitely more comfortable than they had ever been in England or Germany, bombed-out store owners having provided them with so much of everything that one company commander even had lace curtains in his bathroom and a rubber duck in his bath.

For four months they had had no social life at all, except for one exhilarating afternoon when they all travelled to Armagh to watch their scratch Rugby team thrash another Army team 55–0; but for four months they had also protected much of Belfast from the wrath of the I.R.A. and thousands of Catholics from the viciousness of both Protestant thugs and Provisional militants.

They went home to find that their wives were tired and their children didn't know them. And no sooner had they gone than, on a wall in the Markets, one of the incurably feckless locals daubed the slogan: 'BRING BACK THE TAFFS'.

★   ★   ★

Nine months later the Taffs were back, but not in Belfast. This time they were to serve in the border regions of South Armagh, which is known to the Army as Indian country.

Even in peace-time, law and order have never really prevailed between northern Eire and Southern Armagh—not when an enterprising man can get a drink after hours, or evade paying his car taxes, or do a spot of profitable smuggling just by crossing the border. And once the disturbances began in 1969, and the few police-men stationed there either departed or were shot, the I.R.A. made South Armagh their own.

Ever since Ireland was divided in 1921, South Armagh had taken no pains at all to conceal its sympathies with the I.R.A., to which it had contributed generations of recruits. Now that hostilities had been renewed, its predominantly Catholic population—which had never bothered to differentiate between Official and Republican I.R.A.—openly proclaimed its Republican ambitions, blatantly flew the tricolour in towns like Crossmaglen and became the willing accomplices of terrorism.

To combat this rural guerilla warfare, techniques very different from those used in Belfast were required. In Belfast the potential danger was the parked car: on the placid country lanes of South Armagh it was the waiting milk churn.

In Belfast parked cars were likely to be packed with dynamite which would be detonated by a time mechanism; but at least it was possible to control parking and thereby render the unauthorised car conspicuous. In South Armagh milk churns packed with explosives were constantly being detonated by a man a quarter of a mile away lying in wait for a passing army patrol. Nor was it possible to keep milk churns off the roadside. It was where farmers had always left their milk for collection, and always would.

In Belfast a sniper attempting to escape the soldiers on whom he had fired fled from backyard to backyard, and those who pursued him had little more to fear than the abuse of the women in the houses they entered. In South Armagh the sniper operated in open country, across which he could lead his pursuers into minefields or ambushes and from which he could at any time find swift and easy immunity in Eire.

In Belfast, the entire city centre had been segmented, and, because the Army watched and knew everyone in its own little sector, it was dangerous for a wanted man to appear and difficult for him, once spotted, to escape. In Armagh, there were literally hundreds of crossing points along the border which made segmentation— even had it been feasible—pointless, and everyone watched the Army, so that it could not stay in any one place for more than half an hour before it was fired upon, and could not use a secret observation post a second time without the risk of being blown up.

In Belfast it was ultimately the Army who dominated the City's streets with road blocks, check points and observation posts: in South Armagh it was always the I.R.A. who dominated its rural lanes with mines and ambushes—the more so since civilians in cars frequently drove straight through Army check-points (secure in the knowledge that the law forbade the Army to fire on them) and into Eire.

In Belfast the gunman's victim was removed as quickly and decently as possible. In South Armagh the gunman's victim was frequently booby-trapped and liable to be left lying round for hours, or even exploded.

In Belfast there was a degree of telephone and radio security while the Army stalked the I.R.A.: in South Armagh there was no security at all as the I.R.A. stalked the Army.

And finally, in Belfast every responsible citizen, of whom there were many, was obliged to admit that the Army's main concern was to protect his life and property. In South Armagh the entire Catholic community never ceased to complain that the Army's measures were interfering with everything it held most precious, from its farming to its nocturnal drinking, from its trading to its weekly dances and bingo sessions.

With all these problems the First Battalion coped admirably. Rather than cause added ill-will, they imposed no curfew, so that the locals could continue to enjoy their drinking, dancing and bingo.

Aware that hostile ears listened in to all their telephone conversations, and most of their V.H.F. radio exchanges, they chattered unintelligibly in a mixture of Arabic, double-Dutch and Welsh.

Acknowledging the I.R.A.'s daytime control of the roads and the border country-side, they used helicopters to swoop in on any objective, or to investigate any report of a shooting, or of a bomb, or a mine. And having landed they did what had to be done in twenty minutes, or faced the risk of fire from I.R.A. men called up by the nearest farmer. If they *were* fired upon (or if they *did* find bombs or a minefield) they took care *not* to react in the obvious way, because more often than not the obvious way was the one that lured the unwary to a further trap and certain death.

Not to leave the initiative in the enemy's hands, however, they patrolled vigor-ously at night and systematically built up their intelligence dossiers on every farmer and each member of his family in every house, town and village. And using all this information, they brought a tremendous psychological pressure to bear on the local community.

Thus, the junior leader of a patrol—a corporal—would question a suspect, having first checked back by radio with the Intelligence Room in his Company headquarters and given the suspect's name, the number of his motor car and its make, 'So you're driving a new car, Mr. O'Brien,' he would then remark. And continue; 'How much did you pay for it? . . . Where'd you get all that money from when you've just bought all that fertiliser? . . . Where's the old one?' And all the answers would be noted down and added to the dossier when the patrol returned.

To the guilty, the confident statement of one known fact often implied possession of all the other facts. 'Hello there, Mr. Mallon. I see you were drinking with Liam Machin the other night,' would frequently unnerve the Mr. Mallons of Crossmaglen, Forkhill, Bessbrook or wherever.

Should Mr. Mallon then lapse into total silence, he would be taken and held for interrogation, because the Irishman who refused to talk had long since come to be recognised as the most suspect of all.

Guilty or not, Mr. Mallon would know his rights and the local I.R.A. boys would be checking that they were not infringed. By the terms of the Northern Ireland Emergency Powers Act, a suspect could be held by the Army for only four hours before being either released or handed over to the police. Let it be one second longer and the I.R.A.—who had been known to use a stop watch on these occasions —would play merry publicity hell.

Thus, for four months, the vicious game, full of vicious tricks, was played. South Armagh, a gently green and wooded land, was not so beguiling as it looked.

For decades it had been so steeped in hatred that now its farmers used fertiliser less to improve their crops than to make explosives. The true South Armagh was the night-time one, when the warm fields and gentle hills grew chill with mist, under cover of which Irishmen planted their cunning traps and Welshmen, in anonymous vans or on foot, usually led by junior N.C.O.s, patrolled incessantly.

In Crossmaglen, the I.R.A. set a mine and detonated it as a foot patrol entered the town square. Because they were well led, well trained and properly spaced, only one Guardsman was killed. That was the price paid for four months work that yielded little more than a mass of splendidly documented and cross-referenced intelligence.

The First Battalion returned to London duties aware that in both urban and rural Ulster the only Catholic homes unlikely to have produced a terrorist since 1969, or even a dynasty of terrorists since 1921, were those in middle-class suburbs occupied by families who were sleek, comfortable and unconcerned.

Equally they were aware that, just as Ulster, in the words of a Major General, 'has produced the most jacked up peacetime army ever', so it has transformed the I.R.A. into the world's most efficient terrorist organization. Similarly they were sadly aware that each time they returned to Northern Ireland they found the situation not better but worse.

To their tribal memories of service in two World Wars, of containing terrorists in Palestine and dissidents in Aden, was now added the recollection of a distasteful job well done in Ulster. As much as possible they had ensured that the philosophy of fair do's prevailed.

Unfortunately, in guerilla warfare, fair do's do not prevail. On 27 August 1975, the I.R.A. planted a bomb in a discotheque opposite the barracks of the First Battalion Welsh Guards in Caterham. Those barracks stand on the site of a Martello Tower which once looked anxiously across the Sussex Downs toward Brighton, awaiting the onslaught of Napoleon's threatened invasion. Today's enemies cannot be spotted from a tower and do not advance across open Downs. Rather, they wait for the Army's pay day, then plant a bomb in the discotheque of an Army pub.

Five Guardsmen were critically injured. Four of them lost legs, one of them— twenty-one years-old and the Rugby team's scrum-half—lost both his legs and an arm.

'Send us back and let us sort them out,' begged his battalion; but they were sent to Cyprus instead, to stand between irreconcilable Greeks and Turks, peacekeeping for the United Nations.

*The Regimental Badges
of the Irish Guards (left)
and the Welsh Guards (right)*

TRADITION

27 'The Guards Never Forget'

WHEN CHARLES II went into exile a number of his supporters accompanied him. To this day, Grenadiers remind Coldstreamers of their perfidy in having once served under the regicide Cromwell.

When Queen Anne died childless—in spite of prodigious efforts—in 1714, a distant German cousin succeeded her; but some of George I's new subjects, preferring an exiled Catholic Stuart to a reclusive Protestant German, sought to restore the Stuarts to the throne. Among them were officers in the Scots Guards who, whenever the Loyal Toast was drunk, would wave their glasses above their finger bowls—thereby toasting not King George but 'The King across the water.' Since the last Jacobite uprising was crushed in 1745 there have been no finger bowls on the dining tables of the officers of the Scots Guards.

The Life Guards, for their part, rarely drink the Loyal Toast at all. Having rallied round Charles II when he was in exile, they explain, 'It isn't necessary. Our loyalty is beyond doubt.' And add, after a moment's thought, 'Unlike that of the rest.'

On 14 April 1814 the Guards captured Toulouse and the French counter-attacked from Bayonne. Both were then advised that Napoleon's abdication had ended the war three days earlier. A hundred and fifty years later, to the day, a memorial service was held in France and among those deputed to attend was a major from the Coldstream.

Instructed to go to Biarritz, he readily agreed because he thought that 'a few hot days in the Lebanon at someone else's expense would do me the world of good . . . I was quickly told that I was a very ignorant officer and that Biarritz was in the South-West corner of France . . . and that I had better quickly acquire a history book and read all about the French sortie from Bayonne . . . for I was to be the sole representative of my regiment, which took part in that engagement, ably assisted by the Grenadier and Scots Guards.'

Wearing a straw hat, the major set off by train, but soon realised that his history book was 'far too boring to read', so, 'trying hard to conceal the fact that I knew nothing about any of the battles of 1814, let alone the sortie from Bayonne,' picked the brains of the Grenadier and Scots Guards officers also invited to the ceremony and found them 'absolute mines of information.'

Apparently the French garrison at Bayonne had in fact received a message from Marshal Soult advising them of Napoleon's abdication, but had decided to attack the 2nd Brigade of Guards anyway—probably, the major decided, because they considered Soult's message 'just another dirty British trick.'

The engagement that followed was fierce and bloody; and since that day there have been no hostilities on French soil (Waterloo having been contested, by mutual consent, on Belgian soil) between Britain and France.

Two days of celebrations marked the sesquicentenary of this particularly pointless battle. There were two lunch parties, four wreath layings, three church services, a Vin d'Honneur, several band concerts and a two hour address in French which, the major recalls, 'fortunately I did not understand,' because, 'they seemed to think *they* had won.'

At Hougoumont, on the right wing of Wellington's line at Waterloo, the château did not fall because its main gate was forced shut in the face of a storming attack. The hero of that occasion, in the eyes of the Coldstream Regiment, was Sergeant Graham. In whose honour, every year since, a few days before Christmas, the Sergeants of the Coldstream Regiment perform the ceremony of Hanging of the Brick.

All clad in fancy dress, the sergeants process round their barracks behind the Corps of Drums, chairing their oldest member, who carries a brick, which hangs from a chain and symbolises the wall of Hougoumont Farm.

Arrived at the Mess, the Brick is hung over the bar, the oldest member makes a speech, the bar stays open so long as the brick remains hanging and anyone who touches the brick must buy drinks for everyone else. Strangely, however, the Life Guards also celebrate the Hanging of the Brick,—not, needless to say, to pay homage to the Coldstreamers, but simply because they always have. The custom's origins, they explain, are shrouded in the mists of time. Useless, though, to tell the Coldstreamers that: though what they remember may sometimes be wrong, nothing will make them forget it.

Father and Son: Yeoman Warder and Scots Guardsman. The
father served 21 years in the Scots Guards, and the son 22 years

In 1838 two battalions of doubtless disgruntled Foot Guards were sent to Quebec to control its rebellious Frenchmen. On sentry duty at the Citadel one autumn morning, a Coldstream soldier saw a goose, pursued by a fox, fluttering toward him. Obliged to watch this unequal contest in silence—for to have shot the fox would have been to bring out the entire guard—he was more than surprised when the goose, seeking the safety of his sentry box, wedged itself between his legs.

Undeterred, the insolent fox sought to snatch the goose away: so the soldier bayonetted the fox. Whereupon the grateful goose adopted the soldier and the sentimental Coldstreamers adopted the goose—which they christened Jacob.

Some months later, on a wintry night, Jacob and his saviour were on guard duty when the soldier thought he heard a noise. 'Who goes there?' he challenged; but no-one answered. The soldier marched up and down his lonely beat for several minutes, Jacob waddling loyally behind him, until he was convinced that there was no-one out there in the snow and the darkness. Then he stood at ease again in front of his sentry box.

At which moment Jacob hurled himself into the air and, wings furiously flapping, momentarily repelled two armed intruders. The soldier bayonetted the first and shot the second. Two more ran up; and Jacob flapped recklessly round both while his friend fired yet again, and the guard fell out, and the Frenchmen fled.

Next day Jacob was the hero of the garrison, whose officers subscribed for the purchase of an inscribed golden collar which he wore proudly round his neck.

Returning to London with the Regiment, Jacob resumed his duties with the sentinels at the gate of the old Portman Street barracks. As each sentry walked his beat, Jacob walked behind him; and as the sentry saluted officers, so Jacob stood to attention. The Duke of Wellington admired him; children loved him; and he died on duty—run over by a van at the barrack gate. Though buried with all honours, his head and neck were preserved, and can now be seen, complete with golden collar and a Francophobe look in his glassy blue eye, at the Guards Museum—where, to be frank, he really looks rather nasty. But the Coldstreamers don't think so, because to them, who refuse to forget, he is as lovely as Uxbridge's artificial leg or Evans' skull is to the Household Cavalry.

In 1885, at the battle of Abu Klea, Colonel Burnaby was killed. An eccentric giant of a man, he had heard that the Household Cavalry's composite Regiment was on its way to avenge the murder of General Gordon so, abandoning his private explorations elsewhere, he had marched alone through the desert night to join them.

Approaching their position in the darkness, he would certainly have been shot had he not been smoking a cigar—which the Mahdi and his supporters never did. When the dervishes attacked next morning, he was hacked to death. His cuirass, boots and state sword are on display in the Household Cavalry Museum, not so much to commemorate his courage as to honour his swagger, which his regiment found admirable.

'A Cavalry soldier is no damned use unless he swaggers,' proclaimed a corporal major of the day; and certainly every officer in the Life Guards and the Blues did his best to conform—if only by buying enormously expensive uniforms and owning at least two black chargers. One of them even rode his charger into Pooles, the tailors, to demonstrate just how badly his riding breeches fitted. Burnaby was of that breed; and when troopers visit their museum today, and look at his boots, they remember a giant of a man striding across the desert, cigar glowing in the darkness, to join his Regiment in a battle that would kill him.

Irked perhaps by 250 years of Grenadier jibes at their 'perfidy', the Coldstream Regiment, in 1909 submitted a claim for no less than thirteen additional Battle Honours to a special committee at the War Office. Top of their list was Dunbar 1650.

The point of claiming Dunbar as an honour was that, if granted, it would establish beyond dispute Monck's impeccable *loyalty*, in a war against Scotland, to the de facto government. It was not, admittedly, the King's government, but it *was* the de facto government; and anyway the Coldstream have never been averse to publicising their unique link with the all-conquering Model Army.

'But don't you think', the special Committee objected, 'that the Scots would find such an award highly offensive?'

To which the Coldstream Colonel replied that it had, after all, happened 259 years ago, during which time 'Stuart susceptibilies have greatly diminished in Scotland'. Unconvinced by his arguments, and unmoved by his wit, the Committee decided against him. Should Scotland pursue her present nationalist path to its logical conclusion, however, there can be no doubt that the War Office will hear more of Dunbar from England's Coldstreamers, whose memory is elephantine.

Scots Guardsmen likewise forget nothing. Salamanca was added to their list of battle honours a mere 139 years after they fought there; but even more revealing was an incident that occurred during World War II. In 1941, when they were stationed in Syria, two of their tractors were stolen. Before they could pursue the matter further they were despatched to the Western Desert where they fought long and bitterly until it was decided to rest them a while and then train them as anti-tank gunners. To this end they were sent to the hutted camps of Qatana, in Syria.

Three days after their arrival at Qatana they despatched a platoon to look for the two stolen tractors, which were believed to be hidden somewhere beyond Palmyra, more than 200 miles to the north.

Two days later the lieutenant in charge of this expedition sent back a laconic report revealing that he had liberated the two tractors and fifty tons of hoarded wheat, and taken prisoner 400 tribesmen and one sheik. The tractors had been found interred in the desert and the sheik was insisting that they must have been there since the time

The Regimental Mascot of the Irish Guards: an Irish Wolfhound

of the Romans. Their Regimental pride restored, the Scots Guards began their training as anti-tank gunners.

In 1949 they proved themselves no less meticulous. During a bad ambush in Malaya, Left Flank of the 2nd Battalion lost an officer, a sergeant, a lance sergeant and a Bren gun. The men were irreplaceable, but somewhere in the jungle was a Chinese bandit with a Scots Guards' Bren gun. A month later F Company staged their own ambush—and recovered Left Flank's Bren. It had been shortened, to lighten it, and lubricated with Brylcream; but it was indisputably Left Flank's Bren gun. Today it is one of the Battalions many war trophies.

And so, by raconteurs, word of mouth, museum displays and histories the corporate memory of the Household Division and the family memory of each of the squadrons and battalions within it is kept fresh and alive. Each regiment has its individual traits, ascribed to it by the others and accepted by itself. The Household Cavalry are incorrigibly languid, the Grenadiers infallibly correct, the Coldstreamers efficiently relaxed, the Scots aggressive loners, the Micks recklessly Irish and the Taffs quite charming.

Ask each of them 'Is it so?' and each will answer, 'Yes.' Ask them about the rest of Her Majesty's forces, and they will feign surprise that anyone should imagine that there was anyone else. Press them and they will resort to such frivolities as, 'Like the Navy, you mean? Hopeless in the morning, helpless in the afternoon!' Accuse them of being outrageously élitist and they will tell you, 'Of course we're an élite. But so are the Marines, and so are the Greenjackets, and so are the S.A.S. And the one excuse we all make, and it's the only one that's valid, is that for us élitism works.'

It works because of their sense of family, their regimental pride and their determination to forget no one and nothing. A 1975 letter to the Coldstream Association illustrates the impact of the inter-relationship of these three qualities. '*We think*,' it ran, '*we've located the oldest living Coldstreamer. 7456 George Alma Farrow is over a hundred years old and living in Canada . . . . His father was a Coldstreamer who fought in the Crimea, and therefore gave him the name of Alma.*'

28   *The Household Division Today*

TODAY THE Household Division has lost none of its traditions, none of its snobbery and none of its pride.

It sees nothing strange in calling an officer's horse a charger and a trooper's horse a horse, because it always has done—just as it has always kept the coat of that horse or charger free of dust and scurf, its mane a hand's width in length, its eyebrows and whiskers trimmed, its hooves clean and its tail snugly pulled into the rump.

The Household Cavalry see nothing anachronistic in the continued presence of farriers armed with a sixteenth century axe on every ceremonial parade. Its horses still need a monthly shoeing, it points out; and when one asks what a sixteenth century axe has to do with shoeing twentieth century horses, it replies that behind

Major General P. J. N. Ward, C.B.E., until October 1976 Major General Commanding Household Division

the axe blade there is a long spike (or pole) with which to kill horses wounded in battle—hence the expression pole-axed. And one is expected to be satisfied with that!

The Blues are still proud of their title 'The Old Ones,' which refers to their conservative habits and Cromwellian past.

Blues and Royals and Life Guards are proud of their capacity to take turns at manning huge tanks in Germany (as part of N.A.T.O.'s Army) and smaller, faster, more vulnerable armoured cars at Windsor (as part of Britain's Army). As tank men they train to thrust brutishly ahead of their own infantry, crushing the enemy's infantry or demolishing his armour. As armoured-car men they train to probe ahead even of the tanks, each car linked to the other by radio and all linked to Headquarters.

If ambushed an armoured car will lay smoke and seek escape rather than battle—if necessary reversing precipitately out of danger. A tank can also lay smoke; but it is more likely to do so in order to recover one of its stricken companions than to provide cover for its own flight. It is not really equipped for flight. It is equipped to inflict, at considerable range, from a huge gun, horrific damage.

Major General John Swinton, Major General Commanding Household Division from October 1976 (Photographed when commanding 4 Guards Armour Brigade)

Armoured cars will also be used—and have been, in Malaya, Aden, Cyprus, Ulster, all over—to subdue terrorists and maintain peace in a guerilla type war by setting up road blocks and escorting convoys.

So the Blues and Royals and the Life Guards commute in turn between Detmold in Germany and Windsor in England, switching from tanks to armoured cars and back again, and ever prepared in their armoured car capacity to serve N.A.T.O. in Norway or Turkey, to support the U.N. in such trouble spots as Cyprus, and Britain in places like Ulster.

Their regimental relationship is not, however, always wholly sisterly. Though they share a pack of bloodhounds and seventeen horses in Germany (for hunting, of course) the Life Guards tank crews detest, for example, the tradition established by the Blues and Royals of wearing dark polo-necked sweaters to keep out the dirt. 'Black Nasties,' they call them, and never cease to lobby their officers against them.

Neither regiment on the other hand, seems in the least ashamed that few cavalry generals before the twentieth century could handle any command bigger than a regiment; and neither the Blues nor the Royals object to their amalgamation in 1969, the Royals being able to trace their pedigree back to the defence of Tangier, which is far enough, and the amalgamation having anyway worked, which is the Household's one criterion of success.

Nor are the Foot Guards any less self-assured. Each regiment still prides itself upon its total poise and sang froid. When the Scots Guards and the Guards Parachute Company found themselves sharing long houses with tattooed head hunters in Borneo (during the confrontation with Indonesia) no one even commented on the baskets hanging from the rafters and full of human skulls, nor on the bare breasted maidens pounding maize outside, nor on the fact that in one such dwelling a photo of the Queen hung beside an advertisement for Moss Bros. It takes savoir faire to ignore basketsful of human skulls, bare maidenly breasts and the incongruity of Her Majesty sharing top billing with Moss Bros. But the Guards learn it the hard way—by remaining impassive in front of their own ill-informed compatriots.

'Don't they look smart?' a woman spectator remarked to her companion as they surveyed the Guardsmen who lined the Mall one Birthday Parade.

'Yes,' agreed the friend. 'But so they should. They don't do anything else.'

'Madam!' snorted a bearskinned sergeant, not turning his head, but very audibly nevertheless. 'A month ago we were hunting bandits in Malaya.' But he was an exception. Normally the Guardsman will not bother to explain that he is a soldier as well as a performer.

Largely this stems from arrogance—the arrogance of the professional, or the snob. 'Well, of course *our* colonel,' a Mick reminds, 'is a Rumanian Prince.'

'Well, yes, we *were* disbanded in '75,' admits an ex-member of the Guards Parachute Company, 'but the S.A.S. still takes in Guardsmen. And the S.A.S. are now doing *military* free falls from 45,000 feet. Use oxygen as they free fall for 32,000 feet, by which time they're doing 160 miles an hour, and then three minutes to the ground under the canopy. It was done quite recently in the Oman.'

'Sir Richard Steel, the essayist, was a Private Gentleman in the Life Guards before he started *The Spectator* with Addison,' one is apt to be told from the turret of a Chieftain tank in Germany.

'Rex Whistler was in the Welsh Guards,' confide the Taffs; but not in the presence of a Grenadier, who would only go one better by pointing out that *his* Regiment has produced two Prime Ministers, Winston Churchill and Harold Macmillan.

The Household Cavalry are proud of the fact that they are the only troops allowed to bear arms inside Royal palaces, they alone being assigned the duty of lining the staircase, their swords drawn, at Buckingham Palace, Windsor Castle and the Palace of Westminster. Equally they are proud of the fact that a trooper's horse costs half as much as a small car, and an officer's charger a third as much again. Moreover, they point out, the sheepskins that cover a trooper's saddle are made of four lambskins. The officer's sheepskin, of course, is in fact a goat skin. And the saddles, of course, are all specially fitted to the horses, just as the buckskin pantaloons are specially fitted to the thigh and leg of the rider. And officers' swords, of course, are lighter than the troopers', and their helmets better lined, their boots more elegantly shaped, their cuirasses more heroically sculpted (and edged in velvet as well) and their tunics festooned with gold plated cord—all of which is exactly as it should be, thanks to George IV.

The Brigade of Guards is proud of the fact that it marches at 112 paces a minute—except of course for the Grenadiers, who do an eccentric 116.

The Grenadiers are proud of the fact that they alone of all the Guards march correctly at 116 paces to the minute.

Everyone is proud of the fact that at St. James's Palace there are allegedly hundreds of volumes of French cartoons and delicate pornography.

No one was old enough to fight in World War II, which has become history. No one recalls ex-Grenadier Winston Churchill's dictum that in World War II 'the Allies floated to victory on a sea of oil': still less does anyone bother to deduce that that is why guardsmen continue to serve as desert troops in Sharjah, thereby endearing Britain (or so H.M. Government hopes) to the oil rich Trucial States.

In the event of another such war (which Household officers discuss only if provoked) they are not entirely sure whence will come their next 'sea of oil', but they do not doubt their regiments' capacity to function perfectly as air-portable troops, anti-tank troops, ski troops, desert troops, jungle troops, guerilla troops, nuclear troops, reconnaissance troops or tank crews. In the meantime they will train hard in Germany for that which they seldom discuss, attempt the impossible in Ulster-type situations without demur, and perform impeccably as ceremonial troops in London.

For the implementation of all these duties, they readily confess, 'the officers are *not* what matters: what matters is the strength of the N.C.O.'s.'

'What one is aiming at,' a past Major General sums up, 'is an organisation that works—in which everyone gets on with everyone else—in which the men are proud of being part of an élite.'

A hundred years ago Gronow the ex-Grenadier wrote some strangely topical words. 'I have lived,' he wrote, 'through a period characterised by sanguinary wars and huge national debts, and have remained in this world long enough to calculate their results.

'I am afraid we must often be content with that empty glory which lives only in the pages of history. A battle fought fifty years ago appears very often of no more utility than the splendid tombs of Necropolis. Events and objects for which men by thousands were brought together in deadly combat assume, a few years afterwards,

While the Foot Guards march, the Household Cavalry
await their turn to rank past the Queen—
Trooping the Colour, 1972

mighty small proportions; and those who have taken part in deadly struggles at a later period marvel at the enthusiasm which then animated them.

'I am no believer in that era of happiness which some divines imagine to be so near at hand; nor do I imagine that the next two or three hundred years will witness the sword being turned into the reaping hook of peaceful industry; but what I *do* hope for is that nations will know each other better than they did of old.'

Were the Household Division of today to appoint a spokesman to express its views on empty glory, past battles, deadly struggles, present crises and future hopes, he would probably echo Gronow's sentiments to the letter. And why not? They were written about Waterloo, which to the Guards—Foot and Horse—was only yesterday.

Index